Prayer
for the Day

Prayer for the Day

365 Inspiring Daily Reflections

WATKINS

Sharing Wisdom Since
1893

This edition first published in the UK and USA 2014
Watkins Publishing Limited
PO Box 883
Oxford, OX1 9PL
UK

A member of Osprey Group

For enquiries in the USA and Canada:
Osprey Publishing
PO Box 3985
New York, NY 10185-3985
Tel: (001) 212 753 4402
Email: info@ospreypublishing.com

By arrangement with the BBC
The BBC logo is a trade mark of the British Broadcasting Corporation and is used under licence.
BBC logo copyright © BBC 2005
Radio 4 logo copyright © Radio 4 2011

Design and typography copyright © Watkins Publishing Limited 2014
Foreword copyright © Richard Harries 2014
Introduction copyright © Philip Billson 2014
Scripts from the BBC Radio 4 series *Prayer for the Day* copyright © BBC 2014
Biographical Index of Contributors copyright © Watkins Publishing Limited 2014

10 9 8 7 6 5 4 3 2 1

Designed and typeset by Georgina Hewitt

Printed and bound in the Finland

A CIP record for this book is available from the British Library

ISBN: 978-1-78028-855-0

Watkins Publishing is supporting the Woodland Trust, the UK's leading woodland
conservation charity, by funding tree-planting initiatives and woodland maintenance.
www.watkinspublishing.co.uk

Publisher's Note: Scripts may not be exactly as broadcast, but are always substantively so.

Contents

Foreword

〰️

by Richard Harries

There are millions of people, of all faiths and none, who like to pause for a few moments at the beginning of the day and reflect on what lies ahead. For many it will go further than this, to include a period of conscious recollection of themselves and their deepest beliefs. That is why so many who listen to the radio in the mornings welcome *Prayer for the Day*. They appreciate something different from the usual rush – the reminder that there is another dimension to life.

Most of us are pretty sluggish in the morning and our own thoughts can feel tired and stale, so it is always good to gain fresh insight into the wonderful but difficult process of living. For some there is a particular pleasure if that thought turns naturally into a prayer. When I used to do *Prayer for the Day*, I appreciated the challenge of focusing what I wanted to say into a very short prayer – ideally one that might return to the mind at odd points later in the day.

Prayer means different things to different people. For me, it is about trying to relate my life, in all its aspects, to God. This includes thanksgiving, praying for people I know in need, and trying to be responsive to the leading of Divine Love in the day ahead. At the heart of this is an attempt to be still and wait on God. 'On you alone, O God, my soul in stillness waits,' as the psalmist put it. In that stillness we allow God to dwell more fully within us, and work through us.

Many will find this book a real help in nourishing their spiritual lives. Words that are only heard can quickly be forgotten. Here are words that can be read, returned to again, pondered over and made one's own.

I welcome the fact that each passage is short. For a passage serves its purpose if it soon turns what is read into thoughts of our own, and if those thoughts are able to find a focus in prayer.

Richard Harries (Lord Harries of Pentregarth) was Bishop of Oxford from 1987 to 2006. The author of many books on the interface of Christian faith and wider culture, he contributed to Prayer for the Day *for a number of years.*

Introduction

by Philip Billson

Each of these parcels of under 300 words started life running across my desk for checking. My Thursdays and Fridays are punctuated by this regular job. *Prayer for the Day* is part of Radio 4's quasi-liturgical dawn sequence. Before it comes a quirky and fascinating historical piece voiced by the announcer about what happened 'On this Day' – a theme we quite frequently carry on into *Prayer for the Day*. It is followed by a change of gear into *Farming Today*.

I have to consider how the text will be heard in that sequence at 05:43 on a particular day the following week. Will it sound out of place if X or Y has died? Or if there's another major episode in whatever conflict is at the top of the news agenda? Is there a particular group who might hear what is being said differently from how the author intended? Very rarely do we have to pull an episode, and that is thanks to the dedication and sensitivity of all those who contribute.

It is a pleasure to be able to introduce a book which presents the best of *Prayer for the Day*. All our presenters are preachers or teachers of one kind or another and this book feels like a contemporary tribute to the homilist's art – representing the distilled wisdom of years of ministry of whatever faith tradition. Some pieces are quite teasing, like the one that begins with a crossword clue (June 8), or revealing, like the senior Roman Catholic cleric who begins by telling us that as a young man he set his sights on the most beautiful girl in class (July 16). Others tell an amusing moral tale, such as the boy who sent his brother's pet hamster into the sky in a model airplane but didn't confess for years (March 12).

Some of the most moving tell a powerful story. One in particular stays in my memory. You'll find it on April 7. It's a story of self-sacrifice between two young brothers. One of the brothers was Albrecht Dürer, and from that moment in his life came his painting *The Praying Hands*.

Philip Billson has been Series Producer of Radio 4's Prayer for the Day *since 2004.*

January 1

Graham Forbes

Happy New Year! You might be thinking it's time to get up; a fair number, certainly in Scotland, will be thinking it's probably time to head for bed. Later on today I'll be in Pitlochry. Famous for its theatre and salmon ladder, this highland Perthshire town celebrates the New Year in style. At midday today the high street will be closed, a dance band set up on a stage, and the street dancing begins. The local butcher produces pies to feed the 5,000 and soup to drive away the cold. And we dance. Dashing White Sergeants, Gay Gordons … some may even attempt a Highland Fling. And all shapes and sizes dance, from the very old to the very young and all in-between — even the traffic wardens have been known to dance. The dress code, rather like the dancing, might be best described as mixed. I, like many others, will be wearing the kilt, but with wellington boots and a woolly hat for extra warmth. And we dance into the New Year. I know not everyone might feel like dancing, and yet Jesus, who knows all of life's joys and pains, is called 'the Lord of the dance'. Your dance of life this coming year may be as frenetic as this lunchtime's highland flings or as serene as a slow waltz, but it is the Lord of the dance who leads us, I believe, and it is to him we now pray:

Lord Jesus, Lord of the dance, the first and the last and the living one,
You have brought us safely to the beginning of another year.
We thank you for the blessings of the past.
Renew our courage and strength in the present
And direct our ways in the future in the dance of life.
Amen.

BROADCAST TUESDAY 1 JANUARY 2013

January 2

Kelvin Holdsworth

At New Year I ask people in my congregation to bring something with them to church for a special blessing. I ask them to bring their diaries and at the end of the service they all hold them aloft as I ask God's blessing on them. It is a way of getting people to think about how they will use their time in the year ahead and to think about how to consecrate some of that time for the greater good. These days, time is one of our most precious gifts. In a busy world, the offering of a few hours to someone or something that needs time is a gift of great richness.

These days, when I ask people to turn up with their diaries, they arrive clutching all manner of things. Spiral-bound notebooks are still in evidence but there are just as many electronic gadgets. Tablets, mobile phones and even the odd laptop are held on high as I ask God's blessing on the seconds, the minutes, the hours and the days ahead.

The Biblical Book of Ecclesiastes famously says that for everything there is a season, and a time for every matter under heaven. A time to be born and a time to die. A time to love and time to hate; a time for war and a time for peace.

When I bless those diaries at New Year, I hope for life-giving times, peacemaking times and joyful times, full of friendship and love.

God of the universe, fill our time with opportunities to do good. Help us this year to usher in a world which is sustainable and just, and prompt us to bring about a more even distribution of the world's riches. Amen.

BROADCAST MONDAY 2 JANUARY 2012

January 3

George Stack

How long do New Year resolutions last? My experience is, not very long. Go to the gym in the first week of January and you'll see the place is packed. Ninety per cent of the people there have made a resolution to adopt a healthy lifestyle. There is a noticeable increase in joggers pounding the streets. Weight problems will be solved by the latest diet, and a more regular lifestyle will produce a healthy mind in a healthy body. Hardly a month later and most of the short-term enthusiasts have gone. The lack of experience, perhaps the lack of dedication, certainly the intensity of the onslaught on the body, leave people physically and mentally exhausted and maybe a danger to themselves and others!

Many years ago I began a new job and was given a very good piece of advice. 'You must remember that this work of yours is not going to be a sprint. It's going to be a marathon.' I am still learning how to pace myself. Setting priorities and goals that are realistic yet challenging is a challenge in itself. I have learned a great deal from the Rule of St Benedict. Benedict was the founder of Western Monasticism in the fifth century. His Rule for living and working in the community is as valid today as when it was first composed. There are thousands of monks, nuns and laypeople who follow that Rule throughout the world. One of their mottos is *Laborare est orare* – 'To work is to pray.' But it is this instruction in the 64th chapter of the Rule that I really find relevant: 'The Abbot should arrange everything so that the strong have something to strive for and the weak are not disheartened.' None of us is completely strong or utterly weak. In some aspects of life we need to be challenged to avoid complacency. In our weakness we need support in order to be helped to grow day by day.

A prayer of John Henry Newman:

Wherever I am, nothing is wasted. If I am in sickness, perplexity or sorrow, these things can serve the Lord. God does nothing in vain, therefore I will trust in the Lord. Amen.

BROADCAST WEDNESDAY 3 JANUARY 2007

January 4

Richard Hill

Today is Sir Isaac Newton's birthday. Born in 1643, he became one of the foremost intellectuals of his time. He has certainly left his mark in the world of mathematics and physics. In a 2005 Royal Society poll of their members, Newton was deemed more influential than Albert Einstein.

When I was a Physics undergraduate, I was in no doubt about the importance of Newtonian Mechanics. I spent many long hours doing calculations based on his methods. In spite of all his genius and everything he achieved, Newton knew that there was still much to learn. He said, 'I know not what I appear to the world, but to myself I seem to have been only like a boy playing on the seashore, and diverting myself in now and then finding a smoother pebble or a prettier shell, whilst the great ocean of truth lay all undiscovered before me.'

Comparing his mathematical advances with those of Descartes, Newton wrote to the mathematician Robert Hooke, saying, 'If I have seen further it is by standing on the shoulders of Giants.'

He was a deeply religious man for whom there was no division between science and faith. One recent biographer says, 'He believed he was doing God's work.'

I think humility was a real mark of his greatness, along with his faith. Our celebrity culture could learn a few lessons from Newton. The Bible says, 'Do nothing out of selfish ambition or vain conceit, but in humility consider others better than yourselves.'

Father, we thank You for those who have blazed a trail for us to follow. Show how we might stand on the shoulders of giants and glimpse a little more of Your creation. Amen.

BROADCAST FRIDAY 4 JANUARY 2008

January 5

Jenny Wigley

When I was a teenager, I was a regular reader of the kinds of girls' magazines that had a problem page. It seemed somehow reassuring when you're growing up to discover that others had even bigger things to worry about than you! Yet I was aware I knew nothing about the 'agony aunts' whose guidance was being sought. Were they people whose lives were as wise as their words?

There *are* times when advice can stand alone, but often the value we place on someone's words can't be separated from the *person*, and all that she or he stands for. Because of what they've endured or achieved, they become people worth listening to. That's what true wisdom means.

Someone I once knew really embodied that kind of wisdom. Her name was Angela. She lived alone in a one-bedroomed flat, unable to walk more than the few steps from her kitchen to her living room. Yet she counted herself as richly blessed. She had a bay window which looked over a little park – she could sit and watch people coming and going, and the children playing. And she had time to keep in touch with her friends – she wrote a letter to someone every day.

Angela was a person who knew how to count her blessings – and how to share them. She had learned that wisdom of which Jesus spoke when he said that a disciple who is truly taught becomes like their teacher. Jesus had taught her well; and she was now teaching me.

A lovely prayer which sums this up for me was written by a thirteenth-century bishop, Richard of Chichester:

Thanks be to you, our Lord Jesus Christ, for all the benefits which you have given us, for all the pains and insults which you have borne for us. Most merciful Redeemer, Friend and Brother, may we know you more clearly, love you more dearly and follow you more nearly, day by day. Amen.

BROADCAST TUESDAY 5 JANUARY 2010

January 6

Bishop Angaelos

Today is the Feast of the Epiphany — commemorating the story of the strange visitors from the East arriving in Bethlehem to present their gifts of gold, frankincense and myrrh to the infant Jesus and his probably rather startled parents.

There is so much we don't know about these Eastern visitors. Though we might sing 'We three kings of orient are' with great gusto, we don't know if there were really three of them; the Bible doesn't tell us they were kings but describes them rather mysteriously as Magi and it is hard to say with certainty precisely where they are supposed to have come from.

However, the story of those travellers tells us much that we can know with great certainty. Their story shows us that God is there for everyone, even people different from us. Spirituality seems to be something that human beings from different traditions have in common. Consciousness of God seems to disrupt and undermine any barriers and boundaries that religious people might put up. The visit of the Magi suggests that perhaps we need to learn about all that is holy from those with whom we least expect to share common values and experiences. God is amongst those who differ from us.

Gold for the holy refugee family on the run from Herod. Sumptuous incense to mark the birth of the most special child. Strange and bitter myrrh to keep us guessing what God has in store in the future.

Loving God, the Magi were guided by the star to where the infant Jesus lay. Guide us by the light of Your love to walk pathways of peaceful discovery and make journeys beyond the boundaries of our expectations. Amen.

BROADCAST FRIDAY 6 JANUARY 2012

January 7

Andrew Graystone

The outspokenly atheist philosopher Bertrand Russell was once asked what he would say if, after he had died, he found himself face to face with God and had to justify why he hadn't believed in him. Russell replied, 'I'd say "Insufficient evidence, God! Insufficient evidence!"'

There are plenty of believers who could echo Bertrand Russell's complaint that God, assuming he wants to be known, has a funny way of going about it. Of course, the problem is, if Bertrand Russell or you or I are allowed to define what sort of evidence *would* be sufficient, then God ceases to be the judge of the earth and becomes the subject of a scientific experiment. That kind of evidence just doesn't work for this kind of God.

The season of Epiphany is the time when many Christians think about the revelation of God – the ways in which God expresses himself to the world. St Paul, writing to the church in Rome, said that 'since the creation of the world, God's invisible qualities – His eternal power and divine nature – have been clearly seen, being understood from what has been made, so that human beings are without excuse'. He seems to be saying that God *has* revealed himself – that he *has* provided sufficient evidence, not just for a chosen few but for every human being. The implication is this: if we don't get a clear picture of God, the problem is not with God's transmission but with our reception.

Thank You, God, that You have chosen to reveal Yourself to the world. All too often my heart grows cynical and my eyes grow dim. Help me to recognize You today in the people I meet, the things I see, the experiences I have, so that at the end of this day I may know that I have spent it in Your company. For Jesus Christ's sake, Amen.

BROADCAST WEDNESDAY 7 JANUARY 2009

January 8

Jenny Wigley

In TS Eliot's poem 'The Journey of the Magi', he allowed himself to wonder how the encounter with the Christ-child might have affected the lives of the Wise Men. He wrote of them returning to their homeland, no longer at ease there, in the old way of living. He believed that moment with Jesus had changed them forever; they had been granted a glimpse of the divine, and they never forgot it.

What the Bible describes is a unique event, and yet it's also just a particular example of every human encounter, which holds the possibility for something creative to happen, for people to meet one another and be changed in the process. It's one reason why people come together to study the scriptures, or gather in church for worship. They're responding to Jesus' promise that 'when two or three are gathered together in my name, there am I in the midst of them', a promise that something unseen yet significant is taking place.

So in worship, for example, Christians believe that God's creative power is at work, graciously receiving our imperfect offerings, transforming them and us by His presence. What happens in the course of worship can be summed up in the way it ends. At the Communion service, the congregation is sent out with the words, 'Go in peace, to love and serve the Lord.' We've spent time with one another and with God; now we're sent back into the world to do God's work.

We cannot really know whether the Wise Men *were* changed by their encounter, but we can seek to ensure that we are as open as they were in their search for truth, so that we may learn to live by the light of all that we have seen and heard.

Lord Jesus Christ, come among us today; shine your light in our darkness; fill our hearts and minds with new understanding, that we may reflect your love in lives of service, and bring to the world the promise of your glory. Amen.

BROADCAST FRIDAY 8 JANUARY 2010

January 9

Bishop Angaelos

Many Christians struggle to seize opportunities to make the love of God tangible in their lives and the lives of those around them. We look at ourselves and sometimes see only weakness, feeling we have nothing to give. Orthodox Christians, of course, can feel especially powerless when we think of family and friends caught up in parts of the Middle East. Yet if we look closely, we have an abundance of gifts that we can share with others, here and far away.

In chapter 6 of the Gospel of St John, the Lord prays for his disciples, saying: 'I have made you known to those You have given Me out of the world...' As Christ reveals the Father to humanity, we too are called to do the same with one another. This can be realized in the way that we interact, and how we react to each other's pain and celebration.

How often do we ask about each other, how interested are we in others' lives and experiences? Do we give others love, importance and priority? Do we have time for one another in our fast-paced and ever-changing world, or do we get caught up in the daily routine and social networks that have now almost become our primary means of communication?

As Orthodox Christians, we believe that setting aside time in our busy schedules to sanctify our thoughts, actions and selves through contemplation and interaction with God will lead us to share the love and joy that we have freely received from Him.

Lord, may we bring joy to Your heart in sharing Your presence and love, giving freely to one another as we have received from You, expecting nothing in return. Amen.

BROADCAST WEDNESDAY 9 JANUARY 2013

January 10

John Holdsworth

When King Hussein of Jordan made his historic trip to Tel Aviv on this day in 1996, few doubted that this was an important moment in the modern history of peacemaking. It came just fifteen months after the peace treaty between Israel and Jordan brought to an end over 40 years of war and hostility. Neither the treaty nor the visit were without controversy. There was opposition on both sides but the leaders were courageous enough to continue.

This has been the pattern of peacemaking since the end of the bloody twentieth-century era in which, if we learned anything, it was that war is the most unsatisfactory way of establishing peace. If disputes are not to be resolved by a trial of strength, then we have to find alternatives. And what we have witnessed is a series of bold initiatives by governments and individuals to break vicious circles. These initiatives have included acts that some have seen as weakness.

Modern peacemaking involves doing what was once unthinkable; it means talking to enemies, forgiving old wrongs, adopting new trust, abandoning short-term expediency, seeing the good in the other, rejecting caricatures, relinquishing power. What we all accept as the iconic moments of peacemaking have had some or all of these characteristics: the release of Nelson Mandela, the Good Friday Agreement, as well as the historic peace moves in the Middle East between Egypt, Jordan and Israel.

This approach is absolutely central to the Biblical understanding of right relations between individuals, communities or countries. That peacemaking list reads almost like a biography of God, and perhaps that is why it should matter so much to establish peace in this way.

Heavenly Father, Prince of Peace, inspire all those who this year will be in a position to make a difference for world peace, and grant us the will to live in peace with all people. Amen.

BROADCAST WEDNESDAY 10 JANUARY 2007

January 11

George Craig

The first time we took my younger son to a beach, the walk from the car park took a very long time. The trouble was that he was terribly excited about using his new bucket and spade and every patch of sand we came to on the path seemed to him like journey's end. We told him there was more to come, but he was pretty happy where he was and didn't see any need to move on. Left to himself he'd have spent a happy afternoon digging on a grubby path, never seeing the real beach, and not have minded in the least.

Many of us who have embarked on the journey of faith have very similar experiences. I'm sure I'm not the only person who has been reluctant to accept that the experience of God that I've been comfortable with for years may not be the whole story.

We may experience a particular form of faith and we settle down to enjoy it, oblivious of the fact that there is much more, further on – and sometimes deeply suspicious and resentful of those who try to tell us about it. It can feel as if they're questioning the reality of our faith. So we don't listen.

And that's a pity, because God does not call us to a life spent sitting comfortably where we first met Him. He constantly calls us on to bigger and better things. He always has more for us to discover about Him, more for us to do for Him, but, above all, more for us to enjoy in Him.

My son's face when he eventually saw the real beach was a picture: delight but also sheer awe that anything so good could be so vast. And that same sense of delight and awe can be ours if we're just willing to trust God's promise that, however good we may think it is where we are, it's a lot better up ahead.

Lord, it must grieve You that so many of us settle for so small a part of what You have in store for us. We pray for the gift of faith that will draw us on, trusting in Your promise that the best is yet to come. Amen.

BROADCAST FRIDAY 11 JANUARY 2008

January 12

~

Denis Rice

I'm ashamed and sad that I remember very little of my school history lessons. Most dates have gone. The names of kings and prime ministers have survived but, as Eric Morecambe might have said, not necessarily in the right order. When the family are conscripting a team for club or pub quiz nights, I qualify only as a last-ditch reserve. But one historical tale has stayed vividly with me. Indeed, vividly enough to suggest it's more legend than fact. It's the story of King Robert the Bruce and the spider.

Despondent and deeply discouraged, Bruce was hiding in a cave. How was he to find the resolve and the hope to face the enemy of despair in himself, and the real enemies outside the cave? He notices a spider attempting to climb. Time and again the web breaks, and the spider falls and has to start all over again. Eventually it reaches where it wanted to be. Reflecting on this inspiring piece of nature study, Bruce summoned the resolution to go out again and face his foes.

As an adult, many years later, I realized that Bruce's musing on his spider was a very early example of how to meditate, of how to find a way into prayer. I was being introduced to what is known as 'object meditation' – though Bruce's spider might protest at being referred to as an 'object'. Very simply, a quiet focus on some everyday object can lead us into a surprising journey of reflective prayer. It may reveal paths and possibilities, which a tussle with too many prepared words can obscure.

Father God, open our eyes, our hearts and our minds to Your presence in all that surrounds us. May we find moments of stillness, through which our ways may become clearer and our hope and trust may grow surer. Amen.

BROADCAST MONDAY 12 JANUARY 2009

January 13

Nick Papadopulos

It's customary to lament these dark January mornings and to long for the coming of brighter days. Well before sunrise we fumble about in the winter blackness. We can't find our slippers; we can't find the keys; we can't find the kettle; we trip over the cat. It's utterly unlike the summer months, which seem so far away. Darkness means gloom and despair; light means hope and optimism.

These natural sentiments are particularly understandable to early risers at the beginning of a new year, when financial uncertainty and family worries seem to crowd in and disturb us. None of this is very cheerful to contemplate – until we remember the words of the Psalmist: 'darkness and light to you are both alike.' Dark or light, summer or winter, nowhere is far away from God.

Picture a church filled with burning candles at this time of year. The warmth of their glow is bright, and it captures for many of us a powerful sense of God's loving presence. Outside the church it is dark. Yet whether we are inside, basking in candlelight, or outside, groping in the shadows, that presence is constant. Sometimes it is as evident to us as a dancing candle-flame; sometimes it has to be searched for. But it is always there.

God,
Darkness and light to You are both alike,
And You look upon us when we cannot look upon You.
Be present to us this day.
In light, in dark,
In joy, in sorrow,
In hope, in despair,
Desert us not.
Amen.

BROADCAST FRIDAY 13 JANUARY 2012

January 14

Martyn Atkins

Without doubt some great human beings have served as Christian missionaries. Take just one, born this day in 1875: Albert Schweitzer. A lover of music, particularly Bach, the son of a pastor, a medical doctor, a writer, thinker and Nobel Peace Prize winner — it's quite a CV!

His Nobel Prize related largely to what Schweitzer called 'reverence for life'. He believed that reality is ethically neutral and that we could and should choose the moral structures that shape our communities. Our view of the world, he argued, must derive from our understanding of life, and not vice versa.

He urged reverence and respect for *all* life; most certainly for human beings, and particularly for those with leprosy and sleeping sickness, but also for animals. Indeed, 'reverence for life' extended to everything that God, the creator of the universe, had made and makes. And critically for Schweitzer, such reverence for life came about most naturally when we entered a spiritual relationship with God. This prayer for animals is often attributed to Schweitzer:

Hear our humble prayer, O God,
For our friends the animals,
Especially for animals who are suffering;
For animals that are overworked, underfed, cruelly treated;
For all creatures in captivity that beat their wings against bars;
For any that are hunted or lost or deserted or frightened or hungry;
For all that must be put to death.
We entreat for them all mercy and pity,
And for those who deal with them
We ask a heart of compassion, gentle hands and kindly words.
Make us, ourselves, to be true friends to animals
And so to share the blessings of the merciful. Amen.

BROADCAST TUESDAY 14 JANUARY 2014

January 15

Michael Ford

When I worked in a frenetic BBC newsroom, I was no stranger to shifts that kicked in long before the world had woken. But, strange as it might seem, I often felt more like a monk than a journalist. Getting up at 3.30 on a cold January morning and spending half an hour in silent meditation certainly gave my journalistic life a monastic rhythm.

In some ways, the life of a monk and that of a journalist could not be more dissimilar, but I've always sensed deeper connections. The journalist is trained to see what others don't, to piece together the clues, to hear what isn't being said. In traditional terms, the monk is called to perceive 'what eye has not seen nor ear heard,' offering contemplative insights into spiritual ways of seeing and listening.

When I was on the late shift, before the last news bulletin of the day, I used to take a prayerful stroll around the large empty TV studio close to the radio suite. It seemed to possess all the wonder and mystery of a dark monastic church or a vast cathedral.

The great American contemplative and journalist Thomas Merton said that we find solitude not by fleeing from our own community but by finding God right in the heart of the community we're part of. In true prayer, every moment is a new discovery of a new silence — a penetration into the heart of eternity where all things are made new.

So, wherever we find ourselves this morning, we ask God to bless our silence and accompany us through the solitude of our own lives. Whatever this day yields, may we be open to discerning the presence of God in unexpected places. Amen.

BROADCAST FRIDAY 15 JANUARY 2009

January 16

Mark Coffey

A year ago I went along to a national Brittle Bone conference with my two-year-old nephew who suffers from that condition. He's going to have an uphill struggle in life to walk, and there are unique burdens and joys his mum and dad face. It was instructive to see this network of parents linked up by web forums and now sharing resources and addresses; to see an eleven-year-old demonstrate to my young nephew how his adapted wheelchair worked and then see his own delight in manoeuvring around a mini version. Yet the thing that I learned most clearly was not to be fearful of asking for help and not to disdain others who cannot cover up their neediness.

The American theologian Stanley Hauerwas writes that those with physical and mental disabilities are prophetic. And, as with the prophets of old, their wisdom makes us uneasy. Unable to conceal their neediness, those with disabilities remind us of the insecurity hidden in our own attempt to deny our reliance on others. We so often want our bodies, our thoughts, our worlds, to be under our control. Yet only in relinquishing our self-sufficiency can we experience the cooperation and love of others. The great tragedy of our desire to be independent and self-secure is, as Mother Teresa said, the modern disease of loneliness. And in the communities that grow around those with disabilities, something prophetic is said about humanity. We are creatures, not creators. We need God and we need one another to flourish.

Loving God, we lift up to You all who have disabilities — in hearing, in sight, in limb or in mind. We pray too for those who care for parents, partners, children. Meet their needs and grant them the strength to persevere with love and kindness. Amen.

BROADCAST WEDNESDAY 16 JANUARY 2008

January 17

Johnston McKay

On 17 January, probably in the year AD 356, St Antony of Egypt died. He was the first of a group who are called the 'desert fathers', because they lived far away from cities, out in the desert. Antony, who came from a well-off family, like many since, gave his inheritance away and at the age of 21 became a hermit. He lived, so they say, to the ripe old age of 105.

When the Roman Emperor Constantine, who had made Christianity the official religion of Rome, once sent a letter to Antony, asking him to pray for himself and his two sons, there was some astonishment that the Emperor should get in touch with a humble hermit. Antony replied that they should be more astonished that God had got in touch with all of us through his Son.

The former Archbishop of Canterbury Rowan Williams is a big fan of the desert fathers, and in a book of his about their faith I came across something St Antony said: 'Our life and death is with our neighbour. If we win our neighbour, we win God.' Rowan Williams says that none of us can find ourselves without the neighbour, not just because no man or woman is an island but because the way each of us sees things can get in the way if we try to impose that on someone else. Winning our neighbour and winning God isn't like winning an argument with our neighbour and someone loses. It's not about persuading our neighbour to think like us. It's about the reality that some of us call God being far more important than what we think we know about Him. Sometimes we need to let go of others for the sake of their freedom. We need much more to let ourselves go, so that we can then love our neighbour as ourselves.

Loving God, help us let go of ourselves so that You may speak through us to another. Amen.

BROADCAST MONDAY 17 JANUARY 2011

January 18

Kelvin Holdsworth

Today is the anniversary of the birth of AA Milne. That makes it the birthday of Winnie the Pooh as well.

Later on today, I'll be marking this as Winnie the Pooh Day. I'll pour myself a cup of tea and reach for a dusty and slightly battered copy of *The House at Pooh Corner*. The pages are yellowing now and some are in danger of dropping out and scattering all over the floor. Those, of course, are the best-loved pages – the ones I'll want to read most. Pages that remind me that tiggers don't climb trees and that breakfast is best if it begins and ends with a honey pot.

I'll also cast a glance in the direction of my own bear. He too is looking slightly battered by the passage of time. But there he sits on a high shelf and looks down at me on many a day when I forget that he is there.

It is a strange custom, making models of bears and giving them to children for comfort – the wildest and most dangerous animals of the forest given in love. They provide comfort and security and offer small hands something to grasp hold of. All the best bears are given with love, tenderness and delight. Gifts given like that remind us of all that is good about being human.

If Pooh and Piglet, Eeyore and Kanga and all the rest remind us of that, then Pooh Bear's birthday is definitely worth celebrating.

Somewhere in an 'enchanted place on the top of the Forest a little boy and his Bear will always be playing'. And in some enchanted place deep within us, we all need to know that we are already loved.

Loving God,
Hold us and comfort us through all that this day brings.
Help us to find enchanted places
And people to love.
Amen.

BROADCAST MONDAY 18 JANUARY 2010

January 19

Calvin Samuel

What does God require of us? This is not an open-ended question. One well-known response drawn from the Old Testament Book of Micah, chapter 6, verse 8, is this: to do justice, to love kindness and to walk humbly with God.

Walking humbly with God, I suggest, is a critical element in the pursuit of unity. Yesterday marked the beginning of the Week of Prayer for Christian Unity. Traditionally, it takes place within the octave of Saints Peter and Paul, the eight days from 18 to 25 January.

Unity, of course, should not be confused with uniformity. Indeed, it is primarily in the absence of uniformity, when confronted by diversity, that unity is most needed.

In the Durham context where I live and work, unity in diversity is a daily and ongoing challenge. I lead Wesley Study Centre, a Methodist Theological College, which is situated in premises shared with Cranmer Hall, an Anglican Theological College. Our students include Methodists and Anglicans, as well as Roman Catholics, Baptists, Pentecostals, Salvationists and Congregationalists, to name but a few. One or two students from non-Christian faith traditions enrich some of our postgraduate courses.

What does it mean to be in unity with those with whom we do not necessarily agree, whilst remaining true to our convictions? That is the million-dollar question. This is, of course, a question that is of relevance not merely to Christians. It is a question with which many parts of our world are concerned.

What seems clear to me is that without costly conversation shaped by humility, unity will remain but an elusive goal.

Merciful God, forgive us when we fail to listen,
Challenge us to engage in costly conversations,
And lead us into justice and peace. Amen.

BROADCAST SATURDAY 19 JANUARY 2013

January 20

Johnston McKay

It's said that everyone who is old enough can remember where they were when they heard that President John Kennedy had been assassinated. I don't know whether it's just as true that they can remember where they were when they heard the ringing rhetoric of his Inaugural Address, on this day in 1961 – 'And so, my fellow Americans: ask not what your country can do for you; ask what you can do for your country.'

Our family had just got a TV set, and I was a university student, and I was captivated by the idealism and stirred by the rhetoric and hopeful for the future. And so I watched that inaugural address in our basement kitchen with my father. Every time I enthused, he told me he had heard it all before. Every time I waxed lyrical about John Kennedy, he told me he had been just the same about Franklin Roosevelt in the 1930s.

I remember that at the time I was angry at what I thought was his cynicism. Now I realize it wasn't cynicism at all. It was something much healthier. It was scepticism. John Kennedy once said that all politicians have to choose between the inherited blunders of Adam and Eve. In other words, the choices our leaders have to make are seldom between black and white but between various shades of grey. Which is why political rhetoric always dissolves when it has to be steeped in practical decisions.

But I'd rather live in a world where idealism finds itself crucified by reality than one where reality is never tested against the vulnerability of idealism. A poet once said, 'I have spread my dreams under your feet; / Tread softly because you tread on my dreams.' That January day in 1961, John Kennedy couldn't have known how many dreams he had spread.

Loving God, show us that a dreamer can be killed, but not the dream, when it is Yours too. Amen.

BROADCAST THURSDAY 20 JANUARY 2011

January 21

Richard Frazer

Not long ago I was given some time off and I walked 1,000 miles through France and Spain to Santiago de Compostela, that great destination for pilgrims in the northwest of Spain.

I am now convinced that pilgrimage is the best metaphor we have for the spiritual life. That's maybe why nearly every religious tradition uses pilgrimage in some form.

You travel light as a pilgrim; and it reminds you of just how much unnecessary clutter we accumulate in our lives.

You anticipate gifts from strangers, who, if you are open and welcoming, will offer you hospitality and friendship that is quite inspiring; and it reminds you of just how cautious, guarded and narrowly closed off our lives can often be at home.

You take care of your feet and attend to your physical well-being on a pilgrimage because you know you'll never make it to the end if you don't; and it reminds you of how often we overdo it in life, not really paying heed to what it might take to stay the course.

I could go on listing the lessons I learned on that pilgrimage, but my friend the poet Jay Ramsay put it well when he said that 'those who have more on the inside need less on the outside'.

Amen to that.

Dear God, our bread sharer and companion on the many journeys we make through life, walk with us through this day and all our coming days and remind us what is really important, for we so readily forget. Help us to rethink what we need, to cherish friendship and to care more thoughtfully for ourselves and others, and for the earth, for Jesus' sake. Amen.

BROADCAST TUESDAY 21 JANUARY 2014

January 22

Kelvin Holdsworth

Someone asked me the other day what is the first memory that I have. I was able to tell them and to date it exactly. I'm a child of the time of the space race, and my first memory is of being taken outside on a dark night to look at the moon. 'Look,' I was told, 'there are people there.'

I was three years old and was probably more excited at staying up late and being taken outside into the mysterious darkness than I was at being told that there were men on the moon.

Today happens to be the anniversary of the launch of *Apollo 5* – the first time the lunar module was tested in space flight. It was just one part of the process that allowed human beings to reach for the moon and come back safely.

Exploration seems somehow to be built into our psychology. Most people probably want always to stay at home and live a quiet life in safety and security. But human life consistently seems to throw up adventurers in every generation who want to go where no one has gone before, see things that no one has seen before and experience things that no one has ever previously known.

Perhaps that means that there is also an inner adventurer in each of us. For even those of us who stay at home have new things to face with each day that dawns. As new challenges come our way, let us pray that we may accept them graciously, tackle them boldly and be kind to all we encounter on the pathways of our own adventures.

Guiding God, as this day unfolds, inspire us with fresh insights, challenge us with new experiences and reassure us that your love never changes. Amen.

BROADCAST FRIDAY 22 JANUARY 2010

January 23

Richard Frazer

The world is full of experts and we certainly need them, especially when it comes to dealing with our teeth! But I am getting increasingly doubtful about our solution-focused approach to every problem and challenge.

A friend once commented on a woman we both knew who was always rushing around doing good works and sorting other people's problems out. He said to me once, 'You can tell the victims of her kindness by their hunted look.'

That was a pretty harsh thing to say, but I have come to see that fixing other people's problems can be a very convenient way of ensuring that we avoid fixing ourselves. Also, it doesn't always follow that if you think you have a solution for someone's problem you are going to make a lot of difference by pointing out what you think they need to do.

A solution-focused approach can often fail to take account of the truth that it is sometimes our actions, our lifestyles and our lack of self-reflection that might have contributed to the problem in the first place.

We talk about the future health of the planet as though the remedy were a mere management challenge when, quite probably, the only way we can really make a difference is by radically rethinking our lifestyles.

There's a wonderful and very simple prayer that was attributed to a Chinese student: 'O Lord, transform the world, but begin with me.'

Loving God, we remember how easy it is to point out the speck in another's eye and fail to see the plank in our own. Give us the humility and self-awareness that enable us to see when we are part of the problem rather than the expert with the solution. In Jesus' name. Amen.

BROADCAST THURSDAY 23 JANUARY 2014

January 24

Edward Kessler

Sometimes our lives are darkened by the fear of ageing. By bleaching our hair, lifting our faces and dressing in fashionable clothes, we hope to stay young forever – to ward off the inevitability of death. We hope that by joking about Zimmer frames and care homes we will keep them at a distance. Worse, we treat the old without respect; we do not consider them to have a view, to be of relevance. They are a spent commodity. A burden.

There is one way to prevent the encroachment of death into the realm of life, and that is by truly living each day, by refusing to view ageing as equivalent to dying.

We can honour the old among us. Look at Moses and his brother, Aaron, who appear before Pharaoh to demand the freedom of the Israelites. In what looks like an unnecessary digression, the Book of Exodus records that 'Moses was 80 years old and Aaron was 83, when they made their demand on Pharaoh' (Exodus 7.7).

Why does the Bible reveal something so mundane as their ages? Because old age is a source of pride.

In the words of the Talmud, 'at 80 – the age of strength'. What is the strength of 80 years? Surely a teenager is stronger?

But the strength of 80 is the wisdom that comes from experience and completion. Having run much of the course of life, having seen the follies and passions of the human heart rise and subside, having seen their own and their friends' dreams fulfilled or disappointed, an adult of 80 years is finally able to look at the human condition with proper scepticism and compassion.

We pray that in old age God may plant us like cedars in the divine courtyard. Amen.

BROADCAST MONDAY 24 JANUARY 2011

January 25

Calvin Samuel

Many years ago I listened to the Bishop of Jerusalem speak movingly of the challenge of being a Palestinian Christian and of Israeli-Palestinian relations. He pointed out that for many, 'Palestinian Christian' seems an oxymoron.

Nonetheless, he reminded us that Arab Christianity can be traced to the pages of the New Testament. Careful readers of the Biblical Book of Acts discover in chapter 2 that on the first day of Pentecost when the disciples spoke in foreign tongues, among those who heard them declare the works of God in their native tongue were Arabs.

Some years later, I was listening to another bishop. Former Archbishop Desmond Tutu was speaking at King's College London. He spoke movingly of the challenge of being a South African Christian in the wake of apartheid and in the midst of the Truth and Reconciliation Commission.

Perhaps the most memorable part of the evening was Tutu's response to the question of why it was that he thought that South Africa had not descended into bloody civil war after the end of apartheid. Tutu's view was this: South Africa was probably the most prayed-for country in the world in the twenty years or so leading up to the end of apartheid. It is those prayers of God's people all over the world, Tutu argued, that made reconciliation conceivable.

It is that same conviction which lies behind the practice of observing this Octave of Prayer for Christian Unity. The prayers of God's people all over the world make reconciliation conceivable.

Generous God, who is more ready to listen than we are to ask
And whose promises exceed all that we can desire,
Teach us to be bold enough to pray for reconciliation in Your world.
Amen.

BROADCAST FRIDAY 25 JANUARY 2013

January 26

Leon Litvack

On this day in 1853 Charles Dickens wrote to the artist Clarkson Stanfield, to console his friend on the death of his son. He said, 'I am truly concerned to receive your mournful intelligence … I am sensible that it must be a shock to an affectionate heart like yours. I heartily sympathize with you, my dear friend, in resigning him to the mercy of God, in whom we all trust humbly, according to our several ways.'

I'm one of the editors of Dickens's letters, and in my study of such a vast and fascinating subject I'm struck by how Dickens had the capacity to conceive damning indictments of religious institutions and clergy, but could be deeply earnest and steadfast in his personal faith. He wished to communicate something of this to his children — particularly his sons, who, he felt, did not live up to his great expectations of them. When his youngest, Edward, was departing for Australia, Dickens wrote to him to say that, while he didn't wish to harass his family about 'religious observances, or mere formalities', he did beseech his dear boy 'Never [to] abandon the wholesome practice of saying your own private prayers, night and morning. I have never abandoned it myself, and I know the comfort of it.'

The words are quite striking, and speak to Dickens's sincerity about his personal faith. He added, 'The more we are in earnest as to feeling it, the less we are disposed to hold forth about it.'

Heavenly Father, as we think about the messages and examples we pass on, to our friends, our family, and to all those who touch our lives, may we do so with loving kindness and respect for one another, and a deep awareness of how much we owe to You. Amen.

BROADCAST THURSDAY 26 JANUARY 2012

January 27

Naftali Brawer

Growing up in Montreal in the 1970s, I encountered many holocaust survivors in our community. I once heard one of these men share a personal experience that will remain with me for the rest of my life.

He had been a starving fifteen-year old in Auschwitz in the depth of winter, harvesting sugar beets for his Nazi oppressors. He described the experience in vivid detail – the gnawing hunger, the threadbare pyjamas soaked through by the driving rain, the body lice swarming about and the near-total exhaustion. The cruel irony was that, despite the fact that the inmates were literally starving, they would have been shot on the spot for daring to take a bite out of a sugar beet.

Late one afternoon he threw caution to the wind and began slipping sugar beets into his pyjamas. Somehow he managed to slip his arms out of his pyjama sleeves and tie knots at the bottom of each sleeve. He then filled the sleeves with sugar beets. That night he managed to get back to his barrack undetected by the guards.

Later, when the lights were out, he unloaded his precious cargo and began making the rounds through the barracks, offering beets to his starving fellow inmates. He literally saved lives that night.

When I think of the inhumanity of the holocaust I can't help but think of this man. In a heroic act he chose to put others first. Through his story I have learned what we can be. Lower than an animal or loftier than an angel. Capable of unspeakable cruelty as well as the ultimate nobility.

Father in Heaven, on this Holocaust Memorial Day help us to think not only of its villains, but also of its heroes; the men and women who illuminated the darkest of nights and who restore our faith in humanity. Amen.

BROADCAST TUESDAY 27 JANUARY 2009

January 28

Mark Beach

There's a first time for everything, and this is my first Prayer for the Day, so Hello and Good Morning.

Doing things for the first time is a part of life: those first faltering steps to the admiring coos of parents and grandparents, the first time we fall in love and the first time we realize that we can no longer bend down to tie up our shoe laces. Well, I've had the first two but have not got quite as far as the last.

Many of us have watched as children, or young relatives, take their first steps through life. We watch very carefully knowing what will result if they choose a particular action but also knowing that we can't live their lives for them, they have to make up their own minds about what to do and what to say. Those of us who are parents will know how this pulls at our heart strings, but we just have to let them get on with it.

Maybe the coming week will bring a first time for you – a new job or even a new relationship. Go gently as you step out into the unknown, and may the adventure that is today bring you peace and happiness. Maybe it's a first step for somebody you love: bring them before God for his blessing.

Almighty God, help us to live to the full the adventure that today may bring. In familiar tasks may we have a freshness of vision; in the taking of first steps let us tread carefully but with courage. May we be guided in our footsteps by Jesus, Your Son, our Lord. Amen.

BROADCAST SATURDAY 28 JANUARY 2012

January 29

YY Rubinstein

In November I received a very exciting invitation to come and speak in Edmonton, Alberta, in the west of Canada. The fellow who called to invite me explained proudly that Edmonton is the most northerly city in North America. Somehow, I did not combine those two facts, 'Most northerly city in North America' and the month he wanted me to come, 'N-o-v-e-m-b-e-r'. It gets cold in the winter in Edmonton; very, very cold; as cold as -20 Centigrade! That's Siberia cold.

And research shows that cities in locations with few daylight hours and long dark winter nights have a very high incidence of alcoholism and depression.

Well, there is a Jewish festival that falls in the month of January, when days are short and grey and, as my Scottish Granny used to say, *dreich*, or wet and damp. The festival is called Tu B'Shevat, the fifteenth of the Hebrew month of Shevat, but it has another name: 'The new year of trees'.

Although you can't see it, January is the time of the year that sap begins to rise through what looks dead and barren wood to prepare a new season of growth. Only a few weeks later, buds and new life make themselves visible.

There have been times in my life that have caused me to feel cold and depressed, in my own *personal* Siberia; plans failed to materialize, promises made were not kept, trusted friends let me down. Sometimes winds have blown very cold indeed.

But not every failed plan or broken promise turned out badly in the end. That's why there should be a celebration for the new year of the trees. A message of encouragement is appropriate.

God, remind me of the promise in those branches when my own life grows cold and that a new beginning and warmer days may only be a short time away.

BROADCAST WEDNESDAY 29 JANUARY 2014

January 30

Naftali Brawer

The story is told about a man who joins one of the strictest monasteries. So strict is this monastery that the monks must take a vow of utter silence which can be broken only once every five years, and even then only two words may be spoken.

Five long years go by and our friend is brought before the Abbot to speak his two words. Without hesitation, he says 'food tasteless'.

Another five long years go by and again he is brought before the Abbot, and this time he says 'room cold'.

Another five years go by and again he stands before the Abbot, and on this occasion he says, 'bed hard'.

Upon hearing this, the Abbot, visibly upset, looks the monk square in the eye and says: 'The problem with you is that you haven't stopped complaining since you got here!'

The point of the story is that complaining is not so much about words but about attitude. It's an attitude that betrays so many other negative emotions, such as anxiety, self-pity, lack of confidence, despair.

Jewish wisdom goes a step further and teaches that not only can complaining *betray* other negative feelings but the act of complaining itself can actually *elicit* negativity. This is the idea behind the Yiddish adage, *tracht gut vet zein gut* — 'think positive and it will turn out positive.'

What might initially sound like a slightly cute aphorism has deep psychological roots. Life is never perfect and so much of how we experience it depends on our attitude. Positive thinking can actually change one's perspective of reality and one's life experiences.

Father in Heaven, may we find the strength and inspiration to see the world You made in a positive light. Today may we bring hope and happiness to all those around us. Amen.

BROADCAST FRIDAY 30 JANUARY 2009

January 31

Jonathan Wittenberg

Today is the last day of January. For many it's the hardest month. The days are short and night soon falls. The festivals are over and the long winter still lies ahead.

It's easy to forget how harsh these damp and often freezing winter months can be for many, especially if they are homeless or unwell.

If we're old, even getting out to the shops can be a problem and the dark evenings can be endlessly lonely.

Yet I also love late January and the start of February. The snowdrops come in clumps and clusters. They are humble flowers, simple and pure beneath the trees or in the hedgerows. Yet they are the harbingers of longer days and the richer scents of spring. Nearby, the shoots of early daffodils may already have pierced the soil. They should be wary: the snow may yet cover them for weeks.

If I could learn from a plant, I might choose the snowdrop for my role model. It blooms unafraid of the frost. It brings joy when the earth looks bleak. It heralds growth even while the old leaves still lie on the ground. It rejoices the heart and makes the spirit sing once again.

All this it does without fuss, without fancy or flamboyance.

I would like to be such a person who knows how to show the way to hope and warmth, who can lift the troubled heart.

I believe we all have such gifts within us, if only we are mindful of each other, and listen, and care.

God, where there is loneliness and fear, help us to bring confidence, companionship and joy.

BROADCAST THURSDAY 31 JANUARY 2013

February 1

Paul Clayton-Lea

Good morning. We rise today to the first hours of spring. In Ireland of ancient times this was a day dedicated to the goddess of fertility, but she has now been long since baptised St Brigid of Faughart, reputed to be the most formidable woman and evangelist of her age. It was written of her in the ancient Book of Armagh, 'Between Brigid and Patrick there was such a friendship of charity that they had but one heart and one mind.'

It's said of her determination to dedicate herself to her vocation of the single life in honour of Christ and her mission, that as a beautiful young woman for whom her father hoped to make an advantageous match, she vowed to remove one of her eyes and so ruin any possible marriage unless her father acquiesced to her pleading. Her single-minded purpose won the day. Perhaps Brigid's love of nature and God's creatures had revealed to her the strength of spirit that animates all living things to finally achieve their true purpose in life. Brigid's yearning often found expression in one of King David's psalms (Psalm 27.4):

> 'There is one thing I ask of the Lord,
>   for this I long;
> To dwell in the house of the Lord,
>   all the days of my life.
> To savour the sweetness of the Lord,
>   to behold His Temple.'

Lord, may I have the courage today,
To live the life that I would love.
To postpone my dream no longer,
But do at last what I came here for
And waste my heart on fear no more. Amen.

BROADCAST MONDAY 1 FEBRUARY 2010

February 2

Noel Battye

Candlemas is the quietest of the Church's festivals — one whose gentleness derives not just from the infant Jesus presented in the Temple, but also from its image of old age, as seen in Anna and Simeon who welcomed Him there.

Here is old age, not sans eyes, sans teeth, sans everything, bemoaning the losses of life, not filled with reactionary attitudes about the mistakes of a younger generation and the mess they are making of the world, but old age with all the dignity of experience. How very different from *our* world, which wants to be forever young and in control — a world that fears the ageing process and what the years can do to our bodies, and the implication that what happens to the wrinkling body must also happen to the soul or spirit, as it too grows withered, inflexible and unyielding to all ideas different from its own.

But there's none of that either in Simeon or Anna. Here is old age with maturity and warmth, a good vintage mellowed by the years and without a sell-by date, as Simeon welcomes, not a poverty-stricken family not quite conforming to what is expected, but a brand-new and very special life bringing hope, even into the very darkest corners of our world.

Lord, we thank You for Simeon, accepting the years and the consequence of living them,
Simeon, persevering in his prayers to the end, even though the answer was so long
  in coming.
Simeon, the good, devout believer, very much of his own tradition and yet the model
  for all religious faith.
Simeon, whose lifetime of prayer led him to understand that our Lord's vision for the
  world is far bigger and more generous than ours.
So for him and those like him today, we give You thanks, O Lord.
Amen.

BROADCAST SATURDAY 2 FEBRUARY 2013

February 3

—❦—

Sharon Grenham Toze

Good morning. The American writer Elbert Hubbard, who died in 1915, once wrote that 'a friend is someone who knows all about you and still loves you'.

I have known my best friend for almost 40 years, and during that time she and I have grown up, gone through most of the traumas and agonies of complicated adult lives, had children, laughed and cried, and only very occasionally disagreed. We don't see each other much, as we live some distance apart, but when we do get together, the passage of time seems to disappear.

Friends, or the lack of them, is often top of the list of things that are most important to us, alongside romantic partners, family and a satisfying job. Yet we tend to presume that friendships 'just happen'. In fact, psychologists suggest that friendships are every bit as nuanced as dating, and have a central requirement at the core. That's the need for 'self-disclosure'. In other words, we begin to develop a deep and lasting friendship as we gradually reveal the truth about ourselves, our lives, our hopes and dreams, as well as our failures and fears. Never an easy thing to do.

And whilst social media seem to encourage 'over-sharing', it can so easily lack real intimacy. It's probably no accident that many people of all ages report feeling lonelier than ever these days.

So God of love, we pray today for the opportunity to show real friendship to someone else — the giving of our time, our attention and our true selves to another. We're grateful for the friends we do have, and we bring our feelings of isolation and loneliness to You, who know exactly who we are, and love us just the same. Amen.

BROADCAST MONDAY 3 FEBRUARY 2014

February 4

Leslie Griffiths

I enjoy going out to restaurants — eating with friends is for me one of the greatest pleasures of life. I love the conversation, the opportunity to relax, and, of course, I enjoy the food. But there's a little more to it than that. I was raised in poverty and it was always a struggle for my mother to put food on the table at all. My only eating out was when I took my free dinners in the school canteen. I didn't eat meat at home until I was well into my teens.

And yet, how can I ever forget the Sunday teas of my childhood? We regularly invited a Mrs Reidy. She was a widow, gnarled, beaten down by life. I never discovered her claim on my mother's affection or the reason for the Sunday bash so lavishly prepared for her. She seemed to belong to several worlds we knew nothing about. But she always took pride of place: my mother sat her in our one posh chair. I've been in many a devout home where an empty chair is kept around the meal table with a sign on the wall proclaiming that Jesus is to be considered the unseen guest at the meal. In our home, Mrs Reidy, for all her visibility, took the place of Jesus. And those tea parties — with jelly, jam, tea and cake — had all the characteristics of the heavenly banquet we shall all one day enjoy.

Dear Lord, help us to see how it is in giving that we receive. Stir us today to share our love, to offer a smile, to bid people welcome and, in doing so, to know that we are blessed. Through Jesus Christ, our Lord. Amen.

BROADCAST SATURDAY 4 FEBRUARY 2012

February 5

Gemma Simmonds

On this day in 1953, sweet rationing came to an end in the United Kingdom. People crowded the shops and one firm in London gave 800 school children 150lb of lollipops. My nephew Tom, born 30 years after rationing, was nevertheless brought up to eat sweets on Sunday. As a wily four year old he got round this by persuading visitors, ignorant of this rule, to play a game called, 'Let's pretend it's Sunday', which then gave him licence to raid the sweety tin.

Most of us have cunning ways of getting what we want. But knowing what we really, really want can be a challenge. Many people believe that God's will generally works against our desires. But St Ignatius of Loyola taught that getting in touch with our heart's deepest desire is one of the best ways of discovering God's desires for us. The secret is to be able to tell the difference between wanting a quick sweetness fix for our lives and wanting the deep and lasting satisfaction that comes from co-operating with the God who can be known in the depth of our hearts.

George Bernard Shaw wrote: 'There are two tragedies in life. One is to lose your heart's desire. The other is to gain it.' But Jesus said, 'Ask and you shall receive, seek and you shall find, knock and the door will be opened.' God isn't a dispenser of childish goodies, but plants in human hearts a hunger for truth and a longing for love.

God of creation, You are the origin and end of all our deepest longings. Increase our desire for faith, hope and love and give us the courage and perseverance to ask and seek and knock. Amen.

BROADCAST SATURDAY 5 FEBRUARY 2011

February 6

Edward Mason

These are hard times for most people. Money has become very tight … hard times indeed.

Occasionally, I make a note of my bank balance, savings and how the mortgage is going. This tells me what I'm worth and, as with so many of us, it's a lot less than it used to be.

I once knew someone who counted his money differently, and his wisdom really helps me. He used to say, 'A pound when you need it is worth a hundred when you don't.' It's a very different attitude to wealth.

He and his wife were married in wartime. They had very little, and he used to tell stories about this, perhaps exaggerating somewhat – for example, how they began 'with only one cup between them'. The truth, though, was that they struggled to make ends meet, and I know he and his wife kept their first kitchen table to the end of their lives together. He learned then that to receive any kind of help at the right moment makes even a pound when you need it worth a hundred when you don't.

Although he wasn't particularly well off, for the rest of his life he used to give money away to his family and others – anyone who was trying to succeed in life and just needed a helping hand. If they protested at his generosity, out would come that favourite saying.

Helping other people in this way gave him great pleasure, because he knew it would make a real difference to someone's life. Perhaps, too, he knew that ancient proverb from the Bible, 'Generous hands are blessed hands.'

So, generous God, help me to realize the true worth of my money and make my hands generous hands today. Amen.

BROADCAST FRIDAY 6 FEBRUARY 2009

February 7

Noel Battye

How do you know when you're growing old?

Is it when you go to a cupboard to find something, only to ask yourself, Why have I come here?

Is it when youngsters whizz past you in technology, whereas you've only got as far as texting and email?

Is it when the young fellow at the check-out tells you that very soon he's having a week off work to prepare for his wedding in June? 'And have you got your house yet?' I ask. 'Of course!' he beams, 'And we've got a couple of kids as well!' He was so pleased with things, one could only rejoice with him.

The world is changing all around us and I suppose the question raised is, when do you hold on to old standards and when do you let them go?

When a radio presenter, for example, announces that 'he is sat' or 'he is stood', do you write in on behalf of the English language? Well, maybe so if you're feeling grumpy!

But when a family member forms a partnership about which you have strong reservations, do you speak up? Or do you remain silent because you know it's now too late for that?

Is your desire to protect a purely selfish thing based on a rule-book of your own? Or maybe on other people's perceptions of the family? Would your greatest witness be to go on listening while surrounding them with an endless stream of love and silent prayers? As one who has been a pastor for over 40 years, experience tells me that the last of these works best.

Lord, we thank You for the hope and vision of each rising generation.
And we ask You to bless and guide those whom we remember now before You.
And bind us all together in the circle of Your love.
In Jesus' name. Amen.

BROADCAST THURSDAY 7 FEBRUARY 2013

February 8

※

Mark Coffey

I've recently read a bestselling graphic novel about the life of the philosopher and mathematician Bertrand Russell. Russell was convinced that intelligence could save mankind from itself. One quote attributed to Russell intrigues me especially. It's his observation that, 'So far as I can remember, there is not one word in the Gospels in praise of intelligence.' He's right. Yet as Russell himself readily acknowledged, his hope that reason and logic could help us to behave decently was proven repeatedly in his life to be ill-founded.

The support of academics for the First World War caused him, he wrote, 'to revise [his] views of human nature ... I had supposed that intellectuals frequently loved truth, but I found that not 10 per cent of them prefer truth to popularity.' In his love life, too, Russell was to discover how unreasonable and contradictory he himself could be. When he began a second marriage, to Dora Black, he insisted on a policy of openness regarding sexual partners. Yet when Dora had two children by extra-marital relationships, Russell reflected in his autobiography, 'I found my capacity for forgiveness and what might be called Christian love was not equal to the demands I was making on it. Anyone else could have told me this in advance, but I was blinded by theory.'

I suspect if Jesus were to reply to Russell's criticism that he had little praise for human intelligence, he would once more call upon the simplicity of a child, as he did with his disciples – perhaps suggesting that our greatest obstacle to peace, progress and true wisdom may have more to do with that most ungovernable human condition, pride.

Lord God, help us to grow in both intelligence and humility so as to learn from our mistakes. Amen.

BROADCAST MONDAY 8 FEBRUARY 2010

February 9

Paul Mathole

In a world of ever-accelerating technology, we live in an age of instant opinions
– whether posting comments on blogs or on social networking sites. What
can sometimes seem absent is any sense of mediation within the hubbub of
divergent views. We might think of this as an exclusively modern problem.

John Newton, Christian minister and hymn writer, lived over 200 years
ago, yet was sensitive to the same issue. He writes to a friend about 'engaging
in controversy'. Newton says that putting something in print, you will be met
with three types of response. Those who disagree in principle; those who will
readily approve what you say; and a third category who may or may not be
persuaded but will be influenced by the 'writer's spirit' – the tone and intention
you appear to have in making your point. And so Christians, he writes, 'of
all people who engage in controversy … are most expressly bound by our own
principles to the exercise of gentleness and moderation'.

What is most striking is how he ends. His greatest concern is reserved for the
person who steps into any controversy. He finds there are 'very few writers of
controversy who have not been manifestly hurt by it', whether by pride, an angry
spirit or by no longer seeing what is of primary importance in life. 'What will it
profit a man if he gains his cause and silences his adversary, if at the same time
he loses that humble tender frame of spirit in which the Lord delights?' He
concludes: you will need to watch and pray.

*Lord God, give us a gentle and humble spirit in our engagement with others. Help us to
be quick to listen and slow to speak. Give us the grace to live out a spirit of gentleness and
moderation. Amen.*

BROADCAST SATURDAY 9 FEBRUARY 2013

February 10

Andrea Rea

I have a significant birthday coming up, and I've started to mention it to people as if in the perverse hope that it might just go away. I can't really say that I dread the day itself, but I'm not at all happy about being that age for the rest of the year. I'd quite like to try it on for a day or so, and then go back to being ... well, the age I am now, I suppose. It's not possible, of course, to stop time passing or for that matter to change the speed with which it passes, though I'm told by dear friends and family that time passes more quickly as you get older. Lovely. I'm not only getting older, the time I have left is going faster than before. And me with so much to do.

I'm reminded of an old saying by Henry van Dyke, an American author and clergyman: 'Time is Too slow for those who wait, Too swift for those who fear, Too long for those who grieve, Too short for those who rejoice, But for those who love Time is not.'

He can't possibly have written that just for me, and yet I know exactly what he means. As I suspect we all do. We've all had our share of waiting, and grief, and fear and (I hope) rejoicing. But van Dyke saved the best for last.

Lord of love, help us to know that it is in our loving that the best of our time is spent, with friends, with family, with anyone who loves us, and anyone we love in return. Help us to find time for them and for ourselves, so that even if time passes more quickly with every year, we can make the most of those moments of loving when time really doesn't matter. Amen.

BROADCAST TUESDAY 10 FEBRUARY 2009

February 11

Paul Mathole

It was on this day in 1990 that Nelson Mandela was freed after 27 years of captivity in South Africa. From captivity he would rise to become president of his country.

Nelson Mandela's story fits the rich tradition of 'narratives of ascent' – from the earliest slave narratives to the autobiographies of leading civil rights activists and leaders. The narrator frequently begins in a state of deprivation. Many obstacles are overcome. Freedom and dignity are established. And through self-discovery the protagonist is able to go out and make their mark on the world.

In the same month that Mandela was freed, in a different part of the world, a literary agent in New York made contact with a young black man to suggest he write a book. That man was Barack Obama. The book would become *Dreams from My Father*. Obama, too, understands himself through his own narrative of ascent. In words recorded by one biographer, 'He thought enough of himself and his story that he thought to write his autobiography at the age of thirty ... He knew his story was special.'

President Obama is now established in his second term of office as the first black President of the United States. He is a man who sees himself as walking in the footsteps of many great men who came before him. In fact, during his period of political rise, Obama had kept pictures of his heroes on the wall of his office. Martin Luther King, Jr, at a microphone. Gandhi. A war-weary President Lincoln. And also one of Nelson Mandela, reclining in a gold armchair, his cane at his side.

Lord God, our lives can sometimes seem a struggle, subject to circumstances seemingly beyond our control. Give us a sense of your purpose for our lives, the dignity You have given us and the good works You have prepared for us to do in Your name. Amen.

BROADCAST MONDAY 11 FEBRUARY 2013

February 12

Andrea Rea

I think it would be safe to say that I'm not always a morning person. When the alarm goes, I know that I've set it to give me at least 20 or 30 minutes to stay in bed, before getting up and starting the day. And even if I have a very early start, to catch a flight or make an early deadline, that period of grace is a constant. It gives me a chance to think about the day, breathe deeply and also to say a quick prayer of thanks for the night that's passed and the day to come.

There's something quite luxurious about taking those few minutes to 'put my inner house in order', and it makes it easier to get up and get going when the time comes — a vital buffer zone between me and the rest of life, work and responsibility. I often wish, however, that I could take the feeling of those minutes with me into the day a little more. I know that I get impatient sometimes and allow the stresses of everyday situations to take over, and I'm not always as calm and centred as I'd like to be. It's easy to get annoyed at small things, to overreact and cause even more stress for myself and others. Remembering the feeling of those quiet moments before rising in the morning might just help me to step back a bit from those everyday hassles and give me the presence of mind to wait before reacting, to stop and think, and avoid a conflict in myself and with other people.

God of silence and calm, help me to carry the peace of that early morning time of grace with me into the day. Remind me of the deep breath and the small prayer that brings me peacefully from night to morning and let it stay with me as morning becomes afternoon, and evening brings me toward another night. Amen.

BROADCAST THURSDAY 12 FEBRUARY 2009

February 13

Peter Whittaker

I had a long wait in Belfast City Airport before my plane bringing me back to Yorkshire was due. I watched, fascinated, as the departure lounge filled and emptied, a succession of flights leaving for most of the British airports I knew and some I didn't. What were all those journeys for? Having travelled, would these folk have achieved their purpose? Were people enjoying the journey or just doing what was needed to get it over with?

Many travellers spent their waiting time on laptop or tablet computers and, of course, mobile phones. They were waiting to journey, but already somewhere else in their minds. Even those talking to each other seemed to be electronically connected across the tables of the coffee shop. I saw waves of people, coming and going on journeys electronically and physically. I sincerely hope they all reached journey's end with some sense of satisfaction. I certainly enjoyed watching them, and my flight and onward journey home was smooth and on time!

Many of us will travel today, some of us along familiar routes at set times, already knowing the risks of congestion, late running and other travellers' frustrations; others of us going to places we don't know through unfamiliar surroundings. Of course, any of us could meet challenging moments that will test our resolve. Some of us will make journeys long anticipated. Some of us will make journeys reluctantly because of what awaits us. But, hopefully, we'll all arrive safely at journey's end and be satisfied with the effort we've made.

God of travellers, accompany us on all our journeys today. May the way be smooth and the arrival swift and may we enjoy the company of those with whom we travel, those we meet on the way and the people we encounter at journey's end. Amen.

BROADCAST MONDAY 13 FEBRUARY 2012

February 14

Anna Magnusson

When we were young, our mum used to send us each a Valentine's card – at the age when it mattered deeply if you didn't get one from a mysterious admirer – in a red envelope, with the letters S.W.A.L.K. written on the back. I remember she sent me and my sisters one each for a couple of years maybe, with a cheerful 'Love from Mum' and a row of kisses inside.

I was, of course, bitterly disappointed that it was from Mum, as well as secretly comforted by what I already knew – that she loved me. But at that age, it's the romance of being loved from afar that is exciting; it's the thrill of being a distant object of longing – that's what matters when you're thirteen and it's Valentine's Day.

Then you fall in love. And then fall out of love. And you get older and, maybe, fall in love in a different way and find the person you want to be with. And that's when, it seems to me, love becomes much more interesting, as time goes by. It's like a slim, smooth tree that grows thicker and tougher through the years, beaten by rain and wind. It gets bent and broken in places, all gnarled and lumpy. It's messy and beautiful, bare and ugly in winter, and then green and glorious again when the light returns.

St Paul's words about love have been recited in a million marriage ceremonies, and they've lasted because, for all their poetry, they're about the reality of how hard it can be to love, and what demands it makes on us. Not in a depressing, joyless way – but in a kind of magnificent, extravagant act of faith that, whatever happens in life, somehow love 'bears all things, believes all things, hopes all things, endures all things.' Amen.

For those who reach and miss, may they find their path again; when we dream and are brave enough to put ourselves to the test – may God guide us on our way. Amen.

BROADCAST MONDAY 14 FEBRUARY 2011

February 15

Gemma Simmonds

On this day in 1971 the British Government launched the new decimal currency across the country. While many shops ran dual pricing to help bewildered customers, there were concerns that the new currency would be rejected on public transport. More urgent worries focused on the continued spending of old-fashioned pennies in public lavatories. But in the end people got used to the change and even those of us who do remember thruppences and farthings, ten shilling notes, guineas and half crowns do so with a far-off nostalgia disconnected from present economic reality.

A character in an Oscar Wilde play famously says that a cynic is someone who knows the price of everything and the value of nothing. He went on to say that a sentimentalist is someone 'who sees an absurd value in everything, and doesn't know the market price of any single thing'. We live in a society where everything seems to come with a price tag. News reports often comment on the price of a house where some crime or tragedy has occurred, as if that in itself made the events better or worse to deal with. We hear about the price of a celebrity's shoes or hairdo or car, rather than about the value of their work, or the personal price they pay for doing it. Learning the true value of what is precious in life isn't about putting a price tag on it, but rather about measuring the connection between giver and receiver, and learning how to be grateful for all we've received.

God, our Creator, You are the giver of life and the gift itself. Teach us to value all that is precious in what You have made, and give us hearts that are always thankful. Amen.

BROADCAST SATURDAY 15 FEBRUARY 2014

February 16

Tina Beattie

We know very little about the Greek philosopher Socrates, apart from his central role in the writings of his student, Plato. Socrates died on or around this day, in 399 BC. He was condemned to death by the Athenian authorities, for corrupting the youth of Athens and for failing to worship the Greek gods.

There's always a conflict between those who equate goodness with religious and social conformity, and those who recognize that goodness is potentially subversive, because it's a restless quest for wisdom that refuses to be silenced by the platitudes of political and religious authorities. Today, politicians and preachers still often speak as if the primary task of educators is to produce docile and compliant citizens and believers.

But good teachers encourage their students to challenge and to question, and to cultivate a love of wisdom for its own sake. Wisdom is not about the answers we offer but about learning to ask the right questions, and this involves letting go of our certainties and dogmas. The Hebrew Bible tells us that God's wisdom is a playful spirit among us. The twentieth-century monk Thomas Merton wrote that God plays in the garden of creation, and if we could let go of our obsession with the meaning of it all, we might be able to follow in that mysterious cosmic dance.

Let's lighten up then, and let's go out and play in the world today. Like little children, let's ask 'why?' and 'why?' again, and refuse to settle for that weary adult answer, 'just because'. It's in the joy of questioning that we discover the subversive wisdom of what it means to be fully alive.

Lord, on this new day, help us to be alive to the world, and to discover the playful spirit of wisdom among us. Amen.

BROADCAST MONDAY 16 FEBRUARY 2009

February 17

Anna Magnusson

In the middle of winter, Iceland can be a very dark place indeed. It's bad enough in Britain, waiting for the light to edge back, minute by minute; but in Iceland it's darker for much longer — which is why they cheer things up by celebrating the feast of Thorrablot.

In the Old Icelandic calendar, Thorri was the fourth month of winter, which stretched from mid-January to mid-February. Students started holding these feasts of poetry and song in the nineteenth century, and they survived as celebrations of the traditional Icelandic food which kept people going in the leanest and hardest times. When a precious animal was slaughtered, every single bit of it was used, to be salted, stored, dried or pickled, and food such as sheep's head, blood pudding and dried shark meat were valued for survival.

Celebrating the food that kept your ancestors alive in the centuries of cold and scarcity is a powerful affirmation. It's really celebrating life, and sharing a meal is a potent symbol for renewal. It's at the heart of the story in John's Gospel, one of the times when Jesus appears after the Resurrection. In the grey of dawn, on the shore of Lake Galilee, he sits by a fire cooking fish and breaking bread for the disciples; he gives them food, he talks to them, and they're comforted. They're back in the place where he first called them, and they have to start all over again. Somehow, in the poetry of John's story of the fire and the fish and the bread, it feels ... possible.

For the company of friends, for food on the table, for the renewal that comes from both; for the blessings of life, God, thank You. Amen.

BROADCAST THURSDAY 17 FEBRUARY 2011

February 18

Johnston McKay

For 'Sunday Worship' from St Salvator's Chapel in St Andrews in November, I was looking for a quotation from JM Barrie, who was once Rector of St Andrews University. He once described exactly what happens when you force open a jammed drawer. 'If you are searching for anything in particular you won't find it, but something falls out at the back that is more interesting.' Well, my experience of looking for something JM Barrie wrote partly proved the opposite: I did find what I was looking for but that set me searching for other things Barrie wrote.

'The life of everyone' (he actually wrote 'every *man*' but let's not be exclusive!) 'is a diary in which they mean to write one story, but write another; and the humblest hour is when you compare the volume as it is with what you vowed to make it.' I think that is unnecessarily harsh, because very often experiences force us to alter course. (I have a friend who says, 'When circumstances change, I change my mind: what do you do?')

Often experience takes us on a journey that involves dropping off a lot of the ambitious baggage we carried in favour of a more realistic load; so I've never thought of this season of Lent as a time to give things up. Rather, I like to think of Lent as an opportunity to think realistically about what we would be better off without; wiser, stronger, more positive by ditching.

Which is why I have always found the idea that Christian faith was about abundant life and not debilitating negativity much more appealing. A former teacher of mine used to be scathing about those he described as 'wanting to be far holier than God'. I know what he meant.

Loving God, give us garlands for ashes, and the oil of gladness instead of the spirit of meanness. Amen.

BROADCAST MONDAY 18 FEBRUARY 2013

February 19

✿

Gemma Simmonds

I'm a terrible loser. I find it impossible to keep track of my possessions, spending hours searching for things I've put down, only to forget where. If all the umbrellas, gloves and other lost items of my lifetime were gathered together, I suspect there'd be enough to fill an entire left luggage office.

My family and friends are very patient, often helping me in the search, or at least promising to pray to whichever patron saint they favour as the finder of things that stay resolutely hidden until they appear down the back of the sofa or under the car seat. St Anthony, finder of lost objects, heads the list for most of them, but some prefer St Rita, patron saint of impossible causes.

The distress of losing things and wasting time searching can be very real, and the relief of finding them is a special kind of joy. Perhaps someone in Jesus' family circle was a bad loser like me. He certainly was vividly aware of the distress and the joy that come from losing and finding. He illustrated his teaching on God's attitude to sinners and on the kingdom of God through the metaphor of shepherds searching for lost sheep, merchants searching for fine pearls, women ransacking their houses for lost money and someone discovering hidden treasure. The punch line of his stories is always the joy of finding, the willingness to make sacrifices to recover what's lost. We are God's treasure, God's pearl of great price, and God is willing to pay anything to get us back. This speaks volumes for how precious we are in God's sight, even when we fail.

Loving God, may we never lose confidence in Your love and always remember how much You long for us to turn to You. Amen.

BROADCAST WEDNESDAY 19 FEBRUARY 2014

February 20

John Armes

I received a wine warmer for Christmas. It's February now and, I have to admit, I have yet to take it from its box. I feel very ungrateful.

But perhaps you don't know what a wine warmer is? It's a jacket you put round your bottle of red wine, and once activated it warms the liquid to the ideal temperature. Sounds good, doesn't it? I thought so too until I read the small print. Apparently, once the jacket is used, you have to immerse it in boiling water for 20 minutes before it can be used again. In other words, here is a labour-saving device that actually requires more, not less effort to operate – rather like Fred Flintstone's car that moves by leg power rather than engine power. So far I've always managed to warm wine quite successfully by leaving it standing in the kitchen – boiling water plays no part in the process at all.

The wine warmer comes with another interesting device – an electronic wine breather. Wow! Simply insert three batteries (not provided) and switch the thing on and it 'gently bubbles' air through your wine bottle, so releasing all the hidden flavours. Perhaps next year I'll be given a device to drink the wine for me – and then comment eloquently on the experience.

Sometimes, just sometimes, do you wonder whether technology has gone too far?

I enjoy gadgets as much as the next man, but I'm sure the next man, like me, also prefers to sit back and take his refreshment without first boiling a wine warmer and rushing out to the shops for three batteries. Or, to put it another way, when you're chilling out, who needs a wine warmer?

Lord God, may we learn where technology does and where it doesn't enrich our lives. Help us to enjoy simply the simple things. Amen.

BROADCAST WEDNESDAY 20 FEBRUARY 2008

February 21

Sharon Grenham Toze

My son's just recently finished a round of interviews for entry to university this coming autumn. No doubt, like thousands of others, he found it quite a struggle to try to sum up his inner complexity for a panel of strangers.

The pressure on these would-be students is enormous, of course. Many of them, my lad included, are worried that if they don't get in this year, the potential level of fees after that will be too much for them. Then there's the anxiety about jobs coming from the ever-beleaguered economy. Add to that people of my generation telling teenagers it was much harder years ago, so what are they complaining about, and it's little wonder all they want to do is immerse themselves in Facebook and the like.

The writer of the Book of Proverbs in the Bible refers to wisdom as 'more precious than jewels' with an 'income better than silver, and her revenue better than gold'. I think there's something very important in that for us to remember. Of course, gaining knowledge and experience and insight is the route to employment, and through that to a productive, useful life. But the value of knowledge and discovery is so much greater than the ability to secure a place on a graduate training scheme. The fear of unemployment, or the desire for earning power, may well drive our young people, but what will it teach them about the value they, and others, have in the world?

So I tried to reassure my son — he had a whole lifetime of learning and potential opportunity ahead of him, and the next few years should be a time of discovery, and real joy in himself and those around him.

Lord of all Wisdom, may all our years bring us chances to discover, to grow and to rejoice in the world around us. Bless our young people especially as they face an uncertain future, and may we who are older encourage and reassure them. Amen.

BROADCAST MONDAY 21 FEBRUARY 2011

February 22

Tony Rogers

A feel-good film of the 90s was *Groundhog Day* – about a selfish man who lived the same day over and over again until he got things right. In the process came a transformation from selfishness to love. But life isn't like that – we don't have an action replay each day to help us correct our mistakes. Every moment is unique and unrepeatable.

Another movie from the same era was called *My Life*. It was the story of a man diagnosed with a terminal illness. His wife was expecting their first baby but he was going to die before the child was born, so he set about keeping a video diary that could be left for the child who would grow up with some picture of the dad he or she never knew. It was a great idea, but the reality turned out rather differently. As he viewed the diary, he became aware of all sorts of shortcomings – resentments, long-standing feuds, unresolved business, broken relationships. Naturally, he didn't like what he saw, but it was cathartic. By facing those things, he was able to deal with the problems and die at peace with himself and others. This was *Groundhog Day* rooted in reality.

Lent is a time for resolving to do better. Self-denial, tough as it may be, is a way of slowly coming to terms with the fact that we don't have to be enslaved to long-established practices. The extra chocolate bar isn't essential. So, if we can be trusted to succeed in small things, then other, more central aspects of our living can also come good.

Lord, inflame our hearts with the Spirit of Your love,
That our thoughts may be worthy of You
And that we may love You without reserve in our brothers and sisters.
Amen.

BROADCAST THURSDAY 22 FEBRUARY 2007

February 23

Gemma Simmonds

The poet Don Marquis had a character, Archy the cockroach, who is a natural philosopher. In the poem entitled 'The Moth', Archy reflects on the folly of a moth who is so attracted to light that he ends up burning himself in a light source. When Archy questions the sense of this suicidal attraction, the moth replies that he would rather live a short life of passionate beauty than a long one of boring sameness.

When the moth immolates himself on the bright blaze of a cigar lighter, Archy muses that he would rather settle for half the happiness and twice the longevity; but, he says 'at the same time I wish / there was something I wanted / as badly as he wanted to fry himself.'

St Augustine of Hippo might be called the patron saint of desire. After all, he once wrote a prayer, 'Lord, give me chastity, but not yet.' He taught that being in touch with our deepest desires can lead us to the God who is the ultimate goal of all true desire. Archy the cockroach reflects that passionate desires can lead us into danger, but a life lived without passion is hardly worth living. It must be true passion, the longing for life's deepest potential, rather than pointless craving for trivialities. Perhaps the secret is to find deep joy and satisfaction in the quiet quality of living, as well as in the intense moments, embracing what one writer has called the 'Sacrament of the Present Moment'.

God of all moments, both the quiet and the passionate, teach us to seek and find You at the heart of all our desires, especially in each present moment, since You are the end of all our longing. Amen.

BROADCAST TUESDAY 23 FEBRUARY 2010

February 24

Anna Magnusson

We were sifting through piles of family papers last week: house documents from 50 years ago; TV licences from the 70s; beautifully printed rates bills; long, polite letters between my dad and the bank manager; stacks of old newspaper cuttings; bulging brown envelopes of old photographs; and dusty old cassette tapes that turned out to be recordings my father had made of tutorials with a young IT guy who was showing him – in exhaustive detail – how to use his computer. First, switch on...

Of course, we spent far more time reading things aloud to each other than throwing them out – far more time remembering and re-living, than casting away. There were endless cups of tea, and papers and files and boxes all over the floor; hours spent poring over the documents, and smiling at the photographs; touching the precious things that belonged to the people who've gone, and hearing their younger, unfamiliar voices in the letters they wrote to each other long before we were even born.

We all had dusty, dirty hands by the time we'd finished, but that was at the heart of it: it was the physicality of these old things that was both comforting and sad – holding bits of paper that were 50 years old; touching the ink on a page written by someone long gone; or turning the stiff, cracking pages of old photograph albums where the years are stamped not just on the young faces that are now old, but on the faded colour and curling edges of the photos themselves. There's a deep, powerful need to hold and touch the objects that have outlived the people we love; they hold time, and mark precious lives.

God holds our lives, and those dear to us. May we always have people to cherish and care for, to love and remember. Amen.

BROADCAST FRIDAY 24 FEBRUARY 2012

February 25

Bob Fyffe

Christopher Wren, the architect of St Paul's Cathedral, died on this day in 1723. He never lived to see the completion of his masterpiece, and I suppose that perhaps we would all like to leave some mark on this Earth that says we were here. And yet very few of us can be builders of cathedrals, or great composers, or famous actors.

In his recent letter on Evangelism, Pope Francis talks about Christians whose lives seem like Lent without Easter. He recognizes that we have different ways of expressing joy, but that it always endures. But of course life is never full of joy, since we have to manoeuvre our way around suffering and the inevitable difficulties that life throws at us. And yet, even in the worst situations, though it can sometimes seem very difficult, I believe it's still possible to have a sense of wonder and stillness that goes beyond simply being happy, to something that is much deeper. To maintain that kind of faith in God demands something very profound, which cannot easily be expressed in words. To have a faith that still says 'yes' when life has thrown all it can at you is really to turn worldly wisdom on its head. So today we should give thanks for the millions of people who leave their mark on this world because they refuse to be beaten down and demoralized. To give thanks for the joy that fills so many people.

O God, we thank You for the joy of another day
And for our part in it.
Help us to see You in all things
And to welcome You and the stranger
That together we may share the joy of faith in You
And we thank You for a day well lived.
Amen.

BROADCAST TUESDAY 25 FEBRUARY 2014

February 26

Gemma Simmonds

On this day in 1987 the Church of England's General Synod took a vote that eventually would clear the way for the ordination of women priests. For some this was a great breakthrough, for others a devastating error. In every respect it shifted a major boundary within our culture. Many issues in history have prompted arguments to be used from theology, science or the law to defend positions that later change and are accepted without question.

It can be hard for us to think outside the cultural boundaries of our time, but easy to make judgements about the limited vision of an earlier age. We look back now at issues such as slavery or child labour and can't imagine how so many otherwise reasonable and civilized people accepted them without question. Yet what might there be in our society today that we find quite normal and tolerable but that future generations will judge unforgivable and beyond understanding? There have been many ideas within society that seemed set in stone, yet have evolved into something quite different. The great challenge is to be open in mind and heart to new possibilities. If we are used to seeing something only from one perspective, it can seem impossible to get it into any other focus. But all the greatest innovators in history have begun by seeing things from a new angle which leads them to imagine different possibilities. John Henry Newman wrote, 'To live is to change, and to be perfect is to have changed often.' Change isn't canonized for its own sake but an open mind and heart are gifts worth praying for.

God of our present, past and future, help us to uphold the truth, but always to be open to new possibilities. Amen.

BROADCAST FRIDAY 26 FEBRUARY 2010

February 27

Mary Stallard

The start of the day is usually a scramble for me, as I get myself and my family ready for all our various activities. I've often been proud of my ability to multi-task. I'm proficient at organizing breakfast whilst finding stray bits of school uniform, checking homework, writing notes to teachers and finishing my own chores. I sometimes notice with bemused frustration the less energetic but more focused progress of my partner who carefully gets himself prepared for the day and sits at the table waiting for the children to make themselves ready to leave. I've often thought that my husband really depends upon all that I do, but recently, when work took me away for a few days, the family coped annoyingly well without me.

Perhaps we're a little like the household of Martha and Mary, two sisters who were friends of Jesus. One was so keen to welcome Jesus as a guest in her house that she rushed around doing tasks for him and became worn out, whilst the other showed her love by simply sitting at his feet and listening to what he said.

Jesus commends Mary for her way of being above Martha's busy activity and perhaps he offers a gentle challenge to our culture, which tends to favour productivity and action above making time and space for others.

As something of a Martha myself, I know that being busy can be really creative for me, and sometimes a degree of stress is effective. But I'm growing to realize that the pressure to be constantly active can be quite unhelpful too. It's often tempting for me to think that I'm helping others only when I'm busy on their behalf, but I'm learning that by not doing things I can create space in which others can grow. This in turn empowers them and is healthier for everyone.

Jesus, Son of God, you refused the way of domination and control and instead you show us the path of love and gentleness. Help us to deal carefully with all that is entrusted to us today and to give generously but wisely of ourselves and our gifts. Amen.

BROADCAST TUESDAY 27 FEBRUARY 2007

February 28

Bob Fyffe

I recently attended the World Council of Churches General Assembly where we recalled that Mission has been understood for many centuries as a movement taking place from the centre to the periphery, and from the privileged to the marginalized in society. And so our world assembly affirmed the clear message of the Gospel that God chose the poor, the foolish and the powerless to further the cause of justice and peace. With all the pressures we see around us on the fabric of our communities, there's an urgent need to see the margins of society as the place where strength is found. And those of us who belong to the Church are being called to be a poor Church for the poor. All of us are being called to be messengers of a transforming love that sees through power and status and announces a deep grace and acceptance of one another. Perhaps we are also being asked to look to the margins of our society to see how we might best and most faithfully move forward. It's when we look to the places where others are suffering that we see the way toward our own liberation, through serving others. If we recognize that God is constantly seeking out those who are the least in the world, then we will see where we must follow.

> God of life and love,
> Pull us with You from the comfort of the centre,
> From the security of our own place,
> To the margins where You were born and lived and loved.
> Pull us to the distant and unfamiliar places where life is most raw
> To be set free to serve You and each other.
> Amen.

BROADCAST FRIDAY 28 FEBRUARY 2014

March 1

Mary Stallard

All over Wales today children will dress up in traditional costumes or in rugby shirts, and Welsh people the world over will wear daffodils as a reminder of St David. The clothes and symbols are about identifying with the many stories of a man who left such a mark upon his people and nation that, fifteen centuries later, traces of his work are still evident, preserved in the stones, traditions and aspirations of the communities where he lived.

St David was characterized by the simplicity and authenticity of his life. The overriding passion that drove him was a burning desire to live in such a way that he would communicate to others the good news of God's love and generous hospitality. He devoted much time to travelling to remote parts of the country, speaking to people and showing them his faith by example.

David is also remembered for the rules of discipline he taught those who gathered around him, but although he was strict with himself, he was also generous with those who disagreed with him. One example of this was when Gildas, a churchman and a very outspoken critic, was invited to stay amongst the community and encouraged to 'work things out in fellowship' with them.

David's life illustrates the fact that storytelling can occupy an unrivalled place in the art of communication – not only by simply teaching people to read and write but also, perhaps more importantly, by helping to shape ideas and stimulate vision.

It's a good time for all of us to reflect upon the accounts that have shaped our lives and communities and to think about the stories that our own lives might communicate to others.

Spirit of integrity, help us to be faithful and true in all that we do today. May our lives, like those of the saints and people who inspire us, tell the story of your love and be good news to those who need to hear it. Amen.

BROADCAST THURSDAY 1 MARCH 2007

March 2

Jenny Wigley

I like to think I've enjoyed my ministry wherever I've worked, first as a deacon and then as a priest in the Church in Wales. But there was a time when people asked me what I did and I would reply: 'The nicest job in the world: I'm a university chaplain.' But the nicest was also the most challenging, and the furthest removed from the 'More tea, Vicar?' image of clergy life.

Most of the time the people a chaplain meets have never darkened the door of a church. And most of the time the students at least drink absolutely anything *but* tea! A university or a college can be a pretty fragmented place, so that an important part of the chaplain's work is to weave a common thread, to hold the individual parts and the scattered people together. 'Building community' is part of what any minister is called to do. The difference is that the chaplain is not building a congregation but forming networks, finding ways of linking individuals and groups together.

So particular issues, for example, could make a network – concern for social justice perhaps or for the future of the planet. Sometimes actual differences could bring groups together to enter into dialogue – about science and religion, Christianity and Islam. Or we could each make our own contributions to a celebration or event before going our separate ways.

I spoke of weaving a thread. A better image is choreographing a dance, where the spaces in-between are as essential as its various collaborations. The life of a university reminds us of the need to maintain a respectful distance, and that what we do separately is as much a part of the life of any healthy community as what we do together.

God of community, through our diversity You enable us to enrich one another. Give us wisdom to recognize and rejoice in what is good and true, and to walk in Your light all our days. Amen.

BROADCAST MONDAY 2 MARCH 2009

March 3

Shaunaka Rishi Das

Today in England small groups of Hindus from the Vaishnava denomination gather together to celebrate the saint Sri Chaitanya, who lived in India 500 years ago. Sri Chaitanya is renowned for his beautiful chanting of the names of God, and his inspiring personal example of humility.

There's something about humility. Once you claim you have it, you've lost it. Yet it's such a universal principle, appreciated by every culture in the world. And we all have our humbling experiences.

I have one that happened on live TV news. The interview was going well. One of those 'Where was God during the tsunami?' interviews. Questions were coming thick and fast but I was ready for all angles, on top of my game. Yes, I was as proud as a peacock. Then one of my front teeth, a crown – which had stayed religiously in place for 25 years in my head – fell out in mid-theological flow. There I was defending God, in all my righteousness, only to be reminded that my pride is as false as my front tooth. I survived to tell the tale – we usually do.

But if we can honestly reflect on these experiences, we will find them most instructive. They will help mould good character and nurture wisdom.

We can practise being humble. We can pause with Sri Chaitanya, that exemplar of humility, as he prays for strength to

'serve God and creation in a humble state of mind, thinking ourselves lower than the straw in the street ... more tolerant than a tree ... ready to offer all respect to others and expect none for ourselves. In such a state of mind we can serve the Lord constantly.'
Hare Krishna.

BROADCAST SATURDAY 3 MARCH 2007

March 4

Clair Jaquiss

It sits there shapeless, pale, immobile — and, if not exactly hostile, at least sulking. 'Leave to prove in a warm place,' says the book, 'until the dough has doubled in size.' We don't know how long: it depends on the surrounding temperature of the room, on moisture and sugar and the temperament of the yeast. Making bread can't be hurried. You just have to wait.

The activists fill in the time with other tasks while the chilled-out pause, read the paper and drink coffee.

Save on waiting with a bread machine, then? It's not the same. Yes, but fresh bread for breakfast, waiting for you — a wonderful prospect. And when the process means the house is filled at four in the morning with an irresistible aroma, and you wake with your mouth watering in the early hours and can't get back to sleep, there *is* a bit of a down side.

Like Advent, Lent, with its lengthening days, has something of the waiting about it. We're only part-way through. Here are opportunities for reflection, learning and the deepening of faith by disciplines of fasting and giving. The activists fill the time with good works and studies and projects. But sometimes we have to chill and only plant seeds of faith in our wilderness life and wait.

The bread machine produces the loaf with little intervention from you and me, but there should be a place for the slow pleasures: kneading dough and encouraging flour, yeast and water to become an elastic pillow that, given time, becomes daily bread. And then time spent simply doing nothing but waiting.

Lord, when I am tempted to fill my time with one task after the other, give me the wisdom to trust in You and to meet You in the waiting. Amen.

BROADCAST MONDAY 4 MARCH 2013

March 5

Martin Shaw

Millions of people make the sign of the cross. Some do so at what may seem strange times. A friend of mine made a sign of the cross just as he went into an exam. Why? 'Please, God, may I get the questions I've prepared.' When I went for a small operation, I made the sign of the cross. Why? 'May the surgeon, God, get it right.'

From Novak Djokovic, the World Tennis No. 1, to sprinters on the starting blocks, TV captures all sorts of people making the sign of the cross. Maybe Djokovic feels that Jesus is on his side. Maybe the sprinter wants God to create a sudden following wind. Perhaps he wanted Jesus to make sure he didn't have a false start. Maybe he didn't want to trip and become a laughing stock to millions of people around the world. I've seen singers make the sign of the cross, so afraid of making fools of themselves in public. Or maybe it is simply: 'God, give me courage.'

There are text messages which include the initials OMG: 'Oh! My God!' or even 'Jesus' ... a heartfelt note of surprise or alarm. They may be expletives, but I like to think they're prayers. Everyone prays — it's a basic instinct. When someone asks for help, that's praying. Today many will have difficult decisions or something demanding to face. They will pray, no matter what they do or don't believe. Here's a prayer for them and, maybe, for us too.

> Christ, release the resources of love
> In those who are surgeons;
> Those who train for sporting excellence;
> Those whose creative skills are in the performing arts;
> Those who have difficult decisions to make today.
> May we be alert enough to see Your creative Love in them.
> Amen.

BROADCAST MONDAY 5 MARCH 2012

March 6

Shaunaka Rishi Das

There's a wonderful gesture that pervades the culture of hospitality in India: people put both palms of their hands before their heart and slightly bow their head as they say to us, 'Namaste.'

In its simplest understanding it's accepted as a humble greeting straight from the heart and should be reciprocated accordingly – 'Namaste.' It means, 'I offer my respect to you.' The physical gesture itself is called a *mudra*, a form of non-verbal communication, and is considered to be powerful and prayerful in itself.

On a deeper level of meaning, *namaste* also has emotional and spiritual significance. A good basis of all our social interaction is respect. *Namaste* physically shows respect and confirms it by word. Beyond that, by playing with the syllables of the word *namaste*, we find that it also means 'not me, but you': symbolically giving up our pride in front of another – the most profound meaning of this being, 'The Divine within me offers respect to the Divine within you.' A recognition that we are all spiritual in nature.

So this simple and ubiquitous greeting has a prayerful meaning on many levels of understanding: a simple social interaction; an affectionate well-wishing; and a recognition that everyone is touched by God. As a prayer, it honours the sacredness of each of us and recognizes our equality. By sharing this prayer with you today, I offer you respect, I recognize that I am not more than what you are, and I praise God within you.

You'll miss the *mudra* of me joining my palms together, but I can still say to you:

Namaste. Hare Krishna.

BROADCAST TUESDAY 6 MARCH 2007

March 7

Nigel McCulloch

Today's anniversary of the patenting of the telephone by Alexander Graham Bell in 1876 underlines the amazing advances in communications technology since then. That's not to diminish the wonder that greeted those early electronic methods — reflected in Poet Laureate Alfred Austin's lines about how quickly news of the future King Edward VII's illness was communicated: "Along the wires the electric message came, / He is no better, he is much the same."

Not exactly the high water mark of literary merit! That accolade undoubtedly belongs to what is now usually known as the King James Bible, published in 1611. Its superb language, cadences, poetry are unsurpassed in the English language. To heighten awareness of this 400-year-old treasure among a new technology-savvy generation, I'm helping to put the King James Bible onto YouTube. The aim is to have different chapters read by various people and uploaded onto the site. I've been filmed reading my chapter from the set of TV's famous *Coronation Street*. The soap opera's story lines sometimes reflect a lack of love and charity between characters, so perhaps my choice of Bible reading from 1 Corinthians 13 was especially apt: 'Though I speak with the tongues of men and angels and have not charity, I am become as sounding brass or a tinkling cymbal' — through to its memorable ending, 'And now abideth faith, hope, charity, these three; but the greatest of these is charity.' The meaning is summed up in our prayer for today:

Lord, help us to understand that however gifted or full of faith and hope we are, what matters most is how loving and charitable we are to other people. Amen.

BROADCAST MONDAY 7 MARCH 2011

March 8

Clair Jaquiss

Today marks the anniversary of the death of Woodbine Willie – Geoffrey Studdert Kennedy: the army chaplain during the First World War who ministered among the troops in the worst of times. 'Battles do not make for carefully balanced thought,' he once wrote. 'The brutality of war is literally unutterable. There are no words foul and filthy enough to describe it.'

What could one man do in the face of this unutterable horror? He offered little things, which for those who received them were not little at all: friendship and comfort; the sharing of a Woodbine or two; prayer and presence. He was awarded the Military Cross for helping the wounded in no man's land at Messine's Ridge, in Belgium.

The story's often told about the time when he crawled out to a working party putting up wire in front of their trench. A nervous soldier challenged him, asking who he was. He said 'The Church.'

When the soldier asked what the Church was doing out there, he replied, 'Its job.'

He saw himself in those circumstances as a means of God showing solidarity with suffering humanity. Studdert Kennedy's poetry is equally earthy and earthly – with its blunt speech imitating the language of ordinary soldiers. But it is contemporary, responsive and heartfelt.

His passion for all people who matter to God continued in his ministry after the war, outspoken in his working for justice on behalf of the poor.

Lord, who shares our pain and grief, give us grace today to offer simple kindness and support to those in need, that we may glimpse the glory of God in the face of the crucified Saviour, for Your love's sake. Amen.

BROADCAST FRIDAY 8 MARCH 2013

March 9

Martin Shaw

There's a lady I know on the Outer Hebrides, who has dedicated herself to praying intensively for refugees all over the world, escaping from hunger or violence, or both. She lives an ordinary, indeed a hidden life. When I asked her about it, she simply said that it was her job. As I left her, she reminded me that if I was going to speak about her work, I must not use her name. Whether or not her prayer is of much use, is not the point.

At the end of her novel *Middlemarch*, in praise of ordinary and maybe insignificant people, George Eliot refers to them as: 'the number who lived faithfully a hidden life, and rest in unvisited tombs.'

Thomas Merton, a monk and writer on prayer, wrote an imaginary story of twelve seemingly ordinary people, who don't know each other. Each in their hidden lives hold their arms up, as if they were pillars stopping the world from collapsing. I like to think of them as incognito saints...

Well, someone reading this right now may be one of them and, through prayer, may be stopping the world from falling apart.

Most of us are ordinary and today will come nowhere near an important person, never mind be one. The paradox is that the ordinary, hidden people among us perhaps have a huge responsibility. You and I might as well pray, and who knows what the effect might be.

God of unnoticed loving, Your Presence in those who pray in secret for others, is essential for creation and for the world's survival. Although their tombs may go unvisited, we thank you for their hidden lives which, somehow, have touched and inspired us to join their loving of others. Amen.

BROADCAST FRIDAY 9 MARCH 2012

March 10

Sharon Grenham Toze

Every day in the news we're reminded of the frailty of human beings, physically, mentally, morally. Communities are devastated by natural disaster or conflict; elsewhere there's hard-nosed wheeling and dealing, or maybe kissing and telling. Even on a more mundane scale, we're all vulnerable – how many viruses did you end up with this winter?

But it doesn't feel like a world for the feeble – survival of the fittest rules in the office, the retail market and the bank balances. Very often we feel the pressure to keep on and on, until we reach a point of collapsing in a heap, either metaphorically or, all too often, in reality.

It can sometimes feel as if the life of faith is much the same – keep running after the spiritual prizes, pursue perfection, you're never going to be good enough. Then God seems stern – a taskmaster, a heavenly policeman.

Well, in one sense it's true, we're never going to be good enough – but God's a shepherd, a lover, a parent in many Biblical images. A protector of the vulnerable, a perceiver of beauty in any circumstance. Perfection isn't required – our frailty is accepted and acceptable to God – and should be so to one another too. Far from cracking a celestial whip, God's ready with the ointment, ready to forgive, to soothe and to heal.

'Blessed are the meek, the poor in spirit, the oppressed, those who mourn.' Society's rules are turned upside down – it's not the survival of the fittest, but the salvation of the vulnerable.

And so, loving God, we turn to You this morning and reveal our frailties – touch us with the hand of healing and peace. And may we bring the same to others. Amen.

BROADCAST WEDNESDAY 10 MARCH 2010

March 11

Nigel McCulloch

The quest for happiness is the basis for a new national questionnaire. It's often said that it takes more muscles to frown than to smile – though there are times when most of us have good reason to feel miserable: bereavement; disappointment; pain. Times when we may claim, as Aldous Huxley put it in *Brave New World*, 'the right to be unhappy'. But permanent pessimism, always seeing the glass half empty rather than half full, can be profoundly debilitating.

A friend of mine was granted the Queen's warrant for making the flower arrangements for the Royal Maundy service – with the title 'purveyor of nosegays'. The theologian Jürgen Moltmann used that image of the royal warrant to describe what the heavenly King has appointed Christians to be: 'purveyors of optimism', commanded to express our hope in Christ.

Of course, that doesn't mean being insensitive to depression – or going around with perpetual hearty cheerfulness, which can be hugely off-putting. Things do go wrong in life – and sometimes so devastatingly that hope seems very distant. My grandmother, who had a difficult life, often quoted the hymn: 'Count your many blessings, name them one by one, and it will surprise you what the Lord has done.' Itemizing the good things, however small they are, can add up to more than we expect.

And being positive can help us express gratitude. The medieval mystic Meister Eckhart said that all prayer can be summed up in just two words: thank you. This prayer from Hawaii is longer, but it offers hope and thanks for today:

May happiness, like trade winds, sustain you; may laughter, joyous as breakers, shake you; may strength, like coco palms storm-bent, sustain you; and may the ancient shark of discontent disdain you. Amen.

BROADCAST FRIDAY 11 MARCH 2011

March 12

Sharon Grenham Toze

I remember, many years ago, listening to a BBC radio show which contained a slot called 'Confessions'. Listeners would call in with the details of some past misdemeanour, which they'd never been able to tell anyone before. The listening audience would then vote as to whether the person could be forgiven or not. There are some similar ideas now circulating on various websites, but there was something at the same time comic and tragic about actually hearing people verbalizing their stories.

I remember one man recounting how, as a boy, he was a great fan of remote control model aeroplanes. One birthday he was given a particularly beautiful specimen by his parents, with a powerful engine, and even a seat for a miniature pilot. Now, his brother had a hamster ... Needless to say the plane flew off over the hills behind the boy's house, and neither machine nor rodent were ever seen again.

The boy never told his family the full story – for twenty years they'd thought the hamster had simply escaped; and for twenty years he'd lived with the guilt, until he could bear it no longer, and so confessed to millions.

I can't remember if he was absolved by the audience or not, but, once I stopped laughing, I was struck by how powerful a hold the past really has over us. Whether it's a memory of guilt or joy, past events stay with us, and shape us profoundly. Of course, past experience is what brings us maturity, gives us a framework. But it's when the framework becomes a cage that we so often run into problems: when the past doesn't just shape, but imprisons us, leading us to live less than wholeheartedly, less than generously.

So free us, Lord, from all that would diminish and distort us; give us courage to open our hearts and minds, to admit our weaknesses and be prepared to change. Amen.

BROADCAST FRIDAY 12 MARCH 2010

March 13

George Stack

An interrupted dream is often the result of waking too quickly from sleep, and the result is that it's difficult to recapture the memory of our dream. The twentieth-century psychologist Carl Jung developed a theory of dream analysis. He believed dreams act as symbols, as mirrors from the unconscious to the conscious. One 'archetypal' symbol, for example, is that of a ship on a calm sea. Beneath the surface of the water there is the dark, the deep, the unknown, the repressed. And so, when analysed, that turmoil can be identified and healed.

The Old Testament prophet Jonah knew all about turmoil and the sea. Rather than going to Nineveh, he escaped in a ship. In different ways, each of us is called to 'go to Nineveh'. People have rightful claims on us, on our time, on our expertise, on our love. And a storm develops if we avoid these commitments – just like it did for Jonah. He was thrown from his ship and found himself in the belly of a big fish for three days, 'hiding away' in that womb of sleep. The Jonah in us often seeks to escape back into a warm, protective womb where we're not challenged, where we feel secure, where we don't have to change.

Our daily prayer allows us to see ourselves as God sees us. Accepted and loved, not despite failure and weakness, but because of them.

Lord, you know me better than I know myself. I thank You for the wonder of my being. Help me to see with Your sight the reality of the day that lies ahead. Amen.

BROADCAST THURSDAY 13 MARCH 2008

March 14

Roger Hutchings

For those of us gifted with sight, the act of looking is something we take for granted, from the moment we open our eyes in the morning to the moment we close them for a nap or another night's sleep.

One of my hobbies, which relies on the gift of sight, is drawing and painting. When I first went to a life class and rather self-consciously attempted to translate the shape of the naked model into marks on the paper in front of me, I made the classic mistake familiar to every art tutor. Instead of carefully observing and drawing what I could see, I used my supposed knowledge of the human form to construct an image. It's a bit like a child sketching a stick-man: a body, two arms, two legs and a head, but the relationship between the component parts doesn't necessarily reflect reality! You can tell it's meant to be a person, but it just isn't right. Gradually, over the weeks and months, I had to learn to look, and not to invent.

Drawing and painting isn't everyone's delight, of course. But learning to look is for all who can see. This time of year, perhaps we could look at a daffodil. As I prepare these words, I can do just that, courtesy of a friend who gave me a bunch. The sunlight illuminates the pale petals and the more orange trumpet in the centre, and casts parts of the flower into shadow. It's an everyday sight, but when you truly look, special and beautiful.

Give us Lord, the moments to look carefully, to see beauty in others and in the world around us. And prompt us to celebrate the wonder of Your creation. Amen.

BROADCAST WEDNESDAY 14 MARCH 2012

March 15

Mark Wakelin

The best way for many people to learn is to 'do' rather than just sit down and read or think about the topic. They're interested not simply in a theoretical way, but practically: 'How can I find God in the everyday world in which I live?'

The answer that Jesus gives is, 'Follow me.' He doesn't offer books, or for that matter, quiet days or cosy retreats. He simply suggests that they do what he does. What Jesus does is revolutionary. He gets alongside those who feel on the edge, who are sad or suffering. He finds time for people who are hated because of their lifestyles or their political affiliations.

Following Jesus was as risky as stepping out of a boat and trying to walk on water, something that happened in one of the many stories told about him that leaves me feeling that I'd have made a lousy disciple.

However, in the more mundane world of Muswell Hill, north London, where I live, the truth of his challenges still applies. If you really want to find out what he's like and learn more about him, then the only real way is to have a go. Love others, especially the ones whom it's harder to love. Forgive, which is something that always sounds easy until you actually have to do it. And live life to the fullest, which actually demands a good deal of courage and effort.

By moving out of my depth, I quickly discover I'm in his depths, and realize I've learnt something new.

Help me today, O Lord, to do and not just to think about it, and to find you in that doing! Amen.

BROADCAST THURSDAY 15 MARCH 2007

March 16

Glenn Jordan

The British radio telescope at Jodrell Bank in Cheshire in 1960 set a new space record, making contact with the American *Pioneer V* satellite at a distance of 407,000 miles. Nowadays, of course, with equipment like the Hubble telescope we can look deep, deep into space and back further and further into history. The statistics become truly staggering.

Like the fact that if the sky is clear tonight, and you can find a penny, and hold it up at arm's length and look at it through one eye, that penny is blocking out approximately fifteen million stars.

The Psalmist writes that the stars of heaven are the work of God's fingers – delicate filigree work, not back-breaking heavy construction. The kind of work that requires God's complete attention, enough to select the exact position of each one of those stars, moons and planets.

The Psalmist further marvels that the God who created all this and keeps it moving is the same God who remains intimately attentive to the lives of human beings. In fact, Christians believe that the greatness of God is measured not just in his capacity to create the universe, but in his constant mindfulness of each individual. Even to the extent of being aware of the prayer we now express.

Dear God, in the face of Your marvellous creation, help us keep perspective on our place and on the value of each human being You have brought to life. Preserve us from taking our life for granted and from treating others with disrespect. Amen.

BROADCAST MONDAY 16 MARCH 2009

March 17

Gordon Gray

Today, 17 March, is, of course, St Patrick's Day, celebrated most likely with greater enthusiasm in New York and New Orleans than in Birmingham or even Belfast! But behind the shamrocks and the shenanigans there's the story of a young man, of extraordinary character and influence, in Ireland and far beyond.

I often think of him as I drive from my home in North Antrim to the city of Belfast and look across to nearby Slemish, a steep-sided volcanic plug soaring high out of the Antrim Plateau, the venue for an annual pilgrimage on this day.

The story goes that in the fifth century young Patrick was taken captive by raiders from Ireland. They carried him off from his home somewhere in western Britain to live out a lonely youth of hardship, herding sheep on Slemish. There he found — or was found by —God. After six years he escaped back home. But in a vision he felt himself called by 'the voice of the Irish', returned to Ireland as a missionary, led thousands to faith and organized the embryonic Irish Church. Remarkably, the young Patrick did not allow his bitter experience of captivity to enslave him. He had found two freedoms — of body and of spirit.

Lord God, we pray for all captives, all bound in slavery, all held hostage, all the disappeared — some very young. May they be given a vivid sense of Your presence with them today, and soon be delivered to safety and to home. Amen.

BROADCAST WEDNESDAY 17 MARCH 2010

March 18

Glenn Jordan

I have no idea how it all started, but within seconds my ten-year-old and I were locked in vocal combat. It was something to do with him not wanting to do what I wanted him to do, and it all escalated from there. And the next stage was for him to storm off, slamming the door, and then a strange tension descended on our home. We were momentarily estranged.

I was left wondering how I could so quickly descend into this relational downward spiral.

I'm reminded of how it's often hardest to hold the deep conversations with those who are closest – whether it's talking to our children about 'birds and bees' or simply saying sorry to someone we've hurt or offended.

The prophet Isaiah says that one of the marks of true religion is not turning your back on your own flesh and blood.

So why does staying connected to family seem so important? Perhaps it's precisely because it's hardest to pretend among those who know us best.

In that light, a couple of questions occur to me. Who in the wider community are the people who are rightly my flesh and blood, but I find easier to ignore? And, what would it mean to be oriented toward them and not away from them?

Lord, we pray for our own flesh and blood, even if we have been estranged for some time, and we pray for Your blessing on them wherever they are. And we pray for those who feel alone, abandoned or isolated. May they know You as a parent and one who loves them. Amen.

BROADCAST WEDNESDAY 18 MARCH 2009

March 19

Gordon Gray

The season of Lent is observed more faithfully in those Churches with a strong 'catholic' tradition of adhering to 'the Christian Year' than it is in the so-called 'Free' or 'evangelical' Churches. I'm a Presbyterian, and most Presbyterians traditionally have an historic antipathy to a set liturgy, the lectionary, saints' days, and most festivals. As for Lent, their emphasis has been that Christians are called to restraint and repentance all the time and not merely for an annual six-week fast. Well, I wonder!

But this week I've been reflecting that, whether or not we choose to engage in a period of more demanding spiritual discipline and self-denial, life itself thrusts us into stressful situations which test us to the core and force us to dig deep, find fresh resources, and reassess our priorities — what we might call 'Lenten experiences'. While I was thinking along these lines, some words of St Paul in his Second Letter to the Corinthians came to mind. He's been listing the hardships he and his companions have been through, from imprisonment to hunger, and then he says: 'Dying we still live on; disciplined by suffering we are not done to death; in our sorrows we have always cause for joy; penniless, we own the world'.

So, Lord, grateful as we are for the many blessings of our lives, may we learn to sit light to material things and find a deeper peace and happiness in the security of Your love. May we find joy in helping ease the distress of others. Amen.

BROADCAST FRIDAY 19 MARCH 2010

March 20

Judy Merry

The American humorist Erma Bombeck once said, 'A child needs your love most when he deserves it least.' We're understandably concerned when children behave badly — and at the moment the question of what they deserve when the behaviour is extreme is exercising politicians, psychologists and social workers.

When my children were small, they were looked after by a childminder — and at the time she was fostering a boy of three or four. One day I was picking the children up and this boy was in a really bad mood. He was kicking and shouting. You couldn't even call it a toddler tantrum — he was uncontrollable. The childminder was calm, but firm — and she said that, underneath all the bad behaviour, was a very unhappy child.

Loving a child doesn't mean indulging them — or allowing unacceptable behaviour to go unchecked. But to give a child consistent love and clear boundaries takes time and patience. Week by week, month by month, I watched that little boy change. The shift was imperceptible at first, but eventually he learned how to stay calm and control his feelings. Then one day I realized that the turbulent behaviour had all but disappeared — and he seemed, not just better behaved, but much happier too. He was fortunate in having someone who was prepared to love him when he seemed to deserve it least.

Jesus taught his disciples that loving someone when they give you little or no cause is similar to the grace of God: the fact that he loves us even when we don't deserve it. In Lent we're encouraged to think about our shortcomings. Now, we can simply dwell on how undeserving we are — or we can work on being transformed into the sort of person who can, in turn, show grace to others.

So we pray that we might know we are loved by God — even when we behave badly. And may we have the patience and understanding to love others when they least deserve it. Amen.

BROADCAST SATURDAY 20 MARCH 2010

March 21

Anna Magnusson

It was when I was out for a walk that I felt it. It made me pause, the way you would if you thought someone was behind you. The sky was a pale, watery blue, and I could hear the sweet twitter of birds in the leafless trees. The ground was damp and muddy after the rain, and the air smelt fresh and somehow green.

I stopped, and looked around. There were small yellow dots of flower on the gorse bushes, and plump brown buds on the tree beside me. I realized it wasn't cold. And then I felt it again. A stillness in the air, a sense of presence. And I realized what it was: spring was coming.

I felt a ridiculous spurt of happiness. How is it that we live through the seasons, year after year, decade after decade — and still feel that flash of surprise when the change happens? Our lives are shaped by countless beginnings and endings, in the natural world, in our families and relationships, in everything we create; but we never grow used to them. We still feel the excitement, the fear, the happiness, the loss that's in every beginning, and every ending.

As a child I felt an almost physical delight reading the passage in *The Lion, the Witch and the Wardrobe* when the icicles begin to melt and patches of green appear in the snow; and then someone whispers, 'Aslan is coming.' Something was beginning, something was about to change. And to feel that quiver of excitement and apprehension — that is, above all, to feel alive.

God of beginnings, with every breath of this new day may we walk forward to embrace life, and find the open door. Amen.

BROADCAST SATURDAY 21 MARCH 2009

March 22

Ann Holt

Have you ever said, 'I'm washing my hands of this?' I think we all have in moments of exasperation.

Picture this scene from the King James Bible. The crowd is baying for Jesus' blood, and Pilate has a dilemma. He knows that Jesus is innocent, but to free him risks a riot. Matthew's Gospel tells us that Pilate gave in to the crowd's demand for Jesus' crucifixion, taking a bowl of water and washing his hands, saying, 'I am innocent of the blood of this just person.' He was seeking to absolve himself of responsibility for the most pivotal act in history.

When we want to absolve ourselves of responsibility, we often say that we are washing our hands of something.

But responsibility can't be dropped with a gesture. Pilate had to grant permission for Jesus to be buried and placate the Pharisees who feared that the body would be stolen. The responsibility for Pilate's actions just would not go away; and nor will *our* responsibility.

Responsibility for and commitment to others can be hard to face. But those who shirk this responsibility may find themselves increasingly isolated and alone.

Elsewhere in the Bible, having murdered his brother Abel, Cain retorts, when challenged by God, 'Am I my brother's keeper?' The answer to this question today is 'yes', whether that's parents' responsibility for children or a global responsibility to preserve the planet. None of us can wash our hands of that!

Lord, today, however tempted I may be to wash my hands of some troubling responsibility, help me to face it instead. Amen.

BROADCAST TUESDAY 22 MARCH 2011

March 23

Judy Merry

Have you ever tried Googling yourself? A friend asked me that not so long ago. I hadn't even thought about it, but he said I'd be surprised what came up. He was right — it was the passing references on websites of people you'd barely met which was surprising. And if you think your name would draw a blank — don't be too sure. You might be surprised at what someone else has said about you in cyberspace.

So why don't people hesitate before putting information about others onto the web? Maybe it's because — these days — a lot of people live their own lives very publicly. Social networking sites are full of confessions, embarrassing photographs and, of course, a lot of trivia — things many of us would feel were unwise or pointless to share with the world.

Recent cases in the media suggest that many of us are concerned about the erosion of privacy in our society. I know that when I tell someone something in confidence, I expect it to stay that way.

The nineteenth-century poet Lionel Johnson wrote about his deepest and darkest feelings in a poem called 'The Precept of Silence'. In the final verse, he says that he does not speak of his secrets, 'Save to one man, and to God.' Lionel Johnson was a devout Catholic — and the 'one man' was his confessor. The confessional is one of the few places where it's accepted that heavy secrets are told to another person — and not passed on. And the person confessing is asking forgiveness from God — not from another human being.

But this is also an example of absolute trust between two people. And these days that's a rare and precious thing.

So we pray that we might resist the temptation to speak where we should be silent.
May we respect the privacy of others and be someone in whom they can place their trust.
Amen.

BROADCAST TUESDAY 23 MARCH 2010

March 24

Anna Magnusson

There's a beautiful description in Tolstoy's novel *Anna Karenina* of the city early in the morning, seen through the eyes of a man in love. Levin is on his way to propose marriage, and he's so excited that he can't sleep and wanders the streets for hours until the time of his appointment. He is moved by everything he sees – children on their way to school, the silvery-grey pigeons, the little flour-dusted loaves of bread on display outside a baker's. 'Those loaves, the pigeons and the two little boys seemed not of this earth ...'

Levin saw ordinary things, utterly transformed by his full heart into vivid newness. Love can do that. So can starting again, embarking on a new phase of life, launching oneself into unknown territory. You see through fresh eyes, because you have altered your perspective on what is familiar and known. The Greek poet CP Cavafy calls it 'Ithaca' – that hope, that dream which drives us to keep journeying forward, through new and unexplored places. It can be hard and frightening, but 'full of adventure, full of knowledge' – and, whatever befalls us, worth the risk, he says, because 'Ithaca has given you the beautiful voyage./Without her you would never have taken the road.'

God, Your love and compassion are new every morning. You bring us again to light when we lose our way in darkness. You walk beside us on the unfamiliar road. Grant us clear eyes to see beyond what we think are the boundaries of our abilities, and full hearts to carry us there. Amen.

BROADCAST TUESDAY 24 MARCH 2009

March 25

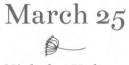

Nicholas Holtam

Most of us love to listen to music and it is even more fun if we can sing or play with others. All over the world people do this, though it sounds very different in China or India compared to here. When I was growing up I sang in a church choir, and I love listening to the cathedral choir in Salisbury, where I am the bishop. Salisbury is also the home of the Royal School of Church Music, supporting church choirs all over the country. Music and church worship go together.

This week many people will be performing or listening to one of the great Passions by Bach from either St Matthew's or St John's Gospel.

Bach was one of the world's finest musicians. It seems inconceivable that he would ever have been held in less than the highest esteem. So it was a surprise to discover that when, in 1723, he was appointed Kantor, director of music, at St Thomas's church in Leipzig, he was the third choice, behind Telemann and someone called Graupner, both of whom, for very different reasons, turned the job down.

Bach was a creative genius who worked incredibly hard. I have often wondered if the circumstances of his appointment meant that he felt he had something to prove, and prompted his phenomenal output. In 1730, disenchanted with the conditions at St Thomas's, Bach sent a memorandum to the church authorities setting out his minimum requirements for well-regulated church music. Their response was to threaten to reduce his salary. When later he asked for a rise, they told him that if he wanted to earn more he could go elsewhere.

Today, dear God, open our eyes to the potential of the people we meet that we may see the most difficult of them as creative people who are made in your image. Amen.

BROADCAST MONDAY 25 MARCH 2013

March 26

Richard Littledale

In a recent year in March I went on a little pilgrimage. It wasn't a pilgrimage as commonly understood – since it ended not at a great cathedral or a shrine … but at a supermarket! Three years earlier, when this particular building was opened, there was a great hue and cry in the press. Finding myself in the town at the heart of all that controversy, I decided to call in. It certainly is an astonishing sight. Soaring high above the surrounding shops, this particular supermarket is elegantly built of brick and sandstone. The main doorway is arched, and there are stained-glass windows just above the cash tills and behind the freezer cabinets. The pulpit may be gone … but this supermarket was once a church.

As a Christian, I found myself in a dilemma. The building had been treated with respect and its original solid beauty allowed to shine. That said, my heart sank a little as the saints in the stained glass looked down no longer on the heads of the faithful but on the baskets of the busy. You have to ask, though – is God better served by tearing a perfectly good building down than by re-using it like this? At least it is open to the whole community – unlike other old churches which have been turned into night clubs or private homes. If I had the choice between looking at stained glass or looking at cardboard adverts hanging from the ceiling whilst I queue, I know which one I would choose. To me, shopping is a necessary evil – but I would rather have some inspiration whilst doing it.

O God, we pray today for the ability to find You in unexpected places. May we find You clothed in the ordinary things and tucked in amongst the very stuff of life. Amen.

BROADCAST WEDNESDAY 26 MARCH 2014

March 27

Tina Beattie

I was travelling on a train into London late at night recently, when the guard announced that we wouldn't be stopping at several stations owing to a problem with the train. A young man came raging through the carriages, shouting and swearing because he had missed his stop and would be late getting home. As the guard approached, we braced ourselves for an ugly confrontation. But the guard commiserated with the young man and offered to let him use his mobile phone to phone his wife and tell her why he'd be late. When she clearly didn't believe him, the guard spoke to her and explained what the problem was. It was amazing to watch the transformation that came over that young man. His anger evaporated and he apologized to us all for his behaviour. Clearly, he'd been dreading a domestic confrontation when he arrived home, and he had taken his fear and rage out on the rest of us.

So often, we hear complaints about the kind of society we live in – how violent or selfish people are, how little sense of community there is. But how often do we pause to recognize the fear, the anxiety, the lack of self-confidence, beneath the masks of bravado and aggression that people sometimes wear? We need to escape from threatening situations in order to protect ourselves. But sometimes we may have an opportunity to reach out with a kind word or a gesture of compassion that can turn a potentially violent situation into a moment of shared human warmth and understanding, as the guard on that train did. The Bible tells us that 'a gentle answer turns away wrath'.

God, may we be people of gentleness and peace as we go about our lives today. Amen.

BROADCAST THURSDAY 27 MARCH 2008

March 28

Mark Wakelin

It's not easy to talk about mental illness in our culture of competence and adequacy. And being depressed, for example, is also complicated, far more than simply feeling melancholy or sad, for your will to cope itself seems to have gone off-duty. The things you might do to make you feel better are the hardest of things to do. Around and around, in ever-decreasing circles, difficult thoughts and feelings subdue your energy lower and lower. And, as they render you increasingly unable to do the smart thing, the healing thing, they simply add to the sense of despair that you will not escape. Worst of all is when you don't realize that this is the worst of all: you don't see yourself as depressed, as you might if you were just fed up, but in the greyness of your feelings you come to believe that this is reality, this is 'normal' and there is no way out.

The minister in me and perhaps the theologian wants to ask, 'in this wilderness, where is God'? The answer is complex, and not always easy to hear. CS Lewis knew this despair when his wife died and he sensed the doors of heaven bolted against him. But God is in there, though illness itself connives to conceal. But God is in there, and sometimes the divine touch is felt through the hand of a friend or family member. Sometimes healing is the hardest of challenges, like a foot that has been sat on so long it has gone numb – the sharpness of pins and needles as feeling returns. Slowly the will begins to awaken and the longing for healing revives.

Lord of all hopefulness, Lord of all joy, come close to those today lost in the wilderness of depression, and to those who walk alongside them, and remind us of light in the midst of our darkness. Amen.

BROADCAST WEDNESDAY 28 MARCH 2012

March 29

Kate Coleman

My housemate sometimes accuses me of selective hearing, particularly when discussing ironing, washing and cleaning duties! And I confess that I have sometimes responded to such concerns without ever really hearing them. I have later been told that I missed some vital piece of information that was passed on to me because, well ... the truth is, I wasn't really listening. I was busy elsewhere, both mentally and emotionally.

In 1788 MP William Wilberforce, arguably the best known member of the Clapham Sect, a group of evangelical Christians committed, amongst other things, to the abolition of the slave trade, set out to get himself heard. Every year for nearly twenty years he introduced anti-slavery motions to Parliament. Wilberforce regularly faced the disappointment of not being heard, largely because economic concerns determined what people were prepared to view as priorities. Wilberforce was, thankfully, persistent.

Hearing and not forgetting are like two sides of the same coin. The epistle of James compares forgetting the important things that we hear to going to a mirror and viewing our reflection only to forget what we look like as soon as we've moved away from it.

Oh God, help us to hear what Your Spirit is saying on a grand scale before lives are lost and energies are spent. Help us to hear the voices of those speaking the kind of sense we don't always wish to engage with. Help us to hear the voices of our loved ones, work colleagues, neighbours and friends in the course of our everyday lives. Help us to hear the silent cries for help in the midst of our busyness and grant us the grace to be Christ-like as we respond. Amen.

BROADCAST THURSDAY 29 MARCH 2007

March 30

Tom Wright

We all face tough and tricky questions, especially when we decide to be different. Some of those questions echo the ones they asked Jesus in the days that followed his dramatic action in the Temple in Jerusalem. Who do you think you are? What makes you think you have the right to behave like that? And, behind those, Is this some kind of revolution? Are you one of those crazy fanatics who's going to get us all in trouble?

The questions buzzed about Jesus' head like wasps. They find an echo in our imaginations as well. Surely, we hear people say, you can't believe in God now we know about modern science? Surely, Christianity has been part of the problem, not part of the solution? Wasn't Jesus just a deluded first-century fanatic? Who do you think you are to suppose you have the right to be different?

Jesus dealt with his questioners in a glittering verbal display. 'Pay Caesar back in his own coin – and pay God back in *his* own coin!' It was a tease, to get them to think about a different kind of revolution. And, when necessary, he could cut the question off at the legs: 'You're wrong,' he said, 'because you don't know your Bibles and you don't know God's power.' And meanwhile the disciples were thinking: that's all very well, but what's he going to *do*? Talking about God's kingdom won't make it happen. We need to win the real battle.

Jesus knew that the questions mattered too. God wants us to love Him with the mind, as well as the heart, soul and strength. Thinking isn't everything, but not thinking isn't anything. The tough questions will come at us, and we need to be ready.

Lord of all wisdom, give us Your sharpness of mind, to see through the confusions of the world and to speak the truth of Your kingdom. Amen.

BROADCAST TUESDAY 30 MARCH 2010

March 31

Edward Mason

In my hand I have a small pottery jug. It's earthenware and unglazed outside, except for the yellowy ring around its rim.

What a casual glance doesn't notice is that it's badly cracked. In fact, if I let go of it, a whole piece of the side would just fall away. I love this jug.

I love it because when I show it to people, I make sure it holds a secret. Inside, I keep a small candle burning. The light is completely invisible apart from where the cracks show a glimmer every now and then.

Our society doesn't much go for cracked pots. We like things perfect: perfect bodies, faces without lines, first-class degrees, champions, health and wealth.

The problem is none of us is really like that. We're only perfect in our frustrated imagination. We know that really we're just clay pots — fragile, with plenty of cracks. And frankly, we can wake up feeling weak and a failure.

Earlier this month, the government minister Shahbaz Bhati was shot for defending the rights of Christians in Pakistan. This looks like failure writ large. Yet his murder and what he stood for reverberated around the world. And how many people do we know in whom suffering and weakness, being truly 'cracked', has revealed an astonishing inner life burning away within them. Without the cracks we wouldn't have noticed what really matters.

So, Lord God, help us today to be less concerned with outward appearances of failure or weakness and more interested in what fosters a flame of life. As You made light shine out of darkness, so make Your light shine in our hearts for the sake of all we meet today who are living in deep shadow. Amen.

BROADCAST THURSDAY 31 MARCH 2011

April 1

Edward Mason

I have on my desk a rather ridiculous red and white hat. More of that in a moment.

On this day in 1999 a world-wide burger chain announced the launch of a new burger for left-handed people. It was, so they said, designed to fit more easily in the left hand. The ingredients were laid between the halves of the bun so that any spillage would fall away from the left side, making it more convenient for consumers.

Of course, it was an April Fool's joke. I say, 'of course', but thousands were taken in – some even asking for the 'old right-handed burger'.

My hat is a jester's hat. Like the left-handed burger, it reminds me that we can all be pretty gullible and, from time to time, need to be ready to poke fun at our all-too-worldly wisdom – a wisdom that sets such store on personal fulfilment and our right to do as we please.

The happiest people I know are those who seem to spend their time doing the opposite of what seems wise. They turn out on a cold evening to serve food to the homeless, they generously give their time to listen to the anxious, and they hardly have money in their hand before giving it away.

It's a foolish way to live, running contrary to all that seems to make sense, and yet their foolishness rebounds in deeply fulfilled lives. It's a way of life that reflects the God described in the Christian scriptures where we read, 'If you think that you are wise in this age, you should become fools so that you may become wise.'

So, Lord God, today help us to risk being generous and loving enough to be called foolish and so learn true wisdom. Amen.

BROADCAST FRIDAY 1 APRIL 2011

April 2

Richard Chartres

On this day 500 years ago the explorer Ponce de León discovered land which he named Florida after the Easter festival of flowers, the *Pascua Florida*, which was being celebrated in his native Spain.

He was in fact searching for the mythic island of Bimini, said to be the location of the fountain of perpetual youth. He found, not the fantasy he was pursuing, but a real place of great beauty.

The Resurrection of Jesus Christ also led on to remarkable discoveries.

One of the final Resurrection appearances was to the friends of Jesus Christ as they were fishing on a lake. It had been a disappointing night, but in the morning there was Jesus standing on the shore inviting them all to breakfast, to 'Come and Dine'.

All the accounts of Christ's Resurrection appearances stress that he could be touched, that he could communicate and share food with his friends. Here is no disembodied spirit offering moonshine for consolation to the hungry, but the risen Christ who taught that we will be nourished and enlightened by sharing our lives with one another.

Christ is still present to be touched and we are still able to share our food with him, because we can see and love him in one another, and especially with those in our world who are hungry. After the gift of the Holy Spirit following his return to the mysterious Godhead, the whole world is full of his presence.

Father, open our spiritual eyes to see the presence of Your beloved Son in one another; help us to be full of invitation so that we can play our part in bringing the whole world to feast at Your table. Through Jesus Christ, Amen.

BROADCAST TUESDAY 2 APRIL 2013

April 3

George Stack

As a Catholic priest living in a very Jewish part of London, I am doubly blessed every weekend. On Saturdays I see large numbers of people walking to synagogues as they mark the Sabbath Day. Every Sunday I witness members of local Christian congregations on their way to church. In this month, moreover, the Jewish feast of Passover is celebrated.

This is the living memory of the liberation from slavery in Egypt of the chosen people. Each generation, each community, each individual person, has to make that journey their own. Exile, slavery, imprisonment aren't just experiences of a previous age or of the Jewish people. In our own time there are significant numbers of people who do not feel free: they fear ridicule or rejection for the things they believe or the way they live.

It is no accident that Christians see the Exodus experience as a sign of the freedom won for us by the death and resurrection of Jesus. He is called the 'Lamb of God' because he is the one who offers himself as the perfect sacrifice to God, atoning for the sins of the world. On the cross, Jesus goes on revealing, goes on loving. Goes on forgiving. The triumph of good over evil, the triumph of life over death, is the measure of God's love for us. True freedom, complete liberation, comes when I realize I am worthy of the infinite love of God.

Open my heart, Lord, that I may experience in the depth of my being the sacrifice you made to show God's love for me. Amen.

BROADCAST TUESDAY 3 APRIL 2007

April 4

Janet Wootton

On 4 April 1968, Martin Luther King was standing on the balcony of a hotel in Memphis, Tennessee, where he was due to lead a march of sanitation workers against low wages and poor working conditions.

A single shot was heard, and the great civil rights activist, whose 'I have a dream' speech still reaches people's hearts today, was assassinated. He was only 39.

During those 39 years, he had changed a nation, and inspired the world. It was no longer possible to ignore the desperate inequalities between black and white Americans, in the life opportunities available to them.

And many wider debates, such as those surrounding apartheid in South Africa, and equality for women, were shaped by the civil rights movement in America. Martin Luther King championed non-violent protest. His aim was not vengeance upon or destruction of the oppressor, but the end of oppression, and a world in which all might flourish.

As with many people who die young, I wonder what his maturer years might have been like. He would have been in his 80s now, with a lifetime in which to have developed his philosophy. What if, like Nelson Mandela, he had lived through and beyond his dream, and seen both its fulfilment and its failures?

Would the path to equality have been smoother, less violent? Would there have been riots in Detroit or Brixton? Would America have a different voice in our own times? How would he have participated in debates about gay rights or responded to today's acts of violence and terror?

God of vision, we thank You for those who shape the thinking of an age, and turn their thinking into action. Help us to build on the vision of a world of justice, and of peace. Amen.

BROADCAST FRIDAY 4 APRIL 2014

April 5

David Chillingworth

When I was a hospital chaplain, I used to sit with people who were passing through very difficult times in their lives. Often I didn't know them – had never met them before, maybe would never see them again. But there I was as they faced the serious illness or sudden death of a dearly loved family member.

Somewhere – sometimes in the quietness of the night hours – the moment would arrive when it would seem right to ask, 'Do you think we should say a prayer at this point?' But of course that was only the first question. The second and more difficult question was, 'What should we pray for?'

You might think that the answer to that would be obvious. Our prayer should ask for everything to go back to how it was. But often we were far beyond the point where such a prayer would be either realistic or compassionate. A lifetime of love, care and emotion had passed in a couple of hours. The place before, where everything was all right, was a far-off country.

So generosity and love would begin to use prayer to explore the possibilities of what might be best – most dignified or most fulfilling – for the person. There are very few people who will not dip into some reservoir of faith in such moments, even if they have seldom or never been part of any religion.

So these words remind us that prayer is the place in which we explore the most generous and sacrificial side of our being.

Father,
Teach us to pray,
Teach us to look at the world through Your eyes,
To see pain and suffering
With deep compassion and love,
So that Your will may be done.
Amen.

BROADCAST SATURDAY 5 APRIL 2014

April 6

George Stack

One of my favourite religious pictures is *Christ of St John of the Cross*, painted by Salvador Dalí in 1951. It's a very unusual picture of the crucifixion of Jesus. When it was bought by the Kelvinstone Gallery in Glasgow, it caused admiration, criticism and controversy. Over the years it has become the object of great devotion.

Dalí was inspired by a pen and ink drawing by the famous sixteenth-century Spanish mystic, St John of the Cross. The cross seems suspended between heaven and earth. The picture is composed of an inverted triangle from arms down to legs, with the circle of the head in its centre. Some people see a reference to the Holy Trinity in this arrangement. There are no nails, no blood, no crown of thorns — another reason why the picture was the subject of much debate. The figure of Christ is seen from above, rather than looking up at the scene from below. The bowed head, the outstretched arms, the tapering legs are like an arrow from heaven to earth. They point to the foot of the cross, which is plunged into the depth of creation. Dalí said the picture was the product of a cosmic dream.

The enduring image is of the crucified Christ, bearing the suffering of the whole world on his shoulders. It reminds us that the cross lies at the crossroads of human suffering, pain and death. Where is God when people suffer?

'Here,' says Jesus, with arms outstretched on the cross.
Lord Jesus, open wide your arms to embrace our broken world. Amen.

BROADCAST FRIDAY 6 APRIL 2007

April 7

Craig Gardiner

Back in the fifteenth century, in a tiny village near Nuremberg, there lived a family with eighteen children. The story is told that two of the children dreamed of pursuing their talent for art, but they knew full well that their father could not afford to send them both to college. The two boys came to a deal: they'd toss a coin and whoever lost would go to work in the nearby mines and support his brother's education. When his studies were completed, they would swap places.

Albrecht Dürer was the brother who won the toss. He went off to study art while his brother Albert worked underground for four years to support him. Albrecht's talent was quickly appreciated, and by the time he graduated he was commanding considerable fees for his work.

The young artist returned home to great celebrations. At the end of the party he rose to drink a toast to his brother for the years of sacrifice. It was time for him to fulfil the vow to support his brother's dream.

Every head at the table turned in eager expectation, but instead of joy they saw only tears of sadness streaming down the face of Albert. Four years in the mine had left him with broken fingers and arthritis; he could hardly hold a glass any longer, never mind a pencil.

To honour this sacrifice, Dürer sketched his brother's broken hands with his palms pressed together. The picture has become widely known as *The Praying Hands*, an image of comfort and hope for many seeking strength from God.

Lord, none of us ever find success by ourselves.
Thank You for the friends, the family
And the strangers, too,
Who have helped us along the way.
May we be available to help others we meet today.
Amen.

BROADCAST MONDAY 7 APRIL 2008

April 8

Anna Magnusson

At school I struggled mightily in Chemistry with the point of potassium permanganate, and ploughed through a textbook called *Physics is Fun*. Alas, it never was for me. Since then I've realized this was because I could never connect the dreary diagrams and formulas to the world around me. Nobody ever made a *story* out of science and said: Use your *imagination* — *this* is how extraordinary the universe is.

Years after I left school, I discovered that brilliant scientists could write about science in a way that brought it alive, like a novelist creating characters. Physicists, especially, caught my imagination. The scope of the ideas, the narrative, the *questions* — it was all fascinating. Like this thought from Richard Feynman, the Nobel physicist: 'Our imagination is stretched to the utmost in this mysterious universe — not, as in fiction, to imagine things which are not really there, but just to comprehend those things which are there.'

If he'd been my physics teacher at school, I'd have sat right at the front of the class.

The other day I was looking through a book of British trees, trying to identify one I'd seen on a walk, and I came across a section about leaves, which described the process of photosynthesis. I can't remember the science, but I know the *story*: a tiny green leaf turns the energy of light into food. And *that* is wondrous.

God of the infinite universe and the atom — may we never stop searching, or wondering. Amen.

BROADCAST MONDAY 8 APRIL 2013

April 9

Johnston McKay

I joined the BBC's Religious Broadcasting Department in 1987, and in those days if a producer wanted to make a radio programme outside, away from the studios, you had to take a sound engineer, and a whole load of equipment, and it was expensive. But a few years later the very small, portable, digital recording machines that came on the market were of broadcast quality. And they were very easy to use, so that, I was told, 'even someone of your technical incompetence, Johnston, would be able to use them'.

So I devised a series called *A Sense of Place*, in which I took people to places that meant much more to them than simply a geographical location, and asked them to say why they mattered. In one programme, the Bishop of Edinburgh, Richard Holloway, took me to a cottage nestling below the Ochil Hills. It was a cottage he had once owned, and from where he had left Scotland in 1980 to go to work in America. And he talked about how the 'little deaths' of leaving a much-loved place are in a way preparation for the big death that comes to us all.

I think the Gospel writers who tell the story of Easter would have said that our lives are also full of 'little resurrections' which help to prepare for the resurrection which Christians believe is the future for all of us – times in our ordinary experience when hope triumphs over despair, maybe only for a short time; or we find it possible to cling onto faith, even if it is by our fingernails; or we find it possible to let love overcome bitterness or anger.

Father Harry Williams wrote that Resurrection as our final and ultimate future can be known only by those who perceive resurrection with us now, encompassing all we are and do. For only then will we recognize it as a country in whose warmth and light we have already lived.

So Lord, show us the everyday hints and signals of the way You can make everything new. Amen.

BROADCAST MONDAY 9 APRIL 2007

April 10

Anna Magnusson

Many years ago, my brother told me about a boy in his class at school who loved trees. This boy used to wrap his arms around them when he was out walking, and lay his face against the bark. My brother was curious rather than mocking about it, so maybe the boy was lucky and didn't get teased by his schoolmates — but, somehow, I suspect not.

But, really, what's so strange about being delighted and awed by trees? I remember being in a forest of massive sequoia trees in California. They stretched skyward in tapering grey columns, still and silent and utterly overwhelming. It's the deep absence of human sound that I still remember so clearly: an absence that was like a presence of something else, something ancient, and magnificent.

We had an elm tree in our back garden when I was growing up. We climbed it, and played around it. In summer we hung a tyre from a rope tied around its lowest branch and swung beneath the heavy, scented leaves, daring each other to jump off. When the tree got infected with Dutch elm disease, my dad had all the withering branches removed. The bare trunk stood for years, like a jagged white bone, until one day it simply crumbled to the ground. Then the grass grew round it, honeysuckle from a nearby bush crept over it, brambles spread through it. Now, twenty years later, it's a tangle of bits of bark, plants and flowers. It's still alive.

God of the natural world, and the cycle of life and re-birth, may we every day appreciate and tend the wonders of our Earth. Amen.

BROADCAST WEDNESDAY 10 APRIL 2013

April 11

David Chillingworth

It may surprise you if I say that I don't find it easy to be religious. I mean that I'm not particularly pious. And life in the Church often isn't particularly soft and pious either — it's about real people and deep feelings. It can be earthy and difficult.

But around our office we talk a bit about what is sometimes called being SBNR — which means 'spiritual but not religious'. It's very much of our times. People drift away from churches — part of today's trend of not being very interested in institutions and authority and the like. But spiritual? That's different. People seem to be more interested in spirituality that is experience — that changes the way the world appears and transforms life.

I have a lot of sympathy with that. I often say to people that the death of the Church begins when it becomes focused on its own agenda, concerns and interests. Better to focus on the reality of people's lives — exploring the meaning of life as it is lived. That means thinking about big questions like meaning and hope — and bigger challenges like forgiveness and sacrifice.

Prayer fits into that — and research suggests that large numbers of people pray. We may feel that we don't quite understand the meaning of things and how they fit together. But prayer means that we keep turning up in God's presence with open hearts, seeking His will and His healing presence in our lives. We need to believe implicitly that if we turn up, then God will turn up as well to fill us with His love.

Father God,
Give us a daily awareness of Your presence,
Teach us to be faithful in prayer
And always open to Your love.
Amen.

BROADCAST FRIDAY 11 APRIL 2014

April 12

Anna Magnusson

The first words the cosmonaut Yuri Gagarin is supposed to have said when he reached orbit on this day in 1961 were: 'I see Earth. It is so beautiful.' These were the first words in space from the first human to orbit our planet.

Since then, that image of the blue drop of the Earth hanging in the vast darkness has lodged itself in the modern consciousness. To me it's still extraordinary, a thing hard to grasp, that we have travelled beyond the arms of our planet, and come home again.

Eleven years after Yuri Gagarin first saw the Earth from space, Eugene Cernan became the last man to leave his footprints on the moon. He was on the final *Apollo* mission in 1972 and he often talked afterwards about how deeply he was affected by the experience. He described being on the moon as 'standing on God's front porch', and said that when he came back to Earth he was filled with 'a yearning restlessness' which was never satisfied. It's exactly how I imagine you *would* feel: and I wonder how many of the astronauts ever fully came home after their missions.

Or maybe the return to Earth was the most wonderful homecoming they ever had. Maybe you are never so aware of how fragile and insignificant we are, until you have flung yourself into the immensity of the unknown; and maybe it's the magnetic force of love and the unquenchable human spirit that pulls you back to Earth, just as surely as gravity.

God of the heavens and the earth, of the darkness of space and the light of spring, hold our world and the people we love, today and always. Amen.

BROADCAST FRIDAY 12 APRIL 2013

April 13

Johnston McKay

I was once walking along the shore of the Sea of Galilee with a friend of mine who is a Roman Catholic priest called John Fitzsimmons, when we passed a notice which said 'No Swimming'. A little further on there was another sign saying 'No Jumping', which we thought was probably meant to stop people diving into the water. John Fitzsimmons said to me, 'Has it ever occurred to you, Johnston, that the good Lord had to walk on the water because it seems to be the only thing you're allowed to do here?'!

It was on the shore of the Sea of Galilee that St John's Gospel tells us that after Easter the risen Jesus prepared a breakfast for his friends. And St John doesn't just describe the breakfast (which was of fish) but he tells us that the fish was cooked 'on a charcoal fire'.

That charcoal fire caught the imagination of Rowan Williams, the former Archbishop of Canterbury. In one of the very first books he wrote, more than two and half decades ago, Rowan Williams points out that if you turn your copy of St John's Gospel back just a page or two, you will find another charcoal fire. This time it is in the courtyard of the high priest's house where Jesus is on trial. And his friend Peter is there, warming his hands beside the charcoal fire, and when three times people say to him, 'You knew Jesus of Nazareth,' three times Peter denies ever having met Jesus in his life.

And now another charcoal fire. Just to rub Peter's face in the charcoal dust and make him feel lousy? Or for Jesus to say to Peter that there is no way he can escape from his past. He can't pretend that it didn't happen. But here Jesus hands him back his past, purged of all its guilt. Jesus gives him back his memories but erased of their power to destroy him.

Loving God, with You we can live in the present, for the past is forgiven and the future is safe with You. Amen.

BROADCAST FRIDAY 13 APRIL 2007

April 14

Gopinder Kaur

This April, the Sikh calendar commemorates the birth of the Khalsa order of initiated practitioners of the faith. This happened in 1699, 230 years after the birth of the faith's founder, Guru Nanak, in the Punjab region which spans modern-day India and Pakistan.

There's one picture from the rich imagery and metaphor of Guru Nanak's lyrical teachings that has become symbolic of our way of being in the world as Sikhs. It's the image of the lotus flower, which is so often associated with the spirituality of the East. For Sikhs, it reminds us to live like the lotus flower, with our roots in the waters of our worldly existence whilst our spirituality blossoms like petals above, radiating their own fragrance and guiding all our worldly actions. It signifies both attachment and non-attachment to the temporal world and a link to timeless truth.

Guru Nanak was followed by nine consecutive Gurus who further shaped the tradition over two centuries of social change and upheaval. I see this development as embryonic, like the development of human life over nine months in the womb. Then came the birth of the Khalsa order and the faith, now fully formed, was 'born', if you like, into the world. It brought together individuals committed to a life of spiritual discipline whilst living the life of a householder, with a strong work ethic and responsibility toward society and all creation. For Sikhs this was a culmination of the message of Guru Nanak, which found its expression through subsequent Guruships and in the Sikh way of life as it's lived today.

O Creator, may we learn to live like the lotus flower — within the world but not consumed by it — and endeavour to be beacons of spirituality on this earth.

BROADCAST MONDAY 14 APRIL 2008

April 15

Gordon Gray

By chance as I prepared this piece my eye lit on a book on my desk: *In God We Doubt* — John Humphrys' patently sincere, though ultimately unsuccessful quest for convincing answers to questions of faith, posed, for example, by religious extremism or by scientific method.

I've travelled a similar route, though with a different outcome. My questions centred on the Resurrection of Jesus. I can't prove my conclusions, but the source of my conviction was another Doubter, the apostle Thomas. Absent on the evening of Jesus' first appearance to his surprised disciples, Thomas refused to believe unless he could see and examine the facts for himself. Overwhelmed by the reality of Jesus' next manifestation, Thomas' response could only be 'My Lord and my God'.

'Blessed are those who have not seen and yet have believed,' said Jesus. Faith is indeed a 'blessing'; a 'gift'. But behind faith lies the evidence of eye-witnesses, many of whom paid for their convictions with their lives. Down the intervening centuries the Church, flawed as it is, has been sustained both by 'belief' and by a compelling sense of a divine presence.

Lord God, Where there is doubt, may faith blossom; may we this day discern You in a moment of joy, in a compassion not of our own making, in a costly stand for principle, in a gesture of love. Amen.

BROADCAST WEDNESDAY 15 APRIL 2009

April 16

Tony Rogers

For seven or eight years David came to our church. He came in late and left early, lest anyone should spot him or, worse still, talk to him. He came from another tradition, and wasn't sure whether he could leave it behind. When he was with us, he wanted to be back with the people and the worship that were familiar to him. But when he was there, he longed for something different. David would occasionally come and talk about his dilemma, and we assured him that it would not be right to move until he was really happy to do so. David didn't want to lose the friends from the church to which he belonged, and when they assured him that he would always be welcome, he recognized a generosity beyond his expectations.

There's a character in St John's Gospel called Nicodemus, who was torn like my friend David. He was well-known, so he came to Jesus at night, because he was afraid to show openly that he wanted to follow Christ. He was full of questions in his search for the truth, and Jesus listened with patience, without forcing his hand.

I know that when I get excited about something – when, for example, someone is hovering on the brink like David or Nicodemus – I'm in danger of accelerating the process and seem to be more concerned with achieving my desired outcome than in recognizing the importance of giving others the time and space they need.

Lord, help me to approach this coming day with the peace that only You can give. Let me listen to the questions of others, rather than foist my views on them. Let me allow You to work in them as and when and how is best for all concerned. Amen.

BROADCAST MONDAY 16 APRIL 2012

April 17

Gopinder Kaur

We always seem quick to applaud the light. Granted: it's mid-April, the clocks have gone forward and many of us are enjoying the lighter evenings. But doesn't darkness often miss out on some of the good press it deserves?

My grandmother was a real night owl. When the rest of the house became dark and hushed, she would stay up reading, reflecting, germinating her thoughts. And if you shared some of these moments with her, your conversation would be one to relish and remember. It was no surprise to me that she loved gardening. Her childhood passion back in Kenya was to dig up the warm earth with her hands, plant something, pat it all back down and watch it grow. She understood that, like seeds, people and ideas need time for incubation and hibernation before surfacing into the broad light of day.

Surely the darkness is as much part of God's mystery as the light. That idea takes my mind straight to one of our Sikh morning prayers, *Jaap Sahib*, which surges with waves of words and names for God's limitless qualities, because they go beyond all the dualities of our world: *Namo andhkaaray, Namo tej tejay, Namo brind brinday, Namo beej beejay* – Praise to the deep darkness, praise to the brilliant light; Praise to the greatest multitude and praise to the tiniest seed.

Chattr chakkr varti, chattr chakkr bhugtay
Suyanbhav subhang sarbda sarab jugtay
Dukaalang pranaasi diyaalang saroopay
Sada ang sangay abhangang bibhootay

… O Creator, Your all-encompassing magnificence is part and parcel of us too, radiant and forever by our side.

BROADCAST THURSDAY 17 APRIL 2008

April 18

Roger Hutchings

I'm old enough to remember — just! — when Premium Bonds began. I was brought up in a fairly traditional Methodist home, and in the lead-up to the launch of Ernie the computer I think the leaders of Methodism, and certainly my own parents, were quite critical of the plans. Methodists have always been against gambling — partly, I suppose, for moral reasons, but also because so many families and individuals have been, and are being, harmed by their addiction to it. To this day, the Church has very firm rules about even such mild forms of gambling as raffles.

The excitement of Premium Bonds was about large prizes — well, large for this day in 1956: the amounts would seem small now. What began then (and continues, of course, with Ernie's successors) has been added to by the National Lottery, by Europe-wide games, and simply huge winnings, not to mention the plans for a super-casino. What began as a rather jolly encouragement to save has, in modern gambling, become a big industry, making money for private investors, and for the government, and for good causes.

It's not only Methodists who have qualms about gambling, of course. The existence of Gamblers Anonymous is a clear indication of the problems, and there are plenty of examples of criminal activity carried out to overcome losing streaks or enforce the collection of gambling debts. For me personally, it's never been a problem, and I have owned Premium Bonds, though I've not, so far at least, played the Lottery: old habits die hard! So my prayer today is:

Lord, forgive us if our greed rules us, help us to understand the compulsions some face to gamble beyond their means. We pray for those who are addicted, and for their families, friends and colleagues. Teach us all how to use our money. Amen.

BROADCAST WEDNESDAY 18 APRIL 2007

April 19

Tony Rogers

I was nine years old and I was in love — with Grace Kelly. My dad was also in love with her, and to celebrate her wedding to Prince Rainier of Monaco on this day in 1956, we acquired our first television set. A fourteen-inch model which cost 80 guineas. And what is more, its pictures were in black and white, as opposed to some sets from which a bluish or greenish or brownish shade emerged. But we were particular. Nothing but the best was good enough for Grace, even if she was deserting me to get married. That childhood dream came to nought, like many others. My understanding of the true picture was limited then — and it's still limited now. Just because I'm no longer a child, I can't claim to have put childish ways behind me. The Apostle Paul's words about taking that approach are easier said than done. As a flawed and fragile human being, I know only too well that I look for the crock of gold at the end of the rainbow. One day, I imagine, I will wake up, organized, tidy and on top of everything. The desk will be clear, emails answered and phone calls returned. The crock of gold will remain in my imagination as long as I just expect it to happen. It's no more likely than Grace proposing to me! But when I recognize that things are in my control, I can edge forward — slowly but surely.

Father, Your Son Jesus came into our world to share with us the reality of human living. Teach us, like him, to immerse ourselves in the world that surrounds us, to be alert to the needs of others, and to work, under his grace, to be people of good news and good living. Amen.

BROADCAST THURSDAY 19 APRIL 2012

April 20

David Chillingworth

'What, then, shall I do with Jesus who is called Christ?'

They all answered, 'Crucify him!'

Ask the audience — it's a commonplace of today's media. Just dial the number — or send a text — to register your vote. So what if the results are a bit random? Involvement is what counts.

Pilate wasn't running a talent competition. It was much more serious than that. Even in my work in the Church, the buzzwords are consultative, collegial and collaborative. We don't make choices without making sure that we have 'everyone on board'. No harm in that.

But Pilate was faced with a justice call. To make a moral choice — to release the prisoner whom he knew to be innocent — would have displeased both his political masters and the crowd. So he asked the crowd, to avoid the responsibility. But moral courage is not a 'What do you think?' kind of thing. Rather it's, 'This is what I believe to be right, no matter what you think.'

Pilate failed that test. He asked the audience — and the audience gave him the answer he needed so that he could avoid the choice which was both courageous and right.

So his enduring legacy is the phrase to 'wash our hands of this — or that'.

Father God
Give us clarity of understanding
And courageous hearts
When we face difficult and costly choices.
Teach us always to discern Your will
And your truth.
Amen.

BROADCAST WEDNESDAY 20 APRIL 2011

April 21

Jeremy Morris

Not so long ago, for the first time in my life, I became the owner of a pet dog, a cross-breed terrier. He's a lovely pet for the family. And I love my dog. That is, I love this particular dog — perhaps not dogs in general.

I'm wary of the way we can get too sentimental about animals. But at the same time, my dog has a character I adore. I know it's a mistake to think of him in terms that are too human. But he has personality, loyalty, affection, unpredictability and playfulness.

Animals can connect with us. There's an ancient Christian argument about whether animals have souls. I think they probably do. There is, surely, something in them — however remote it may seem sometimes — that strikes a chord in us, and evokes our sympathy.

We all need to be reminded of our connectedness to animals. God has placed us in a world rich with colour and variety. We know, of course, that it's a harsh world, in which — so we say — dog eats dog. The terrier whose affection I admire is also the terrier who would savage small birds and squirrels, given half a chance.

But the world of nature is greater than us, and we're one small link in its chain. Pets remind us of that. The harsh way of nature shouldn't blind us to its beauties.

Awaken in us, Lord, a growing appreciation of the infinite richness of our world, and of all the many creatures it contains, that we may learn to treasure and protect them, now and always. Amen.

BROADCAST SATURDAY 21 APRIL 2012

April 22

David Stone

Once, on a family outing to the Royal Observatory at Greenwich, we decided to visit the planetarium. It was a great way to spend half an hour with a couple of active eleven-year-olds! The resident astronomer took us on a fascinating tour of the sky, showing what would be visible that night – cloud cover and light pollution permitting. It was all pretty impressive. But then he turned off the atmosphere, demonstrating what we would see if that wasn't getting in the way. Instantly, the view that had been amazing enough as it was became scarcely credible. The sky was jam-packed with innumerable pinpricks of light. We all sat there, stunned. We know about the sheer unimaginable vastness of the universe in theory, with its estimated 500 billion galaxies, each of them containing about 300 billion stars. But to see it like that was something else.

Being brought face to face with our ant-like insignificance in the scheme of things is an unnerving experience. But at least we're not alone. Many centuries ago, the writer of Psalm 8 had the same experience. 'When I look at your heavens, the work of your fingers, the moon and the stars that you have established; what are human beings that you are mindful of them, mortals that you care for them? Yet,' he goes on, 'you have made them a little lower than God, and crowned them with glory and honour.'

Lord God of the overwhelming immensity of all that is, all that has been and all that ever will be, as we reflect on the wonder of Your creation, help us to see human beings more as You see them and to treat ourselves and to behave toward one another as people who really matter. Amen.

BROADCAST MONDAY 22 APRIL 2013

April 23

Jeremy Morris

Today is St George's day. Growing up in the 1960s and 70s, I don't remember much being made of this. Yet I see the flag around more and more now. Is this a sign of rising English nationalism?

And is there anything wrong with nationalism anyway? Most of us like to feel we belong, and a nation is just one more level of belonging – family, friends, religion, occupation, region or class perhaps, and then nation, these are reasonable and compatible ways of identifying who we are and where we come from.

But the wider these circles go, the broader and deeper they must be, if we are not to fall into a narrow and blind egotism and make our own needs the centre of the world. If a family is made up of different individuals, with a variety of characters and attitudes, how much more varied – infinitely more – must be a nation!

St George is not only the patron saint of England, but of Russia, Serbia, Portugal, Ukraine, Egypt and Greece, amongst other countries. It is somehow fitting that this Roman martyr, who probably never set foot in Britain, is celebrated in so many different places. It reminds us that, for Christians and many others of faith, there is another country still to which all nations belong, and which George himself served – the kingdom of God.

We can love our families, friends, region and nation. But all these loves belong to our common humanity. They don't cancel each other out, and they should never obscure our love of others and our love of God.

Almighty God, as we remember St George today and his witness to the truth, make us alive to the needs of the whole human community, and all those we meet today. Amen.

BROADCAST MONDAY 23 APRIL 2012

April 24

David Stone

Today's twentieth anniversary of the Bishopsgate bombing, which brought death and destruction to the heart of the City of London, reminds us that recent events in Boston, shocking though they are, are nothing new. Back then one person was killed and more than 40 were injured in the massive blast, which did an enormous amount of damage to the area. Among the buildings destroyed was the tiny medieval church of St Ethelburga's in Bishopsgate. Situated just seven metres away from the bomb, it collapsed owing to the force of the explosion. But St Ethelburga's was rebuilt and stands today as a centre for helping to build relationships across divisions of conflict, culture and religion.

As with Coventry Cathedral, where I work, the decision was taken not to let violence and hatred have the last word but to build something new out of the ruins of the old, something filled with hope for the future. Not that we can ever forget the past, a truth that was reflected in Sir Basil Spence's design of the modern Coventry Cathedral. The ruins of the old bombed Cathedral were carefully linked with the new and are clearly visible through the glass of the great West Screen.

Such an ever-present reminder of the consequences of war underlines the cost and the power of forgiveness. We have to travel from where we are, not from where we would like to be. Forgiveness is about refusing to allow the conflicts of the past to dictate how we handle the future.

O God, the Father of all, whose Son commanded us to love our enemies: lead them and us from prejudice to truth; deliver them and us from hatred, cruelty and revenge; and in Your good time enable us all to stand reconciled before You. Through Jesus Christ, our Lord, Amen.

BROADCAST WEDNESDAY 24 APRIL 2013

April 25

Jeremy Morris

If you asked me to draw up a list of the people who have most influenced me in my life, pretty near the top of my list would come my friends. Friends, I think, have become if anything even more important to us than perhaps they once were, now that for so many people the circle of the family has shrunk.

But you can't make friends unless you are first prepared to welcome them as strangers, and that takes a particular skill which I think *is* in short supply today – hospitality. In many cultures, hospitality to the stranger is almost a sacred duty. In our culture, our busy, self-obsessed lives leave us little space and time to take trouble with people we don't know.

We hear how little we know our neighbours, and how unfriendly particular places are. And when something terrible happens to someone, all too often we hear, either of the victim or of the perpetrator, that they kept themselves to themselves – as if that was a virtue!

Our lives are impoverished by our failure to welcome the stranger. In the Bible the stranger is, with the widow and the fatherless, a symbol of human need. Meeting that need not only helps the other person, but makes us better, fuller, more rounded human beings. It may not be easy to do so, but surely we can find a way of putting hospitality back at the very centre of the way we live, so that the walls of suspicion and indifference that divide our society may be broken down. And who knows, we may even make good friends.

Almighty God, teach us to welcome and respect the stranger, so that our lives may be filled with the spirit of Your peace, now and always. Amen.

BROADCAST WEDNESDAY 25 APRIL 2012

April 26

Stephen Shipley

In the early hours of 26 April 1986, reactor No. 4 at the Chernobyl nuclear power plant in what was then the Soviet Union was operating at very low capacity during a planned shutdown. What the plant personnel didn't know was that the reactor's design made it unstable at such reduced power, and the operators were careless about safety precautions during the test. After a sudden surge, two explosions destroyed the reactor core and the resultant plume of radioactive debris that drifted as far as Eastern Europe and Scandinavia caused the worst nuclear power accident in history. Large areas of the Soviet Union were contaminated and nearly a quarter of a million people had to be evacuated and resettled.

Accidents can have terrible effects. But the question to be asked isn't whether the creation of nuclear energy is dangerous. Rather it's whether the risks are such that it's wrong to use this means of production. There are those who think that to produce nuclear energy is to take on the role of God – it's interfering with the natural order of things. But then there are others who would say that the power in the universe comes from nuclear energy formed in the interior of its stars – that's why they burn so brightly. So when God created his universe, he intended it to be powered by such forces – why then shouldn't his creatures on Earth use the same kind of energy?

These are complex arguments. We're bound to live with risk in one form or another, though naturally we try to minimize that risk, whether it's risk from nuclear power or from having insufficient energy for our needs.

Let's pray then, on this anniversary of a dreadful accident, for grace to cope with the hazards of life so that we are neither unduly fearful nor take undue risks. Amen.

BROADCAST THURSDAY 26 APRIL 2007

April 27

Mary Stallard

Recently I was at the funeral of an older friend who was a much-loved priest. Many people came to the church service dressed smartly in black. Right in the front row was a girl, perhaps four years old, wearing a red, sparkly party dress. Her response to the loss of her granddad had made her want to look her best at his special service.

It's not easy knowing how to include children at funerals, but this child, although perhaps too young to fully understand what was going on, clearly wanted to be there with her family. Her scarlet frock stood out like a small bright reminder of fierce love against the dark background of the grief we adults too were feeling. It was as though she showed an instinctive grasp of the bigger story that the hymns and words were seeking to convey. Her dress communicated a note of joy amongst the sadness, reminding us all of the Christian hope that even in death there is something to celebrate. The story of Jesus tells us that death is not the end, because three days after he died he was raised to a new life, in which we are all invited to share.

We may be conscious of people who are experiencing suffering in their lives today or we may be struggling with painful issues ourselves. Like a child at a funeral, there is so much we simply don't understand and cannot explain about why bad things happen. But if we're open to discovering it, the love of our friends and family members of all ages can speak to us of the goodness and giftedness of life. And of the hope that God has given us.

Holy God, all our lives belong to You, and You promise that suffering and death never have the last word. When we're sad or troubled, help us to know that Your love is stronger than anything we face. Amen.

BROADCAST TUESDAY 27 APRIL 2010

April 28

Cathy Le Feuvre

Recently I attended a very special awards evening where the work that's being done in Salvation Army hostels — our resettlement centres in the UK and Ireland — was celebrated.

The Hostel Plus Awards were an opportunity to recognize the hard work and achievements not only of the dedicated staff but also of the residents.

During the course of the evening, we heard how, with the appropriate help and support, people are turning their lives around — seeing the possibility for a new start.

People who were once homeless, maybe even addicted to alcohol or drugs, are being encouraged to look at life again, to tackle problems and to learn new skills. Some are returning to education and employment. In some centres there are social enterprise schemes where residents are working together to run businesses — it's all part of learning to become confident and independent.

Unfortunately, many similarly disadvantaged people have in the past been excluded, ignored by society. Now, with the help of dedicated and experienced professional staff working for a number of organizations dedicated to helping them, they're learning to live life to the full. In time, many will go on to live independent, productive lives.

Jesus reached out to many people during the course of his ministry on Earth. For him there were no hopeless causes! Time and again he urged his followers to get involved, to be sympathetic to the needs of others, to help those who needed help.

Lord, some of us are struggling with the challenges of life. Thank You that You never give up on us. Fill us with Your love and strength so that we may move forward into a future that is full of potential. Amen.

BROADCAST TUESDAY 28 APRIL 2009

April 29

Mary Stallard

My grandmother Kathleen was one of the feistier residents in a local care home. Almost blind, physically frail and rather forgetful, she was nevertheless a determined woman who liked to feel in control of her circumstances.

We went to visit her soon after she'd moved into the home at a time when she was fretful and confused. Apparently believing that she was still in her own house, Kathleen was angry that people appeared to be intruding upon her space. She didn't seem able to let anyone explain things to her or help her, and kept shouting and pointing, telling everyone to leave her alone. But then something unusual happened. My husband, who's also a vicar, picked up a hairbrush lying nearby and gently started to brush her hair. It was a gesture that challenged the social norms: a younger man, a priest, brushing an older woman's hair – quite an intimate action. But it was exactly what was needed: my grandmother almost immediately became calm, comforted and perhaps distracted by the gentle strokes of the brush against her head. She relaxed and forgot her previous anxiety.

Touch can be a powerful, though sometimes controversial, means of communication. When used well, it can be beautiful and healing, an effective sign of care for another person. There's a story in Mark's Gospel about how when Jesus' life was under threat and when he must have felt lonely and exposed, a woman came to him and against all the rules of the time she touched him, pouring precious perfume on his head. Jesus commended her for this, saying that her simple offering would always be remembered as a model of good and kind love in action.

Tender God, help us to be sensitive to the needs of those around us today. May we use our hands to help and heal, that others may find only gentleness and support from our touch. Amen.

BROADCAST THURSDAY 29 APRIL 2010

April 30

Cathy Le Feuvre

There's a freshness in the air. The scent of spring flowers, the smell of newly mown lawns. Everywhere you look, gardens and hedgerows are coming alive with colour.

It's an exciting time of year, I think. Even though nature may seem to have been asleep for the long winter months, tiny seeds were lurking in the ground ready to grow, the smallest bulbs were lying dormant, just waiting to burst into life. The potential has been there for months, but now the temperatures are right and the sun is warmer; new life is springing up everywhere.

Jesus often told stories – parables – to explain difficult-to-understand concepts. God's kingdom, he said, is like a small seed, or maybe like a pine nut. When it lands on the ground, it's quite small as seeds go, yet once it is planted it grows into a huge pine tree with thick branches. Eagles nest in it.

In the world God wants us to inhabit, even small things have the potential for good. Even those who feel they have nothing to contribute DO have something to give. No one should feel excluded from God's love. Everyone is important. And what WE do impacts on others.

Just as the tiniest seed has the potential to bring colour into a garden, even a small act of kindness can make the world a better place. It might be just popping in to check on an elderly neighbour. Calling a friend who we know is going through a hard time. Saying 'Good morning' or smiling, rather than keeping our head behind our newspapers on the train into work.

Lord, although we may not think we can do much, help us today to bring colour, kindness and love into Your world. Amen.

BROADCAST THURSDAY 30 APRIL 2009

May 1

Bob Fyffe

Our Father – the first two words of the Lord's prayer. They are words that Jesus of Nazareth taught his followers to say. So what kind of Father is he, I wonder?

In his old age, my own father and I have become wonderfully close, sharing more than ever we have before, perhaps in part because my mother has become lost in the silent crash of Alzheimer's.

My own father and I argue, mostly about football and politics, and yes, who's better at table tennis. I wonder if Jesus meant us to think of *God* as that kind of Father. But he said *our* Father. Perhaps that's important.

Not my father but ours, mine, everybody's.

So perhaps the Lord means that he is like all the best bits of everybody's dad all rolled into one.

Perhaps he's good like mine when he carefully holds the cup to my mother's lips to ensure that she drinks plenty.

Maybe he lets us do what we like, but helps us to see that 'doing our own thing' can bring pain to others.

Maybe Our Father even hopes we'll go to church.

I wonder if Our Father laughs when we're all happy together, as my dad does.

But I suppose the best bit is that he is *ours*, whatever our own dad is like, whether we have one or not

So thank you, Lord, for sharing your Father with us.

And telling us that he is our Father too.

Thank you for letting us know that He thinks of each one of us as one of *His* family.

God, our Father, thank You for being Father to all of us. Help us this day to live as one family. Help us to make You laugh with pleasure and to love others in the way You love us. Amen.

BROADCAST SATURDAY 1 MAY 2010

May 2

Alison Jack

Of the Scots words I often heard my mother use when I was a child, two stick in my mind. To *deave* means to annoy, especially with repetitive noise and chatter. It was usually used in the negative – 'don't deave me with your din.' But it could also be used as a warning: 'You are going to deave me if you keep on asking for that biscuit.' If I went too far, the next word would appear: to *scunner*. While this word could mean to cause to feel sick – and my mother sometimes used it in that way, as in 'that mouthful scunnered my stomach', more often it would be addressed at my brother and me, and would signal that she had had enough of some behaviour or other: 'I'm scunnered with you two splashing in those puddles and soaking my legs.'

All children irritate their parents, and others too, at some point. There is something about the enthusiasm of children, the relentlessness of their not yet knowing when to stop doing whatever they are enjoying in the moment; or when to judiciously refrain from demanding the thing they most want in the world. Adults are easily annoyed, and sensitive when the repeated request is impossible, or impractical or ill-advised. Sometimes, for the guardians of the very young who rarely get a break, to be deaved and scunnered is the overwhelming experience of each day; and each day may begin very early indeed. Tiredness and frustration can mean we are more easily and quickly deaved and scunnered by behaviour which would otherwise make us smile or join in. We might all be more sympathetic to the burdens others carry, and less swift to judge the deaved and the scunnered.

Loving God, may those who are worn down by the demands placed on them, whether by children, or other responsibilities, find rest and understanding from those around them today. Amen.

BROADCAST WEDNESDAY 2 MAY 2012

May 3

Peter Baker

Since the UK's first heart transplant took place on this day in 1968, thousands of people have subsequently benefited from the revolutionary surgical procedure pioneered by Dr Christian Barnard. Indeed, the entire medical field of cardiology has been transformed as a consequence. And having undergone recent routine heart checks myself, I'm personally grateful for the advances that have been made in the treatment of heart disease.

The Bible often speaks about the heart. Not that it locates the heart within the chest cavity or identifies it as an organ that pumps blood around the body. In Biblical understanding, the heart is the centre of the human personality. Poets and philosophers have followed suit, regarding the heart as the seat of consciousness, the place where reason and emotion come together to generate action. When Jesus reflected upon the human condition, he reckoned that our life priorities and investments would indicate what we believed important: 'where your treasure is, there your heart will be also.'

The heart then acts as the point of convergence where we process thoughts, engage emotions, and turn all that into behaviours, words, responses. It becomes the moral centre, which is why the prophet Jeremiah warns that we need to be aware that the heart can be deceitful and desperately wicked.

Perhaps for this reason the Book of Proverbs says, 'Above all else, guard your heart, for it is the wellspring of life.' Which seems to be suggesting that just as the physical heart is essential to the healthy functioning of the entire body, so our spiritual, moral and emotional life depends upon a good heart. That's why we must look after, protect and monitor it.

David, the great King of Israel, examined the condition of his heart and with candour took the issue to God in prayer. And so we pray with him: 'Create in me a clean heart, O Lord, renew a right spirit within me.' Amen.

BROADCAST FRIDAY 3 MAY 2013

May 4

Alison Jack

I was recently on holiday in a county which, like many others, puts a slogan under its name on the signposts announcing you are crossing its boundary. The slogan for this county is: 'A place where everyone matters.' If you live there, you will know where I was! I may be sceptical about the value of such slogans in practical terms, but there's no doubting the positive nature of the assertion. And yes, maybe I should tell you that I was in Lancashire! Mattering to others, even to just one other, makes life worth living. If we matter, we are given a sense of worth and importance, there's a connection built on trust and interdependence. In communities where folk matter to one another, there is a greater chance of community spirit and cohesion.

It's when we stop mattering to others, or when we feel we don't matter to anyone, even to ourselves, that we can begin to feel pretty lonely and unlovable. Showing that another matters to us is not always easy, either; and we don't always want to admit that we need to feel we matter. Making these feelings visible can make us feel vulnerable, when we'd rather seem strong. That county's slogan made me think again about whom I matter to, and who and what matters to me. And where does God come into all of this? In the example of the life of Jesus, we seem to have a picture of a person who demonstrated that everyone matters: young and old, woman and man, powerful and weak, those highly visible in public life and those so inconsequential they might as well have been invisible.

Lord of all, today may we know what it means to matter — to You, to ourselves and to others, and may we hold out our hands to those who matter to us, in our families, amongst our friends and in our communities. Amen.

BROADCAST FRIDAY 4 MAY 2012

May 5

David Chillingworth

I talked recently to somebody whose work is in what is euphemistically called 'corporate recovery'. It's the business of managing failed and failing companies. It's the moment when all the uncertainty comes to an end, the creditors call 'time' and hopes, dreams and hard work lie shattered.

And what I heard was the human side of it all — what it's like to live constantly with insecurity. One of the letters in the agony column in my Sunday paper recently was from a man who found that the insecurity he and his wife were experiencing was so great that they couldn't communicate any more — paralysed by fear about his job and how they would cope with mortgage, children and the endless costs of modern life.

In a society where so much of identity and status is shaped by what we do, the loss of work is particularly difficult. Unemployment often brings not just loss of income but loss of status and identity as well. It can be as if we cease to exist.

The challenge, I suppose, is to work out how to invest more in what we are than in what we do. It's another of those balances that we struggle with — the spectrum where we measure being against doing. It's how we value our lives and the lives of others. People of faith work hard at these balances. Time-hallowed patterns of living stress the importance of integrity and the way in which our lives are shaped; tell us that we are more than what we do; remind us that in God's eyes we are worth more than the value other people put on us.

Father
When the future is uncertain
And fear grips us
Teach us the strength of being
And the power of love.
Amen.

BROADCAST TUESDAY 5 MAY 2009

May 6

Bob Fyffe

'For yours is the Kingdom, the power and the glory ...'

These are the first words of the ending of the Lord's prayer. We hear lots about power and glory. Leaders of all kinds, sportsmen and women, financiers, television personalities, people in all walks of life, and yes, even within the church, all like power.

Some crave it, and get bent all out of shape by it.

We all like some power. Isn't it true that often we want to be in charge, to be the leader, to take the front spot, to be most popular, and in the limelight?

Well then, why is it that to be greater, stronger, more popular, wealthier, we end up doing things that hurt ourselves and others?

The Lord said, 'The first shall be last, and the last first.' And he also said, 'The least of them shall be the greatest.'

But before we think 'holier than thou' thoughts, let's also remember that the disciples also wanted power. James and John wanted the seat next to Jesus in the Kingdom. But Jesus taught that the Kingdom of God is not built on power and aggression, jealous ambition or longing for fame and glory.

Jesus showed us what power is about when he washed the disciples' feet, when he served rather than being served. The God we pray to in the Kingdom finds power and glory through birth in a stable, through kneeling at the world's feet, in dying on a cross at a crossroads. In that we see power and glory. We find true greatness.

Lord, bless all the activity of this day, that we may show to others the power of our example, not the example of our power. Bless all who seek to serve others in our communities this and every day. Amen.

BROADCAST THURSDAY 6 MAY 2010

May 7

David Chillingworth

It happens all too often nowadays. You call somebody at work or email them – and the response is that they are having 'time off with stress'. Many people experience the pressures of work and daily life as unrelenting. We're all having to do more with less. Everybody is under pressure. Relationships suffer. Once that begins to happen, it's very difficult to stop. We focus on problems and our response to them. Pressure squeezes the joy out of things, saps energy and initiative and makes people anxious about how they will cope. That's life lacking dignity and grace.

The first answers to that lie of course in management and relationships. But there is a spiritual aspect to it as well. I don't mean something that is holy and hides from the real world, but rather that we need to think deeply about how we are as people. Unhealthy levels of stress can turn us into victims – people who are at the mercy of workload and relationships that don't work.

The Bible is full of stress and pressure; conflict and unresolved difficulties; arguments about authority and leadership. Jesus' disciples found the pressure too great when he was crucified and they just ran away. But in the middle of all that pressure, the messages are about being connected to something bigger, being part of God's wider purpose, living out a bigger picture of life and relationships.

We constantly fail to live up to that – but it is the only counter to the way in which stress and pressure narrow down our lives.

Lord, we think today of people who are experiencing stress and pressure, who dread going to work, who fear for the future. Bring to them and to their relationships Your peace, healing and love. Amen.

BROADCAST THURSDAY 7 MAY 2009

May 8

Lynn Gallagher

Recently I met a man from South Africa called Sali. He described himself as Cape coloured, of mixed race, too black for the last regime, he said, and too pale for this one. He was a very nice man, intelligent, sensitive, with enormous experience and a very realistic view of today's South Africa, and the challenges that face it.

He had wanted to go into environmental management, but that had been in the days of apartheid and he had been told quite coldly 'to my face' that those courses were only available for the sons of white farmers. He still maintains a keen interest in the environmental health of the country he clearly loves. I liked him very much, but he said something which at the time I found suddenly shocking.

'I am,' he said, 'a recovering racist.'

He said it 'to my face', and I was unmistakably aware of the history which made him say this, and the implied antipathy toward me, a white person.

But of course, when I thought about it, I recognized the parallel that he was invoking — that, just as an alcoholic has to accept the fact of his or her condition, and move from that position, so does a person of prejudice. It is an honest and commendable thing to say.

As I think about Northern Ireland and its future, I believe there are a whole lot of us here — most of us, and me included — who should stand up and say, 'I am a recovering bigot.'

Lord, You know that past hurt and damage and injustice and violence are no excuses for prejudice. Grant the integrity, self-knowledge and determination to curb every shadow of addiction to old fears and bigotry. Amen.

BROADCAST TUESDAY 8 MAY 2007

May 9

Andrew Graystone

Five hundred years ago tomorrow a young sculptor called Michelangelo Buonarroti started work on the painting that remains one of the artistic wonders of the world, the monumental ceiling of the Sistine Chapel in Rome, I wonder how he felt, five centuries ago, as he looked up at the vast blankness – 550 square meters of damp grey plaster. We know that he took the commission with great reluctance. He must have realized that he was facing years of back-breaking work at great height. He understood that he would face the scathing criticism of rival painters. And he wasn't even confident he was going to be paid for the job. He could have been forgiven for thinking that the task could never be finished – so it wasn't worth starting. And yet he started work.

The ceiling fresco in the Sistine Chapel took four and a half years to complete. Michelangelo's painting is a work of theology as much as art. It is also a triumph of hope and endurance.

In an increasingly cynical culture we need to cherish the dreamers – people of hope and vision who believe that great things can be achieved and the world can be changed.

> *God of hope, we pray for a recovery of hope in our culture.*
> *That from today's young people You will raise up*
> *Artists who can reflect the truth with love;*
> *Politicians and protesters driven by a vision of a better world;*
> *Comedians with a sense of innocent fun;*
> *And Christian leaders burning with the hope of glory.*
> *Amen.*

May 10

Michael Ford

There's nothing more spiritually uplifting at this time of the year than the sound of the dawn chorus, a mystery of creation that begins in March and reaches its peak in May. Blackbirds, robins, wrens, warblers, thrushes and finches — all take part in an earthly ritual received as heavenly melody.

Birds sing, of course, with the very practical purpose of defending their territory or attracting a mate, and they do so particularly at dawn when the air is still and sound transmission is at its best. Some people might find the symphony wakes them up far too early but, for me, lying in bed and praying with the chorus involves me in a liturgical act that seems to purify the past and sanctify the day ahead — a holy communion with creation that has the power of a sacrament to heal and transform.

The French composer and ornithologist Olivier Messiaen believed birds to be the greatest musicians. Notating their songs across the world, he incorporated transcriptions into most of his music, which was often a theological explosion of joy, divine love and redemption. For him, birdsong symbolized the presence of God in creation. 'In the domain of music,' he said, 'birds have discovered everything. If birds are the source of all earthly music, then as musical symbols of creation they are also messengers of heavenly music.'

O Lord, our Sovereign, how majestic is Your name in all the earth. You have set Your glory above the heavens. Help us to perceive the divine mystery at the heart of all creation and be renewed by it. Amen.

BROADCAST TUESDAY 10 MAY 2011

May 11

Clair Jaquiss

She crashed into our room in the early hours. This wasn't just a child's bad dream. 'There's water coming through the ceiling onto my bed.' If even the most mundane leaks cause chaos, those whose lives have been completely turned upside down by flood must live in grief-stricken bewilderment.

The people of the Hebrew Bible had a problem with water. It was dangerous. For a miracle, the Red Sea nearly trapped the Israelites when they were being pursued by Pharaoh. Water drowned the earth in the story of Noah and the flood. Water needed to be controlled – bounded by land and river banks, at the bottom of wells and kept up above the firmament by God until it was time for it to rain in due season. But when water was out of control, it was chaos. The spirit of God right at the start of the world swept over formless and chaotic waters.

Water has power to erode solid rock, to shape the landscape. And in the hands of the torturer, whether administered or withheld, it can be a cruel and powerful weapon.

Living in the presence of water is a risk: it can leak into the electrics and rot your joists. It can take the lives of those who live alongside it or whose work depends on it. For so many in the world, the simple act of drinking it is dangerous – contaminated with waste and bacteria.

So a prayer for today:

Lord God, the source of life, who has given us such beauty and goodness, help us to use Your gift of water with care, protect those who live and work on the waters of the earth, and help us to work toward the day when all Your children may have fresh water to drink, in the name of the one who is the water of life. Amen.

BROADCAST TUESDAY 11 MAY 2010

May 12

Michael Ford

It's hard to believe that so many years have passed since the Labour Party Leader John Smith died of a heart attack. 12 May 1994 happened to be Ascension Day and, in a service that evening on Radio 4, it fell to me to remember him in prayer.

John Smith was an unforgettable force in British politics, an inspirational figure to MPs of all parties. People instantly recognized his integrity and the respect he showed to those who held different views from his own. He had a gift for being able to cast aside political disagreements without prejudice. Many will remember his unique combination of personal authority and good humour which could leave colleagues in hysterics, perhaps something not witnessed that often at Westminster these days.

For John Smith, egalitarian and democrat, politics was a moral calling. It meant values, principles and ethical beliefs. Christianity influenced his political philosophy and gave him strength.

The politician is buried on the tiny Hebridean island of Iona, which had been a retreat for him from the pressures of the House. It was difficult for him to relax but somehow Iona enabled him to unwind like no other place.

The island is still home to a dispersed Christian community striving for peace and social justice. One of its hymns includes the memorable line, 'Let earthly politics be the stuff of prayer', which was very much John Smith's outlook as well.

So, may the God of Justice keep us silent when the only words we have to utter are ones of judgement, exclusion or prejudice, and may earthly politics always be the stuff of our prayer. Amen.

BROADCAST THURSDAY 12 MAY 2011

May 13

Maggi Dawn

We're thinking this week of the idea of giving. In the sixteenth century, St Ignatius of Loyola asked God to teach him 'to give and not to count the cost, to labour and not to ask for any reward'.

Most of us have felt the effects of the credit crunch in recent years. Some people are suffering real hardship, even losing their homes and livelihoods. But all of us are having to think more carefully about what we have, and how we use it.

But this cloud, however dark it may be, may have an unexpected silver lining. In what remains one of the richest nations in the world, the recession and subsequent fragile economic recovery have raised our awareness of what it feels like to be vulnerable and insecure. We've had to rediscover how to get by without things we thought we needed; we may also be challenged to reach out with generosity to those who've been hit harder than us. And so the vulnerability of economic anxiety may reconnect us with the idea of giving.

Giving is a central theme in Christian theology. God's gift to the world was not religious doctrines or rules, not transactions that demand a payback, but the free gift of himself, without conditions attached, given with the inbuilt risk that he *might not* be repaid with respect and love.

The credit crunch revealed starkly that free gifts and money-for-nothing are an illusion. But if, in financial hardship, we rediscover that the true value of a gift is in giving ourselves, then we'll end up as winners, and not losers.

Loving God, we give You thanks that You gave yourself for us. Teach us what is of lasting value, and to give our time, energy and resources to those who need it more than we do. Amen.

BROADCAST WEDNESDAY 13 MAY 2009

May 14

Clair Jaquiss

A friend was trying to lose weight. She'd come along to the slimming club and was following instructions to the letter. She was serious about this – more exercise, healthy eating, plenty of water.

She came back the next week somewhat bemused. The healthy eating was fine. It was drinking the water and the exercise – plenty of skipping – that was a real problem. Her stomach had felt so bloated with water, jumping up and down was seriously uncomfortable. She discovered the reason that next week. She was supposed to drink eight *glasses* of water a day – not eight *pints*.

The advice that we should drink more water and the understanding of the importance of water to the proper functioning of our bodies are almost commonplace these days. Rehydration is important after illness. Enough water can help your metabolism to work more efficiently and thereby lose weight (but not too much water!). Water is needed for life.

For the poets and prophets of the Old Testament, water was a symbol for the blessing of life itself. Ezekiel told a story about dried-up bones in a valley, that God breathed life back into. And Jesus talked of himself in John's Gospel as the living water – as the water of life itself. God makes life happen, as falling water awakens the growth of seeds in the soil, and God sustains life with the living water of his Spirit.

So we pray for this living water:

O God, who make springs gush forth in the valleys
And gives water to the beasts of the field,
Who waters the earth so that grass grows and trees flourish,
Give us the living water of Your Spirit to renew our lives
And to help us live for You and for each other.
In the name of Jesus Christ, Amen.

BROADCAST FRIDAY 14 MAY 2010

May 15

Maggi Dawn

Life isn't fair. The news is full of stories about violence and murder, illness and economic gloom.

Sometimes it's the actions of others that make things unfair, sometimes it's just the circumstances of life.

When life isn't fair, we often write off the idea of God — for how can a good God allow bad things to happen? Jesus himself knew that life wasn't fair: there will always be poverty, he said. But then he called on his followers to be *more than fair*.

'An eye for an eye, a tooth for a tooth' was a rule introduced in ancient Israel to limit acts of revenge to what was strictly fair. If your enemy poked out your eye, you could do the same back to him — but you couldn't take his life.

But Jesus went a step further. Fair isn't enough, he said. True justice demands that someone has the courage not to demand retribution. If someone pokes your eye out, says Jesus, then *don't* take revenge. Turn the other cheek; and stop the cycle of violence.

To see justice and mercy in our world, we have to become people who will be more than fair. That's not to say we should just let others walk all over us. But the cry for fairness isn't enough to end conflict. Justice costs us courage and effort, and will only be won through searching actively after peace.

Loving God, we give You thanks that You gave Yourself for us. Teach us how to be wise and merciful; when to stand up for ourselves, and when to turn the other cheek. Amen.

BROADCAST FRIDAY 15 MAY 2009

May 16

Sharon Grenham Toze

Over the years, we've celebrated many famous Australians: Kylie Minogue, Greg Chappell, Dame Joan Sutherland ... But it's ironic that one of the most famous names in Australian history should be a British woman whom most of us have never heard of!

Caroline Chisholm was born Caroline Jones in Northampton in 1808. After her marriage she accompanied her husband, an officer in the East India Company, to India, where she was horrified by the poverty and squalor she saw on the streets. Many of the destitute she saw begging were the children of British soldiers. Moved to action, Caroline started a school for them.

When she was 30, Caroline and her family moved to Australia. Large numbers of immigrant women were arriving alone in Sydney, looking for work, marriage and a better life. What most of them found was hostility, prostitution and crippling poverty. After a lot of high-level wrangling, Mrs Chisholm set up a home for some of these women, a kind of long-term reception centre, where they received basic education and tuition in life skills – which in turn gave them a chance at both employment and marriage.

Caroline Chisholm became a Roman Catholic, like her husband, and today is set aside as her commemoration day. Living as we do in a country struggling to work out its attitude to immigration, Caroline Chisholm's simple humanitarian response is salutary. Then, as now, immigrants are doing what we all do, at some level – looking for a better life. Whatever their final destination, they have a right, just as we do, to respect, kindness and dignity.

Compassionate God, Your Son Jesus was, in his life, homeless, a refugee, a wanderer and a convicted criminal. Just as You teach us to open our hearts to him, may we also find room in our hearts for those wanderers and exiles who are his brothers and sisters – and ours. Amen.

BROADCAST FRIDAY 16 MAY 2008

May 17

Peter Baker

'Why are you downcast, O my soul? Why so disturbed within me?' Such honesty may surprise those who imagine that belief in God places us beyond the possibility of personal despair and doubt. Not so. The Psalms, from which that opening quotation comes, are refreshingly real – they sing it and pray it the way that it so often is in our lives.

Psalm 42 is written out of an experience of the most intense sadness of heart. 'My tears have been my food day and night,' the Psalmist comments; and then continues: 'Deep calls to deep in the roar of your waterfalls; all your waves and breakers have swept over me.'

These symptoms sound very similar to what we tend to describe as depression. That is, of course, a very complex and common condition. And as the Psalm reminds us, faith does not make us immune to such overwhelming feelings of vulnerability and disorientation. Life on the ragged edge can be the experience of us all, including those who believe in God.

This is why it can be so unhelpful to tell people to 'snap out of it!' We are multi-dimensional creatures in whom the various aspects of our being constantly interact. And our health, therefore, will usually be the product of treating symptoms at all those levels.

According to the Psalm, faith in God gives the capacity to talk to oneself without listening only to the negative voices of life. We're able to separate the inner person from the outer, which is the product of environment, heredity and circumstance. This soul speak is the route to well-being.

Which is why the Psalmist can address himself positively in conclusion: 'Soul, put your hope in God, for I will yet praise Him, my Saviour and my God.'

Lord, be with all who struggle with the disorientation of their life. And may we each learn the importance of talking to as well as listening to ourselves. Amen.

BROADCAST MONDAY 17 MAY 2010

May 18

Peter Smith

There are times in my life when I feel I'm on a treadmill. It isn't that anything dramatic has happened; I haven't lost my job, I haven't had a serious row with colleagues at work or with my friends or family. But each day seems to be filled with a dull routine, and my day-to-day tasks have become a bit of a chore. My life has lost its sparkle, so I turn in on myself, dejected and ill at ease — sometimes even resentful at the apparently happy and contented lives other people lead. I simply force myself to plod on because I feel the burden of duty, but with no sense of fulfilment or any great meaning to the daily round of things I'm doing.

Eventually I manage to face up to it, and say to myself, 'Smithy, for heaven's sake get a life!' It's then that I often discover that I've been living on the surface, responding to letters and emails, going to meetings — all of which have to be dealt with, of course. But they can so easily obscure the transcendent aspect of my life. I've lost my roots, so to speak, and I feel like a tumbleweed, at the whim of the wind which blows me this way and that.

I'm sure I'm not the only one to feel like that, and of course there's nothing wrong with leading a busy and active life. But when that 'activism' takes over completely and leaves us no time simply to be ourselves, then we can become disengaged from our real selves, and from God who created us. Perhaps then we realize that, once again, we have forgotten the admonition of the Psalmist: 'Be still and know that I am God.'

Lord, give us the grace today to find time for ourselves and our needs, and to find You, so that we will have the energy to joyfully love others, as You have first loved us. Amen.

BROADCAST MONDAY 18 MAY 2009

May 19

Becky Harris

You wouldn't think that the loss of such a small insect could have such a catastrophic effect on the world, but it's true: the delicate food chain we rely on is in danger because of the deaths of billions of bees.

My grandfather kept bees and then passed them on to my father. We would feed them sugary syrup through the winter, and then in the summer take the honey from the hives. It always felt like a betrayal, just helping ourselves to what they'd worked so hard to produce. The bees would smell out the honey in the house and come banging on the windows like the birds in Hitchcock's film. I had nightmares of them getting in and stinging us to death in revenge.

But now bees are in real trouble and numbers falling dramatically. The way we farm has reduced their sources of food, and it's possible that some pesticides might be damaging their brains and interfering with the way they communicate and find food, and so they die.

It seems that in a world where we are so often impressed and dazzled by size and power, it's actually the small things that matter; the small things that can have the most profound effect on everything around them. No matter how insignificant something may appear to us, it seems that there's a use and a purpose for everything.

Creator God, we marvel at Your handiwork in this finely tuned world, and recognize that our lives are linked to the success of the whole of creation. You have placed this world in our care and we pray for wisdom to be careful stewards, resisting choices based purely on financial profit and choosing to live simply, grateful for all that You have provided. Amen.

BROADCAST THURSDAY 19 MAY 2011

May 20

 ~~~~~~~

Mary Stallard

Dealing with anger isn't always easy, as I found out recently on a retreat day
by the sea. I'd been thinking about strong feelings that I still carried relating to
a past disagreement. I found it hard to 'let go' of the rage I still felt. Someone
suggested that I went to the beach and throw a heavy stone into the sea as a
symbolic release of this negative emotion. It seemed like a good idea. So I went
down to the water's edge, selected a suitable rock and hurled it toward the waves.

What I hadn't counted on was my own lack of ability at throwing. Somehow I
managed a kind of boomerang technique, and instead of plunging into the sea
as I'd expected, the stone curved round and landed with a heavy thud back on
the beach beside me. Thank goodness there was no one else there.

Jesus had lots to say about recognizing anger. In his famous Sermon on the
Mount he spoke about the danger of letting anger control our behaviour. He
advised those who listened to notice their strong feelings, and to try to act on
them out of love rather than from hatred — seeking healing with enemies and
making peace with those from whom we are estranged. This is really hard to put
into practice, but Jesus didn't just *talk* about dealing with anger, he also showed
us how to do this.

The Gospels report several occasions when Jesus felt anger, particularly when
he encountered injustice or hypocrisy. He used his emotion in positive ways.
Sometimes he expressed his anger in words of challenge, in healing or making
a point by overturning tables in the Temple.

Jesus shows us that anger is natural and does not have to be destructive; but
like a heavy rock it does need to be handled with care.

*Gracious God, help us to recognize our emotions and to show wisdom and sympathy in
all our dealings. Amen.*

BROADCAST MONDAY 20 MAY 2013

May 21

Mal Fletcher

We probably didn't need a scientific study to tell us that life in large cities is moving at a more rapid pace these days. But according to a recent experiment in 32 cities across the world, people, on average, walk 10 per cent faster than they did in 1994.

I wonder, with a smile, if a similar study had measured brain activity, would it have found us *thinking* more quickly on our feet or more efficiently?

Psychologists believe that these and similar findings reflect the way that technologies such as the internet have made us more impatient, so we try to cram more and more activities into a day.

Thirty years ago, futuristic writer Alvin Toffler correctly predicted a 'roaring current of change' which, he said, would leave people feeling disorientated. In an age when the winds of change blow against us more and more strongly, there has never been a greater need for times of deliberate reflection.

In the midst of a bruising schedule which would leave most of us reeling, Mother Teresa set aside prescribed periods each day for quiet contemplation, meditation and thanksgiving. Whatever she and her co-workers happened to be doing among the desperately poor, they would drop everything for these precious times of quietness.

Mother Teresa often credited these moments of communion with God for her ability to rise above the misery of her surroundings, with joy.

So that we don't end up in a world where, in the words of theologian Jacques Ellul, we build 'faster and faster machines to take us absolutely nowhere', perhaps we too need to take time out?

Lord, help us this day to take the time we need for communion with You and with our thoughts. Help us to slow down long enough to consider where we may be heading next. Amen.

BROADCAST MONDAY 21 MAY 2007

May 22

Peter Smith

When our lives are radically shaken up, through the bereavement of someone close to us, or because we have lost our job or been diagnosed with a serious illness, our lives receive an enormous jolt. The familiar comforts and securities we have relied on suddenly disappear and we can feel raw, naked and isolated.

In our sorrow, amidst our hurt feelings, we can easily despair of ever being able to get back to normality, to feel happy and contented. At such times I have always found great comfort in reading and reflecting on the Gospel accounts of Jesus' passion, death, resurrection and ascension into heaven. The disciples had not behaved well and had much to regret in terms of their infidelity, cowardice and selfishness. They were bereft and were deeply anxious about what the future would hold for them.

But despite their failures through human weakness, Jesus' love for them never failed for a moment, and he gave them words of great comfort and hope: 'I tell you most solemnly, you will be weeping and wailing while the world will rejoice; you will be sorrowful, but your sorrow will be turned into joy.'

I'm quite sure they found that hard to believe, but they discovered in time that it was true. They were able to take up a new life, and one which, despite suffering and difficulties, brought them deep joy and fulfilment. Later in life they must have wondered, 'Why did we doubt? Why did we find it so difficult to believe?'

Well, because if we're honest, we all doubt and we all find it difficult to believe at times. We need the gift of faith and trust if we are to discover the truth and the wonder of God's enduring love for us.

Lord, help us to believe that You truly love us just as we are, and especially when we suffer, and that Your love will never fail us. Amen.

BROADCAST FRIDAY 22 MAY 2009

May 23

Mary Stallard

I spend part of my time working as a chaplain in a local high school where I am learning lots about ministry, often in unexpected ways. When a stray dog was discovered trapped in the school yard, lots of people tried to help to get it out, but it didn't seem willing to go near anyone. When the bell rang for lessons to begin, I thought I'd stay outside and try to catch it. It seemed a caring thing to do, and if I'm honest, it was a bit of a challenge: I wanted to be the one who'd succeed where others hadn't.

After nearly an hour I started to feel foolish: nothing I tried worked. I'd called the dog and whistled for it. I'd stayed still, waiting for him to come to me, and I'd chased him. Eventually he retreated into a thorny hedge and crouched there whimpering. I climbed in after him and I sat in the hedge, talking softly to him. I wondered whether I should give up, but finally he crept toward me and allowed me to grab his collar and pull him out.

By now it was break time, most of the school were outside and saw me muddy, scratched and clutching the wet dog. Far from thinking I'd done a good job catching him, it seemed most of the pupils thought that the dog must be mine! It wasn't quite the triumphant rescue I'd imagined.

By contrast, in the ministry of Jesus we find a completely unselfish model of caring. Jesus deliberately put himself in the way of people in need and risked his reputation and even his life – not to make himself look good but to show people the patient, self-giving care God has for all of creation.

God, give me grace today in any opportunities I have to serve You by helping others. Teach me to recognize my own needs and to offer my friendship with a glad and generous heart. Amen.

BROADCAST THURSDAY 23 MAY 2013

May 24

Gemma Simmonds

One of my favourite pastimes is doing embroidery. I fidget if I sit for too long with empty hands, so whether I'm sitting on trains or in airports or, on rare occasions, watching television, I usually have some project with me. The problem is that this allegedly relaxing hobby becomes so compulsively absorbing that I find myself sitting up half the night just to finish a section of the pattern, so the object of the exercise is rather defeated. And though, like many women, I'm a good multi-tasker, there's always the dreaded moment when I discover I've made a mistake several inches back. It's a terrible dilemma – should I decide to ignore it and carry on, hoping it won't show, or should I go through the agony of unpicking it all to get it right? I was doing a particularly delicate and complicated piece of embroidery while I watched Princess Diana's funeral and missed one stitch. No one else would have known about it, but my eye couldn't miss it. It took me a whole week of unpicking to put it right.

Most of us don't get the chance to undo our mistakes. We just have to incorporate them into the pattern that follows, for good or ill. Muslim carpet weavers, who weave the most wonderful and intricate designs, will put in a deliberate mistake as an act of humility, because perfection belongs to Allah, and not to human beings, however skilled they may be. That sort of humility and freedom of heart is a rare thing to find. But learning to incorporate our failings creatively into the greater pattern of our life is one route to wise living.

Creator God, help us to find the pattern of Your wisdom in all the choices of our life. Amen.

BROADCAST THURSDAY 24 MAY 2012

May 25

Alison Murdoch

Today is the most important day in the Tibetan Buddhist calendar, when the historical Buddha is said to have been born, become enlightened and passed away. In thousands of homes, temples and monasteries around the world, it will be marked by prayers, ceremonies and celebration of the fact that the Buddha's teachings have helped people develop compassion and wisdom for over 2,500 years.

The Buddha's personal journey from wealthy Indian prince to world religious leader began as an act of curiosity — with asking questions. Like any parent, his father wanted to protect him from uncomfortable experiences. But when the young prince saw someone who was struggling with old age, someone who was ill, and someone who was dead, he wanted to know why such suffering occurs, and what can be done about it. Eventually he was so consumed by these questions that he left the palace at dead of night to seek the answers for himself.

'I have no special talent. I am only passionately curious,' said Einstein, another towering historical figure. 'Question everything. Never lose a holy curiosity.' Yet how much time do any of us actually give to life's big questions? Probably very little, until we get ambushed by a major life event such as the illness or death of someone close to us. From morning to night, and from birth to death, we are the masters of distraction.

Special days, whether those associated with the Buddha or with other religious leaders, or our own birthdays and anniversaries, are an opportunity to take a break from the non-stop distractions of daily life and to remind ourselves of what is most helpful and important.

Let's pray that we can each make time to seek the answers to life's big questions, and then to use those answers to bring more compassion and wisdom into the world.

BROADCAST SATURDAY 25 MAY 2013

May 26

Lindsay Allen

One evening I was sitting at the computer talking to my son and daughter-in-law in Canada, when the strangest thing happened. Suddenly, and without warning, the twenty-first century slipped away, the years rolled back, and I found myself enfolded in a world long gone.

A world in which there were no computers, no televisions, no CD players, no dishwashers, no washing machines. A quiet world lit by the glow of an open fire and flickering candlelight.

That's right, we had had a power cut!

Within a couple of minutes some of the neighbours called and we all sat around in the flattering candlelight talking about what we were doing when the power went off and the twenty-first century came to a grinding halt!

Of course, we all knew that in an hour or so, power would be restored and life would return to normal. But what if it wasn't? What if that was the end of the world's oil?

The Bible teaches us that the Earth is not ours to exploit for our own short-term gain. David reminds us in Psalm 25, 'The earth is the LORD's, and everything in it, the world, and all who live in it.'

Our role is that of trustees, not owners, and as such we are entrusted to care for the Earth and conserve its resources — a role we have not always discharged well. Now we are becoming more aware of the impact of our actions, and have started to take steps to conserve this wonderful planet on which we live.

Heavenly Father, we thank You for the wonder and beauty of this world in which You have placed us. We thank You for its wealth of resources and know that You have given us all things richly to enjoy. But we pray now for understanding that we may better care for it, and the wisdom to make provision for coming generations that they too may enjoy its riches. Amen.

BROADCAST THURSDAY 26 MAY 2011

May 27

Mark Wakelin

A journey on public transport can be a fascinating way to see your fellow humans coping with life, though it's worth noting that others are no doubt watching you as you watch them! One lesson to learn is that you see what you expect to see more than you might imagine. If you decide, for example, that 'people today are pretty awful', you will find enough evidence to justify your view. Feet on the seats, chewing gum under the seats, and litter everywhere.

If you decide that 'people today are quite wonderful', however, you will find more than enough evidence for that as well. An honest young man running after someone who dropped a £20 note. A tired commuter giving up her seat for someone who looked even more tired. A kind reminder that a person's shoe laces were undone.

Paul tells us in his great hymn to love that 'love rejoices in the right'. One meaning of this is that you should look out for the good rather than the bad. It sounds a bit strange to say that love is about discipline, but perhaps it can be – the discipline to look for the lovely things rather than the dreadful, to face down the 'grumpy old person within' and notice signs that there is much that is wonderful in the world.

Paul also writes that love 'bears all things, believes all things, hopes all things, and endures all things'. There is something daunting about that – particularly when your experience of public transport is too early in the morning, when facing even your closest friend can be a challenge!

Loving God, give us the discipline today to 'rejoice in the right' and the patience to 'bear all things', and thank You that You bear us, and love us. Amen.

BROADCAST THURSDAY 27 MAY 2010

May 28

Alison Murdoch

'Everyone who is born holds dual citizenship, in the kingdom of the well and in the kingdom of the sick,' wrote the American writer Susan Sontag. My elderly mother is very ill at the moment, and so our family, along with so many others, find ourselves plunged into the kingdom of the sick, with its carers, ambulances and hospital visits.

Even if we pass by hospitals on a daily basis, or are addicted to TV soap operas, many of us have little idea of what they're really like inside. And sometimes the easiest way to respond to things we don't understand is to make a joke of them. Like many children, I used to giggle at old people being wobbly on their feet, without thinking what it would be like to experience that happening to myself. And I may not be the only person who, until the Paralympics came along, found it hard to accept deep down that people in wheelchairs are just the same as me.

I got involved with Buddhism because I wanted to have more love and compassion, and was then taught that the first step is to develop my capacity for empathy and equanimity – the ability to put myself in someone else's shoes, however different they may seem. The silver lining to life's most painful experiences, such as illness, disability and bereavement, is that they help us to develop our capacity to understand from the inside out.

'Be kind, for everyone you meet is fighting a hard battle,' said Plato.

I'd like to offer a prayer for every person and family that is struggling with illness today. May we each develop our ability to listen and to understand what they are going through, so that we are better able to offer them our kindness and our love.

BROADCAST TUESDAY 28 MAY 2013

May 29

Noël Vincent

A week or two ago I heard a convicted criminal telling how his life was changed in prison by a drama workshop on Shakespeare. School hadn't worked for him and he was reluctant at first. Then he discovered that Shakespeare was writing about things he recognized – anger, fear, greed and so on – and he began to discover language in a new way and it released something in him, and he's now a professional actor.

It's just one example of how we can change and grow. Another initiative being tried in prison is 'restorative justice', where criminal and victim are brought together to share frankly their feelings about what's happened. Some are sceptical, but where it works, offenders can get a real insight into the effect their behaviour may have on innocent victims – enough to help them rethink their lives.

Our most natural response to crime – especially violence – is anger. People are suspicious of 'soft' treatment for offenders. The important thing, though, is to achieve change and that's true for all of us – criminal or not. One way of doing this is by exposure to arts and culture. We might immerse ourselves in new experiences – music, the visual arts, drama, novels. Any of these experiences can help us to confront negative or dysfunctional aspects of our own lives. Popular culture is fine, but it's also good to face the challenge of moving outside our comfort zone; to climb our own emotional Mount Everest.

Even if we sometimes feel unconvinced about some modern art forms and contemporary drama, if we persevere we too may discover a life-changing power waiting for us.

God of mystery and miracle, speak to us through our eyes and ears that we may grow spiritually into the people You want us to become. Amen.

BROADCAST THURSDAY 29 MAY 2008

May 30

Alison Murdoch

Do you ever wake up feeling tired and jaded, trapped by the demands and timetables of the day ahead? Or do you ever wonder how to make today meaningful, in the midst of so many others? A friend of mine recently tried a simple experiment. He decided to say a warm and heartfelt 'good morning' to everyone he met that day.

He started off by taking his dog to the park for a morning walk, and immediately got some mixed responses. A trio of junior school girls chimed 'good morning' in a Pavlovian response to his greeting, but many of the adults looked startled, and some annoyed. A man peered warily over his newspaper with a 'do not disturb' expression.

However, on the way back from the park, my friend noticed a change. Before he could open his mouth, a stranger suddenly said good morning to him! Then it happened again. Across the road, he noticed two women with prams saying good morning as they passed each other. All the way back to his apartment, he was amazed to observe people greeting each other with a warm smile.

One of the main teachings of Buddhism is that we have far more power over our lives than we realize, because every positive thing we think, say and do will not only shift our own mood, but ripple out to others. Real happiness in life starts when we cherish others, and the trick is to look out for the opportunity — to make that phone call or cup of tea, to share a smile, or give five minutes of our time.

'We can do no great things, only small things with great love,' said Mother Teresa.

Let's pray that we can each find our own way of bringing more warmth and kindness into the day ahead.

BROADCAST THURSDAY 30 MAY 2013

May 31

Sharon Grenham Toze

Last year my fourth child was born, at home. Two weeks late, she finally decided to arrive in a little under an hour, and before the midwife arrived. Nature waits for no one! Despite being an experienced mother, giving birth without skilled help was very frightening indeed. I think I have never been so relieved as I was when I saw that reassuring uniform rushing through my bedroom door!

But of course, giving birth alone, or with only amateur help, is the reality for countless women around the world. Even in my scary situation, the hospital was only a twenty-minute drive away. For many, it's hours away, if it's there at all. The midwifery services we have in this country are precious indeed; and, despite the recent criticism at national level, thousands like me are very glad they're there.

There are many times in our lives when we have reason to be grateful for a professional to stand beside us. A midwife as we're born, a teacher as we learn, a nurse, a lawyer, a minister, a banker, even an undertaker as we deal with the death of a loved one. They can make big moments in life feel safer, smoother, a little less scary. But we tend to take their services for granted. It's easy to forget the years of training, commitment and personal sacrifice that any professional brings with them. It's not until they're not there that we realize how much we need them.

And so we thank You, God, for the skills of those who ease our lives, often at times of crisis. Remind us of our privilege, in a world where so many must 'go it alone'. And we pray especially today for all who will be born, their mothers and their midwives. Amen.

BROADCAST THURSDAY 31 MAY 2007

June 1

Eugene O'Neill

We all like to feel that we are open-minded and willing to change: I wonder if it's always true?

How unsettled do you — or I — feel when faced with the unfamiliar? Perhaps a novel approach at work; the unexpected strategy in politics; unforeseen ideas getting a grip in society; the face of the new person before us?

Even though the most powerful word in politics is deemed to be 'change', people generally don't like their familiar patterns of friendship, family, work or thinking to change very much at all — as any expert in change management will tell you.

The same is true of religion. By and large, when religions encounter the unfamiliar and challenging — in people, ideas or unconventional ways — they have tended to follow one of three paths: to withdraw in order to remain uncontaminated; to reject and attack; or, sometimes, to engage in an attempt to understand.

The unofficial patron saint of such open engagement is Justin Martyr, whom many Christians remember today. Born of pagan parents in Nablus in Samaria at the beginning of the second century, he was steeped in Greek philosophy. Though his intellectual search ultimately led him to Christianity, he never ceased to believe that honest dialogue between people seeking answers to the questions common to all could advance the search for truth.

He has much to teach a world where some can see dialogue as weakness and difference as a threat.

Author of truth, maker of the human intellect: open our minds to the minds of others. May we not withdraw in fear, nor reject in anger...but trust You to lead us together into greater respect and understanding. Amen.

BROADCAST TUESDAY 1 JUNE 2010

June 2

Glenn Jordan

At 6.17am on this day in 1966 the US landed its first space probe, *Surveyor 1*, on the moon in the Ocean of Storms. Everyone was surprised because they expected the first four or five attempts at a soft landing would fail. Not so, and just over 30 minutes after touchdown the craft started to transmit a series of astonishing photos back from the moon's surface.

Things have moved on remarkably since then. Men have landed on the moon, a space station's being built and the Hubble telescope can photograph distant constellations. I have vague, vague memories of those late 60s heydays when space vehicles, after surviving the most momentous journeys, crashed down into the ocean and were picked up by navy ships and their anxious crews.

Now we have a vehicle that can be used repeatedly to visit space and return just like a conventional aircraft. We can even have the option to have our ashes blasted into space, or the rich can visit the outer fringes of our atmosphere as tourists.

It's easy to lose perspective in the face of the vastness of the cosmos. When I consider the heavens, which are the work of Your fingers, and the moon and stars which You set in their places, what are human beings that You are mindful of us? Good question from the pen of the Psalmist.

Dear God, in the face of Your creation help us keep perspective on our place and on the value of each human being You have brought to life. Preserve us from taking our life for granted and from treating others with disrespect. Amen.

BROADCAST SATURDAY 2 JUNE 2007

June 3

Peter Baker

One of the most iconic public spaces in the world is Tiananmen Square, Beijing, where on this day in 1989, after seven weeks of occupation principally by pro-democracy students who were demanding social and political reforms, government troops and tanks were sent in to disperse the crowds.

Chaos ensued. Ten thousand were arrested; hundreds, possibly thousands, were killed. But amidst the repressive terror, one enduring image captured by the media came to symbolize what these movements for freedom are all about.

On June 5 a lone protester, in an act of unbelievable courage, stood in the way of an approaching tank, holding what looked like shopping bags in both hands, with which he waved the column of tanks away. As the lead tank manoeuvred to avoid him, so the man blocked its path. First to the left, then to the right. In a dance of death, the tank came within feet of him. Yet he jumped on the metal monster and appeared to talk to the soldiers inside. The driver opened the hatch. The protester clambered down and defiantly stood on the square. Then some people rushed to the tank and took him out of harm's way. He was never seen again.

Outside the country he simply came to be known as Tank Man. His status as a hero guaranteed. Inside China he is still not known at all. Was he jailed or killed? Like his identity, what happened to him remains something of a mystery.

But Tank Man made a difference to the way the Tiananmen Square massacre was perceived by the world. Yet we don't know how old he is, where he lives or anything about him. This very anonymity is refreshing in an age of celebrity. He reminds us that you don't have to be known in order to change the world.

Lord God, may we be content to find our identity not by being recognized but by those unnoticed acts of kindness, bravery and compassion that transform the world of other people. Amen.

BROADCAST FRIDAY 3 JUNE 2011

June 4

Katherine Meyer

One of the most classic and long-wearing fruits of the Spirit is faithfulness, that serviceable and enduring refusal to cut and run. Or at least, that's sometimes what we've reduced it to. Surely, at its best, faithfulness is an enviable flair for living with your choices in a kind of expectant creative freedom, and thus becoming a person whom others cannot always predict but can always trust.

Even in its most enduring expressions, however, faithfulness works best with the accessory of knowing how to let go. This is not the same thing as backing out. It's more like knowing how to make more room for the choices you've already made, and for the people you've already chosen.

It's a bit like getting over the idea that there is only one thing you are supposed to do with your life, and if you don't find it, your whole life will turn out to have been a mistake. The less glamorous but also much less anxiety-producing truth is that a decision often turns out to be the right one only as you learn how to live it in a way that makes it so.

And so faithfulness only comes into its own as a spiritual gift when it's paired with the accessory of knowing when to make room. Thus ensuring for the future a spaciousness which is the best-kept secret of those who can be trusted.

God, the Holy Spirit, when neither our lives nor the shape of the choices we've made remain the same, help us to let go of what we thought they would look like, so that they may become something we could never have imagined. This is our prayer. Amen.

BROADCAST THURSDAY 4 JUNE 2009

June 5

Stephen Shipley

One of my favourite paintings — and one that was introduced to me by my father — is by the French artist Nicolas Poussin, born this month in 1594. It's displayed in beautiful surroundings in the Wallace Collection of Art in Hertford House, just north of Oxford Street in the West End of London — and it's known as *A Dance to the Music of Time*. Four dancing girls represent the four seasons of the year, while old Father Time calls the tune on his lyre. The girls dance hand in hand forming a ring but facing outward as if they're inviting others to join them. The figure of Time the musician crouches over his instrument, a sinister rather than a kindly figure — Time that mocks us rather than Time that's our friend. And I suppose, in a strange sort of way, that's why the painting appeals. It's an allegory, intended to alert the attention of the viewer and lead them to reflect on the human condition.

So what does it say to *us*? As life moves on, it asks the question: what sort of person do you want to become; what sort of person do you want others to find you to be. This is a tremendously important choice. The way we are with others reflects the way we are within ourselves — and the way we are within ourselves reflects the way we are with God. So will you, won't you, will you join the dance?

And that's the challenge: how can we be sure? Sure of what? Sure that all will be well. Only by getting into the dance and allowing the leader to teach us the steps.

Lord, guide us in every moment of our lives and give us the courage to dare everything in Your great service. Amen.

June 6

Leslie Griffiths

The year 1968 was a tumultuous one. The death of Robert Kennedy, assassinated on this day in a Los Angeles hotel, came just weeks after Martin Luther King had suffered a similar fate in Memphis. These two brutal deaths seemed part of a civil disorder and revolutionary spirit of the times, representing a real crisis for the United States of America, which was not to be equalled until that September day in 2001 when terrorists flew their planes into the Twin Towers of downtown New York. As well as the assassinations, 1968 saw widespread protests against the war in Vietnam, the civil rights demonstrations beginning to turn violent, and young people everywhere seeming to want new freedoms and to want them there and then.

It was Martin Luther King who had warned his fellow Americans about the dangers of responding to violence with violence, returning evil for evil, hatred for hatred. No one had put the case for Christian love more powerfully than he. This gift of the Holy Spirit of God was, in his view, the only antidote to the violence and bitterness that lurk in the human heart and, once they burst its banks, can sweep away the security and well-being of whole societies. Love alone can rescue us, he claimed, from the never-ending vicious circle where hatred begets hatred and one vile deed breeds another. That's advice that's worth heeding in every age and by all people.

Dear Lord, make us channels of Your peace. Where there is hatred, let us bring Your love; and grant that we may never seek so much to be consoled as to console; or to be loved as to love with all our soul. Make us more like Jesus, we pray. Amen.

BROADCAST FRIDAY 6 JUNE 2008

June 7

Jenny Wigley

I imagine that lots of families have had the kinds of conversations we have as we look at our boys – trying to decide which particular characteristics each has inherited from his mum or his dad. I, of course, take the credit for passing on all the best bits!

But good parents pass on so much more than the genes for blue eyes or curly hair. They encourage their children to develop values and make judgements. And they create a safe space for them to grow. The journey from infancy to maturity is about beginning to make decisions for yourself.

The Christian Church has always used the father-child analogy to speak of the relationship between God and humankind. It's the language of creation and nurture – of a God who makes and shapes the world in love. His children bear his image, each their own person yet each having something that speaks of the divine connection.

In the church where I'm vicar, by September we'll have seen eighteen brides walk down the aisle, most of them on their father's arm. There was a time when dad would have stayed alongside his daughter and her husband-to-be until the place in the service where the priest asked 'Who gives this woman to be married to this man?' But that's not a question we ask any more in the Church in Wales.

A father doesn't give his daughter away – nor does he abandon her. He's brought her to the point when she has made her choice, and is ready to declare it publicly. That's what any good parent would do, and it's what God our heavenly Father does for us as he gives us space to grow and to learn – the freedom to be ourselves.

Loving God, You who are Father and Mother to us all: hear us as we pray for those who share the joy and challenge of parenting that they may bring up their children to choose wisely and to share in Your inheritance of what is good and loving and true. Amen.

BROADCAST SATURDAY 7 JUNE 2008

June 8

Janet Wootton

New translation of *Antigone*? Certainly not.

No, I'm not arguing in favour of the old versions of the wonderful play by Sophocles. That is, in fact, a cryptic crossword clue, 8 letters. If, like me, you are an addict, you will not want the answer just yet.

I always carry a book of cryptic crosswords with me. There are all sorts of times, waiting in queues, enjoying a quiet cup of tea in solitude, when it's useful to have something to keep the mind occupied.

Cryptic crosswords either enthral people utterly or baffle them completely. I like them because they don't depend on general knowledge, but invite the solver to find hidden clues. Is it an anagram, or should we be thinking of similes, as I implied by talking about versions instead of translations?

This is also quite a decent life skill. There are often concealed messages in what people say, and it's useful to be able to pick up an underlying emotion, especially in situations of stress. Being able to see what is hidden can help us to understand how someone is feeling, and so be the first step toward compassion or reconciliation, the negation of hatred – by the way, that's the answer to the clue: 'negation' is an anagram of Antigone!

Our intelligence is a God-given gift, to use, develop and enjoy. If we allow God to weave intelligence together with the gifts of wisdom, understanding and compassion, we may find ourselves able to solve much more than crossword clues.

God of wisdom, we give You thanks for the complexity and power of the human mind.
Help us to use our wisdom and understanding to reach out in compassion for others, and
bring about reconciliation. Amen.

BROADCAST TUESDAY 8 JUNE 2010

June 9

Tina Beattie

At the dawn of history, when something in the evolutionary process jumped the tracks of consciousness, the human emerged as a dreaming ape. Deep in the caves of the world, creatures began to paint. A species had evolved that could imagine the world as other than it is, and from that imaginative leap came the very essence of what it means to be human. Werner Herzog's film, *Cave of Forgotten Dreams*, takes us inside those caves and enables us to gaze on wondrous images through 30,000 years of our time on Earth. He brings us face to face with the most mysterious and haunting questions about the origins and meaning of human life. Some say those were the earliest expressions of religious art.

In the Middle Ages the Gothic cathedrals of Europe were home to some of the world's greatest art. On 9 June 1310, Duccio's altarpiece, the *Maestà*, was installed in Siena Cathedral amidst great ceremony. An eyewitness account tells of how the whole city came together for the procession, and the poor received many alms. The centre panel of the altarpiece shows the Virgin enthroned in majesty, holding the infant Christ, surrounded by angels and saints. It's an image of astonishing serenity, gazing out at us across the centuries with an infinite peace.

Art is powerless to change the world, but great art enables us to imagine a *better* world. That's why tyrants and dictators always wage war on the freedom of art. It remains the most primal and creative expression of human freedom. Without it, we're less than human.

Today, we pray for the gift to see the mystery of God in the beauty of creation, and to reflect that beauty in all our artistic endeavours. Amen.

BROADCAST THURSDAY 9 JUNE 2011

June 10

Jenny Wigley

This week we're thinking about individuals who act as carers, who take responsibility for someone who's vulnerable. But many of those carers would want to speak of what they themselves get out of the relationship, of how they are able to receive as well as give.

There's a whole raft of human experience which uses the language of mutuality, where people care for each other as friends, partners, husbands and wives. Each party contributes to the well-being of the other, rather than one being active and the other the passive recipient of their care.

One of the great things about mutual care is that, at its best, it doesn't do sums! We need generosity and trust to take it in turns to help each other out, so that we're not always checking up on who should do what next. In the end, we'll have seen each other through, done each other proud. We're in each other's debt, but there's no balance-book reckoning to be made, just an experience of life being made sweeter in the presence of the other.

In the Gospel account of Jesus' last moments, he sees his mother standing at the foot of the cross. In first-century Jewish society, she would have needed the care and protection of a male relative in her old age. But Jesus doesn't look for someone to take responsibility for her. Instead he speaks to someone referred to only as the beloved disciple, one of the twelve but not one of the family. He entrusts them to each other: 'Woman, here is your son; son, here is your mother.' The future lies in mutual love, care and respect. That's the community that Jesus bids us create.

Gracious God, we offer to You all that we have, all that we are, all that we hope to be; fill us with the power of Your Spirit that together we may build a community of love here on earth as it is in heaven. Amen.

BROADCAST TUESDAY 10 JUNE 2008

June 11

Richard Chartres

Today is the 500th anniversary of Henry VIII's wedding to Catherine of Aragon. It was a joyful day but alas, as we know, the story did not end well.

Marriage is rightly hedged about with legalities and formalities. It is often described as an 'institution' and we do, of course, need scaffolding in our lives, but the living heart of the matter is something else.

At the heart of the mystery of marriage, there is an exchange of gifts which cannot be priced or bought.

Marriage is a way of life in which at its best, as the poet Edwin Muir says, 'Each asks from each what each most wants to give, / And each awakes in each what else would never be.'

This is the way of married love. We give out of what we have been given, and in doing so we bring one another into fuller being. We should honour marriage and indeed all committed relationships.

The mysterious process of losing ourselves to find ourselves is at work in any honest relationship, but for many people the way of married love is their profoundest entry point.

Marriage is an entry into the mystery of spiritual life, in which we discover that the more we give of self, the richer we become in soul; the more we go beyond ourselves, the more we become our true selves.

God our Father, who hast taught us that love is the fulfilling of the law, grant to those who have entered into holy matrimony that loving one another they may continue in Thy love unto their life's end through Jesus Christ our Lord who liveth and reigneth with Thee in the unity of the Holy Spirit, one God, world without end. Amen.

BROADCAST THURSDAY 11 JUNE 2009

June 12

Marjory MacLean

In these days of long, long light, the longest is in the far north, in the Shetland and Orkney islands, which lie under the biggest skies of Britain and where sunset happens an hour later than in London. Those northern skies are complete lucid domes of drama, where clouds constantly change, and shafts of sunlight zig-zag through the spaces that are left, and strike the land in the unexpected patterns that only quite happen in those places. And the ocean seems to go on for ever, and your sight seems to have no limits because the horizon is so far away that it hardly seems to exist at all. You could almost imagine you could touch America.

As night forgets to happen for these next few weeks, people relish a life that seems bigger and more relaxed. Golfers play matches at silly times, just because they can. Fishermen on the trout lochs lose all track of time because in what Orcadians call the 'grimlings' of long twilight, there is no complete darkness to chase anyone home. In the bays and sounds of Scapa Flow, sail-boats buzz about in races and games late into the evening, distant dots on shiny water to those watching from cliff-top walks.

As I describe these scenes, I'm sure you'll have all sorts of pictures of your own magical places, and perhaps places that are especially magical at this generous time of the year. We all, whatever surroundings we live in, have those moments when we can slow down and drink in what most refreshes and inspires us, and be made better by those little bright pauses.

O light of dawn and dusk, wait with us when we need to take a moment to understand the blessings of our lives, when we need to remind ourselves of what lies deepest inside us, when we need to be refreshed and enabled to live again with strength. Amen.

BROADCAST WEDNESDAY 12 JUNE 2013

June 13

Gopinder Kaur

The early morning is very special to me as a Sikh. We call it the Amrit Vela, the still hours before the break of dawn, an optimal time for prayer and meditation. I know that if I miss the Amrit Vela and wake up just as day's begun, my mind is sure to start whirring with mundane preoccupations before I've even got out of my pyjamas! The Amrit Vela lets me keep all that at bay and experience myself in a different way. It's a part of Sikh tradition that helps us nurture a feeling of being at one with our Creator.

We also refer to the Amrit Vela as the 'ambrosial hours'. In India, *amrit* is an ancient word for 'nectar of immortality'. And for the ancient Greeks, ambrosia was the sweet, fragrant food of immortality given to the gods on Mount Olympus. Ambrosia and Amrit — maybe that similarity is no coincidence, and this yearning for the Immortal is common to us all. Not to stay young forever, no — but to experience that bit of 'who we are' that doesn't die, and savour a sense of timelessness inside us.

And so you find that dedicated Sikhs are dedicated early birds, thirsting for this Amrit-nectar. Uttering the sacred words of scripture, it seems we can almost taste it and sense it in the dewy freshness of the air before dawn:

'Amrit vela sach naou vadiaaee veechar,'
our first morning prayer tells us —

'In the Amrit Vela, meditate on the True Name, reflect on the glorious greatness of the One who is eternally real.'

BROADCAST SATURDAY 13 JUNE 2009

June 14

Marjory MacLean

As a Royal Naval Reserve chaplain, I especially love the quiet darkness of the bridge of a naval ship during the Middle Watch of the night far out at sea. Of course, that's a place of ambiguity for many people, not a place for inspiration, you'd think, at all. And certainly it's functional and a little threatening, and certainly the shadows and silhouettes of military equipment are unmistakable even in very deep darkness.

But from time to time, when two warships pass each other, and two groups of human beings with the same purpose come within reach of each other in one of the world's sea-lanes, a watchkeeper will be sent out onto the bridge wing to send a message the old way, by Morse signalling lamp, to the other ship. It's the nearest thing to touching those two ship's companies can do, and the cold steely reality suddenly becomes warmly human just for a few moments.

Curiously, it gives you a feeling of safety; for in a world where electronic communications have so replaced the tradition of signals from another age, and the protection of information becomes a complicated science all by itself, here is conversation no listening device can eavesdrop, simply one to another. You really feel you've met your friend and you are alone with them.

Light, blinking on and off as it has done for more than a century, continues a friendly conversation and sends the good wishes of colleagues and friends on round the seas of a difficult and dangerous planet.

O light of land and sea, sustainer of a wild and beautiful world, and keeper of those who are asked to give difficult service far from home: protect all those beyond our reach for whom we worry, and keep them away from darkness and danger. Amen.

BROADCAST FRIDAY 14 JUNE 2013

June 15

Gopinder Kaur

We all have pictures of some sort in our homes, either framed on a mantelpiece, or hanging on a wall; pictures we wake up to.

There's a beautifully framed picture I have, a wedding present. It's a photograph of the Harmandir Sahib, otherwise known as the Golden Temple in Amritsar, the most famous of Sikh shrines, shimmering jewel-like in the tranquil waters of a sacred pool. Its architecture reflects the universal interfaith values Sikhs hold dear. A Muslim saint was invited to lay its foundation stone, and its four gateways welcome people of all backgrounds. Entering, you step downward, to a place where humility reigns. At its heart, our sacred scripture is enthroned and revered like an eternal sovereign. As the melodious singing of its verses wafts across the waters, it speaks of Oneness and the divine spark waiting to be kindled in us all. All around there's an almost tangible serenity – not quite a stillness, but something that gently moves and motivates the spirit.

To look at this picture now is particularly poignant, as Sikhs remember the martyrdom of Guru Arjan Dev, our fifth Guru, after days of severe torture by hostile imperial authorities. This was not long after the Guru had completed the construction of the sacred complex and compiled the sacred scripture installed within it. So today, especially, we remember Guru Arjan Dev's prayer:

Tera kia meettha lagai; har nam padarath Nanak maangai.

– Oh Lord, may Your Will be sweet to me;
I beg only for the treasure of Your Divine Name.

BROADCAST MONDAY 15 JUNE 2009

June 16

Clair Jaquiss

So I walked into the DIY shop — and there, tidying the shelves and sorting out the stock, was a young man. He was in his overalls and safety boots and wearing the company logo pinned to his chest and a sign, 'Here to help'. It was good to know I could have asked him about plumbing accessories, electrical tools, grades of sandpaper and window locks. He would have gladly carried heavy things to the car, but how far could I push him? Was he in a position to advise me on a recent job application or where I should go on holiday? Could he offer me anything for a strained muscle or tell me how I was going to pay off my debts? Well, possibly — but I would be unlikely to ask him. It would be unrealistic to expect that kind of help — even if help was what he was here for.

When Jamie Whitaker was born five years ago today — happy birthday, Jamie — he too was 'here to help'. His brother was seriously ill and needed a transplant from a sibling sharing the same immune system. The group of cells that was to become Jamie was found to be genetically suitable. And so he grew inside his mother until he was ready to be born.

The ethical choices in such situations are complex and agonising. Is a boy like Jamie being used only for the help his cells can give? Will that choice and the relationship with his brother and his parents mean that he's less loved — or more loved — or loved differently? Parents with an only child wonder whether a second can be loved as much as the first. I worried about that — but found that love expands to embrace additional children as they grow and become themselves in their own right. So our prayer today is for those facing difficult decisions over the birth and care of children:

Lord, be with them and give them wisdom and guidance — and we offer a prayer of thanksgiving for the skill and technology that enable us to receive the grace to be here to help each other. Amen.

BROADCAST MONDAY 16 JUNE 2008

June 17

Gopinder Kaur

I will never forget the time I heard my daughter's first ever bellow of laughter, in a moment of pure, crystal-clear joy.

One day the great outdoors seemed to beckon, and we set off with little Kanpreet for the Sandwell Valley, which brings acres of countryside to our doorstep in Birmingham. As first-time parents, we were still so conscious of her newness on this planet, as she gazed around and felt the air on her cheeks, floating about, astronaut-like, snuggled in daddy's sling.

We got to a lake and I pulled out our bag of bread to feed the ducks. As they swam toward us, quacking for crumbs around the water's edge, a sudden gigantic chuckle filled the air, full of heartiness and absolute delight, fuelled by a robust pair of baby lungs. Kanpreet was stamping the world with her presence, her bellyful of laughter rising to the skies, as the waddling ducks gathered beneath her feet.

Often it's our elders who remind me that, no matter how much the body withers, the divine light inside us is forever young. Spirituality is not all doom, gloom and seriousness. Liberation is about freeing the spirit to rise up from the grip of our selfish ego. And this we can experience right in the midst of life, coloured by all the joys that make us a child of God:

Nanak satgur bhetiai, puri hovai jugat;
Hasandia, khelandia, painandia, khavandia, vichay hovai mukat.

— O Nanak, meeting the True Guru, one comes to know the Perfect Way.
In the midst of laughter, play, dressing and eating, the spirit can be liberated.

BROADCAST THURSDAY 17 JUNE 2010

June 18

Andrew Martlew

I'm sufficiently old to remember the furore when the government announced that it was going to set an objective limit on the amount of alcohol you could drink and still be fit to drive a car. I was too young to drive, of course. And I'm saying nothing about drink. But I remember lots of men – and I do mean 'men' – saying, 'Rubbish, I can drink ten pints and drive home safely.' And they really believed it – and lots of them did it. Drove, that is, not safely – as the accident figures testified. But there really was a view that such limits only applied to other, weaker people – the speaker was always above such limitations.

Well, the drinking and driving message may have sunk in for the majority of the population, but I'm not sure about the other lesson, that 'the normal rules do apply to me'. And if I'm being brutally honest, I think that's even true of me; there's a bit of me that thinks, 'I'm different. I don't need to follow that advice, keep those rules, open that instruction book.'

Which is probably enough confession for one morning, so I'll just ask, ever so quietly, if it's just possible that I'm not unique in thinking this way. And, if I'm right, whether the world would be a bit of a better place if we all had sufficient humility – and realism – to understand that the normal rules include us, whether we're thinking about the effects of eating, or drinking, or smoking, or even exercise.

Lord God,
We are all your children,
We share our weaknesses with our neighbours,
We aren't supermen or wonder women;
Give us the gift of humility
So that we may accept ourselves for who we are
And Your love for us – with all our imperfections and limitations. Amen.

BROADCAST TUESDAY 18 JUNE 2013

June 19

Gopinder Kaur

I don't think I could ever imagine a world without colour. Even if tomorrow the world turned grey, or I lost the power of sight, I couldn't possibly take the idea of colour away from my mind. Colour is like a language, full of signs and signals, and when we talk in colour it suggests all kinds of moods and states of mind.

India is famous for its tradition of dyeing fabrics, and in Sikh scripture you often hear colour words like *lal, chaloola* and *majeetth* evoking a state of being infused with the deep crimson-like colour of the Creator's presence and love. *Majeetth* is a dye from the madder plant, which takes time and patience to extract, but is renowned for its lasting quality. In contrast, there's the safflower plant, whose dye is quick to obtain and just as quick to fade away. It reminds us to be wary of things that may be alluring, but short-lived and superficial. Even empty religious practice is said to be like the temporary dye which wears off after a few washes; but when it fills us with the profound experience of the divine, it's said we are coloured with the brilliant lasting richness of *majeetth*, which signals the glorious moment of discovering our soul's true colour.

Eh man sundar aapnaa, Har nam majeetth rang ree: 'Oh my beautiful mind, colour yourself in the crimson of the Divine Name.' As any traditional fabric dyer will know, you can't expect even the best-quality dye to be absorbed by any old length of cloth — it has to be specially prepared to become colour-fast.

May we work on our hearts and minds so that, whatever our source of inspiration, it might sink into us like a heavenly dye, and gradually take effect.

BROADCAST FRIDAY 19 JUNE 2009

June 20

Alison Elliot

People have different images of Europe, as I discovered when I attended a church meeting of people from different countries. We were asked to bring a picture or an object that captured Europe for us. A crocheted Celtic cross from the Peace Line in Belfast, a picture of Mostar's broken bridge or Transylvania's soaring mountains. From England, a journal article promising cheaper Volkswagens. A poster about human rights. From Albania, two rough maps, one showing an undifferentiated Soviet block, beside the individual states of the West; the other showing the European Union as a block, next to a fragmenting East.

If you asked me today, I'd offer the picture of children playing on the Soviet War Memorial in Berlin. It's a massive construction, built to welcome a liberating army, but it quickly came to symbolize the oppressive pain of a divided city. The occasion was the 50th anniversary of the Treaty of Rome, in March, and Berlin was partying. Crowds milled around the Brandenburg Gate, bands were playing, the beer tents were doing good business and the sun was shining. Children were scampering over the tanks that are part of the memorial and tourists were photographing their girlfriends under its intimidating arches. Berlin is a city that has ached for centuries and it was good to see it *en fête*.

Let us pray that European leaders remember the importance of reconciliation in a diverse continent that still has its divisions, and that they hold to a vision of Europe as a community of hospitality for those displaced by war and conflict and a sign of peace for the whole world.

Loving God, our continent has witnessed times of exuberant creativity and periods of callous destructiveness. Guide all those who build peace and seek justice in our land today. Amen.

BROADCAST WEDNESDAY 20 JUNE 2007

June 21

Michael Ford

So the longest day has arrived, the time of the year when the sun is at its most northerly point and people congregate at one of Europe's biggest stone circles, Stonehenge, to watch the sun rise. 21 June hails the start of summer in the northern hemisphere and it's an especially important date in the Druid calendar. But although the summer solstice is known as a pagan festival, I know at least one Christian family who've been celebrating with a barbecue and all-night party in Lancashire, where they've stayed up to welcome the dawn. After all, they tell me, Christ is the Light of the World, so what better time of the year to acclaim that?

The name 'solstice' comes from the Latin for sun, *sol*, and *sistere*, which means 'to stand still'. Perhaps, then, there's a sense in which the longest day is a reminder for all of us to step back and stand still – to move back from our routines and pressures to see life from a deeper line of vision. Prayer is all about standing still. As the Psalmist put it: 'Be still and know that I am God.'

Getting up early is one way of entering into such stillness. Although dispelling all those psychological distractions can be tough, if we refuse to yield to their destructive power and keep trusting in the hope of a new beginning, we slowly become aware of the still point within, where we discover our unity with God and with one another. And then the longest day can become the deepest day.

And so, at the start of this new day, we ask God to still our hearts and minds. And, whatever trials and challenges lie ahead, may we stay close to the still point of our lives and there discover peace and replenishment. Amen.

BROADCAST SATURDAY 21 JUNE 2008

June 22

David Chillingworth

In my life as a priest and pastor, one of the most fulfilling parts of the work has always been funerals. That may sound strange. But it's true. Caring for families in the loss of a relative or friend, conducting funerals – there's very little more important. It needs to be done well and faithfully. Otherwise, people can be left with a deep dissatisfaction – with things inside unresolved. It's hard then to move on and pick up the threads of life again.

It took me a long time to realize that loss – or the fear of loss – shapes our lives in all sorts of ways. We tend to crave security and fear change. Illness itself may mean that we can no longer take good health for granted in the longer term. Unemployment, family breakdown, childlessness – they are all in their different ways an experience of loss, a bereavement to be lived through. And, of course, change – or the fear of change – stirs deep anxieties ... about loss of the familiar or of identity or of role.

Hymns often shape the way we think. So Henry Francis Lyte's lines, 'Change and decay in all around I see, / O thou who changest not, abide with me,' may condition us to think that change will always be for the worst. In fact, while change may be painful and unwelcome, it may allow us to break our patterns of life in such a way that new possibilities open up.

As we pray, this morning, we ask that from experiences of loss may come, in time, new and sometimes better ways to reshape our lives.

O God of love,
You hold all things in Your hands.
Heal us as we grieve for what is lost.
Give us courage and hope
As we face the challenges of the unknown future.
Amen.

BROADCAST TUESDAY 22 JUNE 2010

June 23

Clair Jaquiss

One of our school's midsummer treats was maypole dancing. We seemed to be practising for weeks in the school hall – without the maypole at that point. We were expected to use our imaginations. And then the day would come when the maypoles would be set up in the playground and parents would be invited. We donned our costumes and skipped around to a crackly record of some ancient accordion and wove ribbons into a pattern up and down the pole as we danced.

We didn't really have any understanding of its significance. I suspect our teachers probably didn't feel it appropriate to risk engaging in controversy about fertility and phallic symbols with ones so young. For us it was fun and a chance to be outside away from lessons. Midsummer is a great occasion still for celebration in the lands of the midnight sun. It's a good excuse for a party.

But during the Reformation in England, they tried to put a stop to all that kind of fun and midsummer dancing nonsense. But, however frivolous we are, or serious, the Earth still tilts on its axis, the days grow longer and shorter and the sun rises.

Our dependence on the Earth and the rhythm of its days and seasons is perhaps even more established in our awareness than it ever was. We know now about changes in climate and the effect we have had on the Earth's natural rhythms. So we can choose to dance with the harmony of the Earth and encourage others to do so, or run counter to its rhythms and fail to do anything at all. So a prayer for today:

O God, save us from a selfish arrogance that believes we know what is best for the Earth, inspire us with wisdom to care for it. Teach us to stand out of our own light so Your daylight may shine. Amen.

BROADCAST SATURDAY 23 JUNE 2007

June 24

Michael Ford

My brother's just gained access to one of the world's most exclusive societies where, they say, 10,000 secrets are lodged. He's been performing since he was a child and never thought he'd make the grade. But now, after a gruelling audition process, he's been admitted to The Magic Circle. There are only 1,500 members in the world. As you walk past the firmly sealed doors of the society's headquarters near Euston station, you can't help wondering what goes on inside. But now my brother knows. Not that he'd dare betray any magic codes.

I get the impression that many people who struggle today with issues of faith and belief look at religion or the Church in much the same way as an audience observes the art of the magician – as outsiders, viewing what they see with a mixture of admiration and suspicion. And yet to live a spiritual life doesn't depend on any sleight of hand or slick performance. It's not about gaining access to a prestigious club, learning a set of secret rules or becoming part of an elite group.

For surely God isn't some kind of heavenly wizard, waving a wand across the universe as the mood takes him, but a humble, self-emptying creator whose love knows no bounds.

When our time comes to meet our Maker, I somehow doubt we'll have to undergo an audition before the tall, heavy doors creak open. More a case, I suspect, of allowing ourselves to become overwhelmed by the goodness of God who will see us as we are. That day we won't need to play the role of the great illusionist, keeping our darkest secrets behind our back, but we'll have the confidence to discard our masks, knowing that what lies behind will be embraced by God and transfigured.

And so today we pray for those who find their real selves hard to love and ask God to transform our darkness into the light of eternity. Amen.

BROADCAST TUESDAY 24 JUNE 2008

June 25

David Chillingworth

'I have discovered the secret of life and I am going to share it with you now.' It was the moment for wise words in the middle of a wedding service. It was a foolish and unwise thing to say. But I stumbled on.

Of course, I couldn't claim to have discovered the secret of eternal youth or wisdom or how to turn lead to gold. But I have spent a lot of my life trying to find the answer to deep-seated conflicts – problems so deeply embedded that they are beyond the capacity of people of even the greatest good will.

At that point, it seems to me that we are really dealing with things that belong in the world of the spiritual – challenges to heart and mind that go far beyond 'a bit of give and take'. It would be easy to say that I'm thinking of the kind of forgiveness the Lord's Prayer talks about: 'Forgive us our trespasses as we forgive those who trespass against us.'

Actually, I'm thinking about something that comes before we get anywhere near that. If you have been hurt, if you have been wronged, you are entitled to feel strongly. You are entitled to say so. You may even feel that you are entitled to have that put right. At the extreme, maybe you even think about revenge.

That seems understandable to me. And nobody should suggest that hurt and wrong should just be silently endured. Down that path lies injustice. But maybe, just maybe, I've seen times when people have let go of their right to anger, to getting even, to revenge … and that heroic renunciation is what opens up the path to forgiveness.

Father God,
Give us patience with the failings of others.
Teach us how to tread the path
That makes forgiveness possible.
Amen.

BROADCAST FRIDAY 25 JUNE 2010

June 26

Michael Ford

It was hard to imagine that the 35-year-old lecturer and Buddhist, cheerfully welcoming me to his Liverpool bedsit on a beautiful June day, was a former drug addict who'd spent thirteen years in a hell of his own making.

Today is the UN's International Day against Drug Abuse and Illicit Trafficking and I was keen to hear Stephen's story. Indeed, his journey from disintegration to self-empowerment is almost the stuff of movies.

Between the ages of 16 and 29, Stephen lived on a range of drugs including cannabis, ecstasy, LSD, methadone, heroin and tranquillizers. What he remembers most vividly is the crushing sameness of every day, knowing he'd have to go out and 'graft' — get money for the drugs his body was screaming out for and find another dark corner to 'shoot up'.

Then, one day in 2003, something deep inside him snapped and he recognized his utter poverty. The road to recovery through detox and rehab was slow and painful, but eventually he gained a Double First in theology and is now working on a PhD about addiction and spirituality. He lectures at a university and works with families affected by substance abuse. In contrast to his former existence, Stephen says he now leads a life of overflowing fullness, brimming with wonder and excitement.

And so now a prayer from the hand of Stephen himself:

Let us remember all those who are affected by addiction and substance abuse; those who are consumed by addiction themselves, and their families, lovers and friends. May we have the courage to recognize and share in the humanity of the addict, to confront ourselves in their gaze, and to rejoice in the powerful redemptive knowledge that lies dormant in their hearts. Amen.

BROADCAST THURSDAY 26 JUNE 2008

June 27

Catherine Cowley

A writer once described our journey to God as 'dancing madly backward'. This description appeals to me because sometimes I have to undo and unlearn what I've already done and thought I'd learnt. It can seem like going backward rather than inching my way forward.

I also like the image of dance. I sometimes think of my life as the weaving of a carpet with different coloured threads. As I dance my life, these different threads form a pattern. Each strand of my life, all those different parts, has to be given due consideration if the pattern is to be complete. If one dominates, the pattern is distorted. If one is omitted, it soon shows up. Sometimes it seems that one of the threads has become unpicked and isn't lying smoothly with the rest, and then I have to dance backward in order to mend it and set it straight.

But that assumes that I've understood what the pattern is – and that's not always true. I can't always see the pattern. I think it's going one way and then I look back and see that something else has emerged. Something I had thought was a mistake has been incorporated into a beautiful – but different – pattern. Only God sees the whole pattern, and all I can do is to trust that God will take my mistake and make a new pattern out of it, one I didn't anticipate.

Thankfully, Lord, Your creativity can take all our actions and bring good out of them. Help us to trust in You so that we do not become trapped in our 'what might have beens'. Amen.

BROADCAST SATURDAY 27 JUNE 2009

June 28

Frank Sellar

Forgiveness is the easiest thing to talk about and the hardest thing to do. We all like to think that we are generous, forgiving people, but when we have a row with our spouse, fall out with someone at work or get upset by something that has been done against us, forgiveness is the last thing we think about, let alone practise.

When Jesus urged his disciples to pray, 'Forgive us our trespasses, as we forgive those who trespass against us,' he wasn't pointing to some unattainable idea. For he knew what he was talking about.

Throughout his ministry, people made false accusations against him. In the end they mocked and crucified him, yet on the cross Jesus practised what he preached and said, 'Father, forgive them, for they don't realize what they are doing.'

The Apostle Paul in 2 Corinthians says that God made Jesus who had no sin to be sin for us, so that in him we might become the righteousness of God. Jesus accepted on our behalf all the wicked things that people did to him, so that we who deserved only to be condemned might be forgiven, and it's because we have been forgiven so much by God that Jesus now encourages us to pray for the same forgiving attitude toward other people.

Heavenly Father, today if I wake up with an unforgiving heart toward my spouse, colleague or acquaintance, remind me of the extent to which the Lord Jesus has forgiven me on the Cross, and in the light of that, grant me the ability to be willing to understand others, so that I may come to forgive them as much as I yearn to be forgiven by You. And our prayers we offer for Jesus' sake. Amen.

BROADCAST FRIDAY 28 JUNE 2013

June 29

Craig Gardiner

Back in 1995 Commander Robert Gibson, of the American space shuttle *Atlantis*, successfully docked his craft with the Russian *Mir* space station. That such a thing was possible so far from Earth and at speeds of 17,000 miles an hour seemed close to miraculous, but what was more remarkable at the time was the cooperation between these former Cold War enemies.

Symbolic gifts of welcome were exchanged, along with a relief crew for *Mir* and fresh water and air supplies. The Americans stayed to use the Russian facilities for research. This was now the cooperation of friends. The journey to friendship from enmity is often a long and difficult one — whether it happens between two mighty nations, in work with a colleague or in a feuding family.

Peter famously denied he even knew his friend Jesus. He didn't go to the Cross to watch his teacher being executed. After the Resurrection you might expect Peter to be due a telling-off. But instead Jesus found where Peter was fishing and helped the disciples land an unprecedented catch of fish. But the real miracle is not the fish, it's what comes next. Jesus began the awkward conversation with the man who denied him, to restore their friendship.

Moments of reconciliation can seem so close to the miraculous. And there's no doubt we often need God's help in doing it. But it's also down to someone with the courage to make the first approach and then it needs a lot of honest talk and plain hard work from everyone involved.

Dear God,
Where there are broken relationships today
Between nations or families,
Between colleagues or friends,
Give us the courage to make the first step toward healing.
And may we begin by asking for Your help. Amen.

BROADCAST WEDNESDAY 29 JUNE 2011

June 30

Catherine Cowley

One of the parables in the Gospel speaks of a merchant who found a pearl of great price, went and sold all he had, and bought it.

If a tray of pearls were put in front of me, I wouldn't know which was the most valuable. I might pick the largest, which, for all I know, could be a high-class artificial one. Or again, I might choose the one with the nicest colour, or perhaps the shiniest. At best it would be a guess, and not an educated one at that.

This merchant, however, knew what he was doing. Presumably he had spent a long time trading in pearls. He'd learnt the difference between the real thing and a clever imitation. He could spot a duff pearl among the good ones on offer, or one with a subtle flaw. Probably his knowledge was hard-won — he'd almost certainly have been mistaken at times and lost money, but he kept on until now he could tell that this was the one pearl worth everything he had.

When searching for what's really valuable in our lives, what's worth giving everything for — that's when our past choices come to help us. Things which at the time seemed wonderful but we now realize led to a dead end, or which seemed to offer purpose and meaning but now seem empty. But nothing is wasted: all our choices — even our most disastrous — can help teach us to recognize the genuine article.

Lord, as we try to discern which values are real and which are just froth, help us to take time to listen to all our experience so that we can recognize what truly comes from You. Amen.

BROADCAST TUESDAY 30 JUNE 2009

July 1

Roger Hutchings

A friend of mine recently boarded an aircraft – with some trepidation – for the first time in 35 years. A few days later, another friend showed me an app on his phone which showed the current position of all the aircraft of a particular airline flying throughout Europe: the little map was absolutely covered with planes. I'm reminded of these things because I'm due to catch a flight myself today, and for me, as for millions of people, it's become as normal as stepping onto a bus or driving a car. Even just three generations ago, it wasn't so: such has been the speed of change in mass travel.

Yet every journey, however commonplace, can become imprinted on our memories. Obviously we remember the ones that go wrong – as when thousands of people had their flights cancelled two or three weeks ago because of industrial action in France. We remember the very successful business trip, or the visit to friends in some faraway place. And we remember journeys that were new beginnings – maybe to a honeymoon, or a first visit to some exotic resort.

We say various things to those leaving on a journey – 'take care' has become a common one, but 'go well', 'God bless', 'be safe' or 'bon voyage' all convey the hope that the journey will be a good experience. 'May God go with you' is a more 'religious' farewell. All these things are an expression of our knowledge that life is risky, and perhaps if we are people of faith an expression of our desire to pray.

So we pray for those who travel today. May they go in peace and arrive in safety. Loving God, bless our going out and our coming in. Amen.

BROADCAST MONDAY 1 JULY 2013

July 2

Alison Murdoch

Do you ever get frustrated that we don't seem to mend things anymore? Whether it's a mobile phone, a toaster or an overnight bag, my home is full of broken objects that I don't have the time or skills to fix but which I'm sure will be useful some day.

In Amsterdam they've come up with a great solution. A couple of years ago a series of Repair Cafés opened up across the city. Staffed by volunteers, they invite local people to bring along all those broken objects, to be mended free of charge over a cup of tea. Repair Cafés save everyone money, give retired and unemployed people a chance to share their skills, and reduce landfill. Nobody is turned away, and nothing goes to waste.

In some ways a Buddhist centre can be compared to a Repair Café. The Buddha taught that deep down within each one of us, without exception, is an inexhaustible source of compassion and wisdom. Through mobilizing that compassion and wisdom, we can definitely find happiness, and help others to do so as well. It's a gradual process which starts with developing awareness and confidence in our positive qualities, such as kindness, patience, forgiveness and respect, and gradually eliminating the anger, jealousy, grasping and pride which take away our peace of mind. A good Buddhist centre, just like a church, temple, synagogue or mosque, provides the experienced teachers, tools and techniques, and supportive community needed for this task.

Let's pray that we can all, in our own ways, get the help and support we need to strengthen our positive qualities and realize our potential to find happiness and peace, both for ourselves and the people around us.

BROADCAST MONDAY 2 JULY 2012

July 3

Roger Hutchings

Today two friends are staying with us. One I've known on and off for well over 40 years, the other only for maybe ten years. It's interesting to reflect on the ways various friendships begin, and how they persist — or, in some cases, don't! You'll probably be able to think of the story of a friendship of your own. Shared interests can be important, as indeed can be shared values, but neither of these is vital. Often we're hard put to it to explain precisely why a friendship is formed, or why it 'works' year after year. It's one of the real joys of life to know and be known well enough to feel comfortable together even if there have been months or years of separation.

Because of what I believe about God, revealed in Jesus Christ, it's clear to me that we are created for relationship. After all, the idea of three persons of the Trinity is an attempt to express how fundamental is relationship in the heart of God. When we say we are created in the image of God, we must therefore be declaring that the heart of our humanity is also in relationship. Friendship isn't the only way we express this, but it has to be one of the most important. No law can demand friendship. Nobody can insist on being my friend.

Sharing the story of our lives with our friends is a precious gift. There will be moments of shared joy, and moments of shared pain, and the more we are able to entrust friends with our deepest thoughts, the more likely it is that a friendship will last.

We give thanks, Lord, for our friends. Help us to celebrate our friendships and to value them today and every day. Amen.

BROADCAST WEDNESDAY 3 JULY 2013

July 4

Alison Murdoch

On this day in 1954, something of huge daily importance happened in the UK: fourteen years of food rationing finally came to an end. As the London Housewives Association celebrated the end of the 'Kitchen Front' in Trafalgar Square, my mother looked back at a childhood short on hot buttered toast, scrambled egg and sweets. But it was still happy, and the side benefits included no waste, minimal obesity and less strain on the environment.

Two and a half thousand years earlier, the historical Buddha was no stranger to feast or famine. Born a royal prince, he became disillusioned with a life of luxury, and crept out of the palace at dead of night to seek happiness and peace of mind in other ways. The story goes that for many years he went to the other extreme, living in the forest on just a daily grain of rice and a sesame seed. However, his breakthrough came when he realized that neither excess nor denial was the issue, and accepted a cup of milk from a passing milkmaid.

The Buddha's insight was that there's nothing wrong with good food, nor the pleasure we get from it. The problem comes from our unrealistic expectations. How often have you thought, either consciously or subconsciously, that a bacon sandwich, a latte or a bar of chocolate will make you happy? On a temporary basis, it can work. But if we're looking for lasting happiness and peace of mind, we'll need to develop the ability to be content with whatever life brings.

In these times of economic uncertainty, when many people have to change the way they live, let's pray we can do this in a way that nourishes our inner strength and understanding — that real and lasting happiness comes from the inside out.

BROADCAST WEDNESDAY 4 JULY 2012

July 5

George Craig

I have always secretly admired birdwatchers. And I mean the real hardcore ones: those who if a rare bird is spotted will travel anywhere and willingly spend hours – indeed days – waiting for just a glimpse of it.

Strangely, it was that thought that struck me when I noticed that the Tour de France started this weekend. I will admit to being a long-term fan of all things French. And in France, the Tour is certainly something special.

Every year and throughout France, whole towns and villages shut for the day (at least it feels like it) and people enjoy themselves with picnics, dances, circuses – all sorts of fun and games – while they wait for the riders to pass through. But then when the race gets there, it's over in a flash – you'd better not blink or you'll miss it. It almost seems unfair that the cyclists themselves – some of the fittest and hardest working athletes in any sport – should have to put in so much effort for a public that barely glimpses them.

But it strikes me that many things that we celebrate, enjoy or maybe just use, are the result of somebody else's hard work. The obvious example is the medical profession – doctors study for years but we only really appreciate their skills when we need them. And there are many others who we may actually never see but who put in a lifetime of hard work in manufacturing industry, in public utilities and in service industries simply so that something we want, need or enjoy is there for us at the right moment.

So, while we celebrate our cycling idols, maybe we should also find time to celebrate the less glamorous but maybe even more important ordinary men and women who put in so much effort just for our pleasure, safety and well-being.

Father, we give You thanks for people whose steady years of hard work we may never notice – but none the less benefit from. Amen.

BROADCAST MONDAY 5 JULY 2010

July 6

Ibrahim Mogra

This day in 2005, London was given the honour of hosting the 2012 Olympics, beating the long-term favourite city, Paris. It was indeed a momentous day and the nation celebrated. The last time London hosted the games was in 1948.

Olympians from all over the world would bring incredible diversity and would compete in the spirit of friendship. Years of training and hard work would finally bear fruit and win them medals. Their countries would welcome them back home as heroes.

London and other participating cities made us proud. The opening ceremony, the events, the medal ceremonies and the closing ceremony were all magnificent. New records were set and champions were born. Human beings pushed themselves to their limit and achieved great heights. They became household names and many are now earning a lot of money.

But name, fame and money should never become the goal of life. The Qur'an says we were created to worship God. This also means serving His creation. Muhammad (peace be upon him) said, 'The best of people is the one who is most beneficial to others.'

Past Olympians such as Eric Liddell, a Scottish Christian; Harold Abrahams, an English Jew; Muhammad Ali, an African American Muslim, all fit the bill. Their decisions to participate or not to participate, risking all, were motivated by their desire to benefit humanity.

I hope the heroes of London 2012 are also doing their bit and joining the ranks of those who are most beneficial to humanity.

Gracious God, enable us to find true purpose in our lives and make us amongst those who are most useful to others. Amin.

BROADCAST SATURDAY 6 JULY 2013

July 7

Cathy Le Feuvre

We all know St Francis of Assisi as the patron saint of animals and the environment – but this man who lived 900 years ago left another wonderful legacy in the form of prayers, the best known of which begins with the words, 'Make me a channel of your peace.'

This prayer contains many Biblical truths of what it means to be a Christian – among other things, it urges us to give and forgive, to love and to hope, even when there is hatred, despair and darkness.

On this day in 2005 the UK was rocked to its foundations with a series of bombs going off on the London transport network. Some felt it to have been a defining moment in British history, a day which left us with a sense of foreboding, a real insecurity about the future. For some, even, the day left an enduring sense of suspicion, especially of those who look different from us.

But I believe it could have a positive legacy too.

In the immediate aftermath, volunteers distributed water to thirsty commuters. People embraced and cried together at hastily erected peace gardens. In Trafalgar Square thousands remembered the precious lives lost, maimed or otherwise affected. People of differing faiths came together to celebrate and reaffirm the ties that bind us, rather than the differences that divide us.

Being a peace *lover* or even a peace *keeper* is one thing. But God calls us to be more: to be peace *makers* – not just helping to avoid or patch up arguments, but helping to create peace in even traumatic and difficult circumstances.

Lord, comfort those today who are still suffering as the result of violence, and help us all – even today – to be your peacemakers. Amen.

BROADCAST MONDAY 7 JULY 2008

July 8

George Craig

Last year I found myself, briefly and unexpectedly, the owner of two large stained-glass windows. One of my great grandfather's brothers, in the 1920s, made some money and donated a number of gifts to his old village — including these two windows. The building in which they had been installed was being demolished and, after a bit of research, those concerned discovered that I was the closest living relative — so I was asked whether I'd like to have them, and if not what should be done with them.

I couldn't use them; I couldn't find anyone else who could use them. Eventually they went off to be recycled and, I hope, re-used. It was a difficult situation. I didn't want to see them destroyed and didn't want to sell them, but I was also very unhappy that my relative's generosity should simply trickle away. I'm still brooding about whether I did the right thing.

And the whole affair got me thinking more generally about stuff we inherit. I suspect I am not alone in having boxes of things in my house that I'll probably never look at again and certainly won't use — but can't bear to throw away because they once meant something to someone I love.

But there are other things that we inherit, and not all of them are quite so harmless. There are wars being fought today, the main causes of which are grievances that go back centuries. Generations grow up and, out of a sense of obligation to the memory of people long dead, keep inherited prejudices, hatreds and hostilities alive.

As with objects, maybe we need to be more ruthless in letting go of attitudes and ideas that may have once been important but should have no place in our lives now. It won't be easy — but sometimes letting go is the right thing to do.

Father, give us wisdom to recognize those things we inherit that we should keep and cherish and those we need to let go so that we can move on. Amen.

BROADCAST THURSDAY 8 JULY 2010

July 9

Peter Baker

What started as a project by a BBC documentary film maker, exploring attitudes to old age, became a most unlikely entry into the UK record charts.

Tim Samuel's ambition to give the elderly a voice saw the creation of the oldest pop group in the world named The Zimmers! A website video of these pensioners performing their version of The Who's rock classic, 'My Generation', attracted more than 2 million hits in its first few weeks.

Yet with a combined age of 3,000 years, The Zimmers are more likely to have problems with arthritis than their celebrity status. Nonetheless, they tapped into a social anxiety about the way we perceive the ageing process and what our responsibility should be to the elderly.

As their 90-year-old lead singer Alfie Carreta said, 'People seem to think that if you're old, then you're silly and doddery and pointless. Walk down the street, and people don't notice us — we've become invisible.'

But the culture of the Bible is wide open to the value and importance of old age. It recognizes that age can bring wisdom and understanding.

Some of the greatest accomplishments of heroes like Abraham and Moses came during their final decades. They were hardly men who lived with one foot in the grave.

This call to notice older people can be heard in the book of Leviticus: 'Rise in the presence of the aged, show respect for the elderly and revere your God.'

At a time when the focus of so much political and social attention is often on the younger generation, it's important to remember that the care of the elderly, as of all the vulnerable, is a key indicator of a society's values.

Lord, forgive us when we fail to see and hear those who feel they have no role and no voice. May we respect and care for all those made in Your image, giving them the dignity we would wish for ourselves. Amen.

BROADCAST MONDAY 9 JULY 2007

July 10

Cathy Le Feuvre

Jesus advised his followers not to worry about life but to have faith that God would look after everything if we trusted our lives to him.

But *not* worrying about how life is going to turn out is hard, especially if we have really huge concerns – like health, family and relationship problems.

I recently read an article about the 'Science of Worry', which explained that although the ability to feel anxious might have started off as a way of human beings being alerted to immediate dangers, modern worries are very different.

Today we worry more about long-term threats to our livelihood and relationships – issues that may not be immediately resolved, no matter how much we worry about them.

One suggestion for dealing with our anxieties about the future was to set aside some time every day to think about them, and then to forget them.

It might work for some, but not for me. I have a sneaking suspicion what would happen is that in the run-up to my 'worry hour', I'd be fretting about whether I'd remember to worry about everything, and afterwards I'd be worrying that I'd forgotten to worry about something *really* important.

God calls us to a life of trust in Him. He calls us to a life of faith, but he doesn't leave us to obsess about life on our own. We may bring our concerns to God, and just knowing that someone else, who cares about us, is also involved, can help us find solutions.

Today, Lord, we place our worries at Your feet. Give us the faith to believe that You can help us deal with whatever life may throw at us. Help us to listen for Your Voice, and to be prepared to take Your advice and direction. Amen.

BROADCAST THURSDAY 10 JULY 2008

July 11

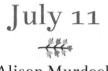

Alison Murdoch

I've always been drawn to the saying of King Solomon: 'death and life are in the power of the tongue.' Or as the comedian Eric Idle said more recently: 'sticks and stones may break my bones, but words will make me go in a corner and cry by myself for hours.'

This emphasis on the power of words is reflected in the Tibetan Buddhist equivalent of the Ten Commandments. Out of ten 'non-virtuous actions', four of them relate to the way we choose to speak: lying, gossip, harsh words and divisive speech.

The first time I heard this, it came as a wake-up call. Few of us would argue that lying is almost always wrong, but the other three are part of daily life. Gossip, harsh words and divisive speech are the bread and butter of the media, and programmes such as *The Apprentice* have turned them into mass entertainment.

This seems particularly sad when the capacity to master language is one of the special qualities that make us human. Every morning we wake up with a fresh choice. Either to share the grumpy mood or hurtful remark that can spoil someone else's day; or else to consciously use our speech as a force for good — to show kindness and concern, to encourage and inspire. If we genuinely want to make the world a better place, paying attention to our use of words is a failsafe way to go about it.

Let us pray that all of us can find a way to speak today that will heal rather than hurt. May we use the power of the tongue with kindness and care. May we find the strength to make this a habit, day after day.

BROADCAST SATURDAY 11 JULY 2009

July 12

Peter Baker

The advent of email has added a new dimension to the way we communicate. Not long ago the British Library tapped into its cultural significance by inviting people to forward a memorable email from their inbox or sent items. From these, a so-called 'twenty-first-century Doomsday Book' will be created, enabling future generations to read what we today find interesting or important.

Given how dependent many of us now are on this form of communication, it promises to be a fascinating snapshot. For it's not just boring spreadsheets or office memos that are coming and going at the press of an icon. Mini soap operas are played out in inboxes across the country every day, from job offers to wedding proposals, big breaks to break-ups. Instant answers, access to information, and all available from virtually anywhere on the planet -email has revolutionized the way we relate to each other and the world.

In many ways this has been a wonderful development. But there can be problems. In our haste to reply, we can fail to allow time for considered reflection. And we certainly haven't got access to those important clues that face-to-face encounters can give. In comparison, an email can often hide more than it reveals. Sometimes there's just no substitute for eye contact when we really need to understand a message.

When God wanted to get through to the world, to reveal his love, he chose to send His Son. For Jesus is the body language of God.

And when the Apostle John came to reflect on that experience, he commented, 'what we have seen with our eyes, what we have looked at and our hands have handled — this we proclaim, the word of life.'

Everlasting God, thank You for the variety of ways in which we communicate. Especially we thank You that we know You because Jesus was the word who became flesh and lived among us. Amen.

BROADCAST THURSDAY 12 JULY 2007

July 13

Alison Murdoch

There was much rejoicing in my workplace recently when the wife of a colleague passed her final medical exams. This was particularly meaningful because it had been her childhood dream to serve others as a doctor. However, she didn't get the right grades as a teenager, so it wasn't until she'd got a PhD in another subject that she was accepted as being bright enough for medical school. It makes me wonder about the balance of qualities we're looking for in our future doctors.

Most of us will know a young person who's currently biting their nails about exam results after years of cramming facts and learning the arcane arts of multiple choice and essay writing. Once again, it's academic grades that will largely determine their future direction and success in life. The message we're giving our young people is that what matters most is intellectual ability, rather than a sense of vocation or a wish to help others.

The aim of Buddhism is simply to help people to be happy, and it does this by encouraging us to develop both a smart mind and a warm heart, in equal measure. The Tibetans offer the metaphor of a bird needing two wings: if it has one without the other, it will never get off the ground. To put it in contemporary terms, a smart mind untouched by kindness can create inhumane weapons and unjust financial systems, while a warm heart without intelligence can make promises that can't be kept, or give away money in a way that harms rather than helps. We need them both.

Let's pray that we can find ways of showing young people that intellect alone will not bring about well-being and happiness, and support them in creating a world in which intelligence is always balanced by kindness and compassion.

BROADCAST WEDNESDAY 13 JULY 2011

July 14

ᛣᛣᛣ

Ibrahim Mogra

The command of kindness to parents in the Qur'an is second only to worshipping God. Parents brought us into this world and looked after us when we were helpless babies. Their constant love, care and devotion helped us to become what we are today. How can we ever repay them?

The Qur'an says, 'Your Lord has decreed that you worship none but Him and that you be kind to parents. Whether one or both of them attain old age in your life, do not say a word of contempt to them, nor repel them, but address them with honourable speech. And out of kindness, lower to them the wing of humility, and say, "My Lord! Bestow your mercy upon them as they cherished me in childhood."'

Islam demands absolute obedience to parents except in unlawful things. The Messenger Muhammad (peace be upon him) said, 'The major sins are to associate partners with God, to disobey parents and to give false evidence.'

The mother who bears and nurses the child through infancy is assigned a higher status than that of a father. Muhammad was once asked who deserved the most courtesy and good manners. He said, 'Your mother.' When asked a second time he said, 'Your mother.' When asked a third time he said, 'Your mother.' When asked a fourth time he said, 'Your father.' He also said, 'Be close to your mother for truly Paradise lies at her feet.'

The Qur'an says, 'And remember We took a Covenant from the Children of Israel: Worship none but God; treat with kindness your parents and relations and orphans and those in need...'

Lord, enable us to remain observant of our duties to our parents and relations, to care for them with love, honour and respect. Amin.

BROADCAST SATURDAY 14 JULY 2012

July 15

Claire Campbell Smith

As a teenager, I felt a great sense of pride to go to the same school in Manchester where Emmeline Pankhurst had sent her three daughters. Emmeline's commitment to the cause of women's suffrage was inspirational to me, underlining the school's philosophy that we girls could achieve anything we wanted, if we put our mind to it and worked hard.

Emmeline hadn't enjoyed such educational advantage: her parents' support of women's advancement in society hadn't yet affected their belief that girls' learning should centre on 'making home attractive' and other husband-pleasing skills. They did send her to a Parisian finishing school, but it was their political activism rather than her education that had already begun to shape one of the most influential women of the twentieth century.

Emmeline was born on this day in 1858, even though she always said her birthday was a day earlier and that she felt a kinship with the female revolutionaries who stormed the Bastille on that previous day, decades earlier.

Again as a teenager, one of the most attractive features I found in the Christian story was the radical attitude of Jesus toward women. He overthrew tradition by treating women as equal to men, just as he did by showing favour to others of inferior status at the time – children, lepers, tax collectors, people with disabilities. To him, these outcasts were created in the image of God and worthy of grace. Today he'd be alongside the addict, the asylum seeker, the person living with AIDS, just as much as with the successful and powerful.

Lord, help us to treat with respect everyone we meet today. May we see Your image in them. Amen.

BROADCAST MONDAY 15 JULY 2013

July 16

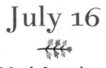

Mark Langham

As a love-sick schoolboy, I set my sights on the most beautiful girl in class. Like all youngsters in love, I tried to impress her with my jokes and cool behaviour. I became, to my mind, the sophisticated sort of person she hung out with.

As you can imagine, I got absolutely nowhere. She saw the act for what it was.

We are often so desperate to impress that we try to be better than we are. Our pride will not allow us to admit the truth about ourselves.

Pride is unwilling to come clean, because deep down we're insecure, or unhappy, with what's there. Weak kings always like to sit in high thrones. Pride is wrong because it's not genuine. Jesus warns us that pride will use up our energy, exhaust us.

Humility, as Jesus makes clear, is not a matter of only seeking the lowest part. He himself told us to let our light shine before the world. Humility is much more about being authentic – being really who we are. Jesus himself was the greatest exponent of this. He was the genuine man, who didn't put on an act.

To be authentic, we need to understand that we're loved by God for who we are – not what we think we ought to be, or what others think we ought to be. What need have we, then, to be other than we are? If we could spend half as much time being ourselves as we do trying to be someone we're not, we would find that peace, that integrity, that brings real joy.

Lord, grant me the confidence that comes from Your love of me, so that I can be truly myself, and shine forth before the world. Amen.

BROADCAST MONDAY 16 JULY 2007

July 17

Derek Boden

This spring, in my part of Ireland, the whitethorn blossom came late. When the bloom did come, it came suddenly, and in what seemed like an instant a profusion of white-blossomed borders graced the roads and the fields. And for those of us fortunate enough to have a thorn hedge in our gardens, we were garlanded with a wealth of creamy blossom. With that profusion of white bloom and with the beauty of the fresh green everywhere, our hard long winter was forgotten.

If every waiting-time brought such compensation, our waiting would be the more bearable. As it is, the waiting is hard to endure. Those test results, whether medical or academic, bring their own anxieties. Most of us don't deal well with the 'time between'. Between the planting and the blossom, between the sowing and the reaping, between the asking and the hearing, how interminable it all seems. How long, O Lord, how long!

It was a line from TS Eliot that gave me pause for thought, as with so many other lines of his. In a chorus from *The Rock* Eliot wrote of taking no thought of the harvest, but only of proper sowing. Good advice, but I'm afraid I'm a 'harvest' person, though as I get older the wisdom of Eliot and others makes me think.

So grant us, O Lord, the patience to do just what lies to hand and to trust that You in Your wisdom will bring to fruition that which is already of Your mind and Your heart. Amen.

BROADCAST SATURDAY 17 JULY 2010

July 18

Richard Hill

'To be free is not merely to cast off one's chains, but to live in a way that respects and enhances the freedom of others. No one is born hating another person because of the colour of his skin, or his background, or his religion. People must learn to hate, and if they can learn to hate, they can be taught to love, for love comes more naturally to the human heart than its opposite.'

These are the inspiring words of prisoner 46664, Nelson Mandela, who was born on this day. Today is being celebrated in South Africa and in many parts of the world as Mandela Day, and it's hoped it will be a growing global initiative to honour and celebrate the former South African President and his legacy.

Mandela Day is an opportunity for people around the world to take some time to make a contribution to the world around them. Not simply celebration, but a call to service.

On a trip to Cape Town I remember standing in Mandela's cell in Robben Island prison, and seeing the quarry where he spent days under the sweltering sun breaking stones. I still marvel at this statesman's lack of bitterness. It is inspiring to think of how he taught fellow prisoners to read and write during his rest periods in the quarry.

In the Bible, St Paul calls us to catch this vision of service. He says, 'Use your freedom to serve one another in love.' That's how freedom grows.

Heavenly Father, teach us to use our freedom generously. As Christ has served us, so help us to serve one another. In Jesus' name, Amen.

BROADCAST SATURDAY 18 JULY 2009

July 19

Chris Bennett

Where I work, in the Titanic Quarter in Belfast, two huge yellow metal cranes dominate the skyline from every vantage point – Samson and Goliath. They were installed decades ago for heavy industrial use in the shipyard, and they are still in use today, but they also have a place in the hearts of many Belfast locals as a familiar part of our city skyline, as iconic as the Eiffel Tower or the Statue of Liberty. I love to use them as reminders of the two fascinating Biblical characters after whom they were named. Goliath, in particular, is often used as the ultimate example of the insurmountable problem. In the Bible story he was a mighty, undefeated warrior, whose arrogant call to battle struck fear into every terrified Israelite. In our day, we sometimes refer to those strength-sapping, sleepless-night-causing, insoluble problems as the Goliaths we have to face.

David broke the deadlock by focusing not on the size and strength of Goliath, but on the power of the God he served. 'It is not by sword or spear that the Lord saves,' he said as he stepped forward. His change of focus gave him courage while the rest of the Israelite army shivered in fear. May we have that change in focus as we face our Goliaths. They may be huge, as overwhelming as that massive crane towering above the shipyards, filling the sky.

But Lord, re-focus our eyes so that we concentrate not on the size of the problems we face, but the greatness of the God we serve. Give us David's perspective and his strength and spirit. Amen.

BROADCAST TUESDAY 19 JULY 2011

July 20

Peter Townley

I was spellbound the other week, listening at a breakfast meeting to the story of the adventures of five teachers, who in 1967, after saving up for two years, set off from Barnsley in a fully laden Landrover and made their way to Kathmandu. They set out from there and trekked to the base camp of Mount Everest. It was quite an undertaking and all organized by themselves. Not only was it the enthralling story of an unforgettable journey across land, it was also a moving tale of the people they met and the Nepalese welcome they enjoyed.

Mount Everest has always held a magnetic fascination for mountaineers, and it is the scene of great achievement as well as tragedy.

Sir Edmund Hillary was born on this day in 1919. In 1953 Sherpa Tenzing and Hillary were the first men to scale Everest successfully. The Duke of Edinburgh was patron of the expedition, and for many people the news of this achievement put the icing on the Coronation cake.

Reading the accounts of these achievements, what is striking is just how much they were team efforts, with none of the advanced technology we take for granted today.

Sir John Hunt, the leader of the expedition, spoke of the comradeship forged through the dangers and difficulties in attaining their goal.

When they reached the summit of Everest, Tenzing made his small offerings to the gods that Buddhists believe have their dwelling there, and beside them Hillary buried in the snow a crucifix, which Hunt had given him to take to the top.

O ye mountains and hills, bless ye the Lord, praise Him, and magnify Him for ever. Amen.

BROADCAST SATURDAY 20 JULY 2013

July 21

Andrea Rea

On this day in 1969 the childish notion of the man in the moon became a startling reality and astronaut Neil Armstrong took his 'one small step for a man' on to the lunar surface and walked.

As a child in 1969, my school class had been learning about the planets, about the speed of light, lunar distances and space travel. Although the moon was relatively close to the Earth when compared to the rest of the solar system, it was still much further than anything we could really grasp. That distance was measured in numbers bigger than anything we could even imagine. What *was* a light year, anyway, if we couldn't ever hope to go that far ourselves? Where was the Sea of Tranquillity, if not in our own backyard?

Then, overnight, something in the nature of those numbers and that distance changed completely. Suddenly, there *was* a man in the moon, and there were footprints there to prove it. Now there were human traces there and live television pictures showing us something that had been the stuff of imagination, from the stories in our textbooks and in our minds only, like a dream.

Today, the innocence and hope of those days seem very far away, as does the moon, if not quite as far as before. One thing that hasn't changed, however, is our need to learn and strive and reach for the stars, wherever we are and whatever those stars mean to each of us.

Great God of our universe, help us to remember that every journey we take begins with a single step and the footprints we leave matter more than we might imagine. Help us to tread lightly wherever we walk, bearing in mind that, even if our destination is light years away, all the 'giant leaps' made by the human race in our own lifetimes began with just one small step. Amen.

BROADCAST SATURDAY 21 JULY 2007

July 22

Richard Hill

When I'm in London, I travel on the bus rather than the Underground. I was going to a meeting last week when I spotted a church in south London. It caught my eye.

It had the usual sort of sign fixed to the front — the church's name, the rector's name and phone number, and the service times. But that wasn't what first grabbed my attention and made me more curious. You see, there was another sign, higher up, clearly visible from the top deck of the bus. Bright letters clearly spelled out the word 'warning', and just to the left of the bold sign was the CCTV camera it was warning about.

The Bette Midler song 'God is watching you ... from a distance' immediately came to mind.

When I pointed the camera and the signage out to my friend travelling with me, he said it should be taken as a warning that inside the building you will find a message of religious imperialism.

Not a view I would necessarily agree with, but one that would probably chime with many people. But it set me thinking. Perhaps the moral of the warning might be that those inside our churches need to be careful what they do with the freedom that's supposed to be at the heart of the Christian faith. St Paul said, 'it is for freedom that Christ has set us free.'

Perhaps all churches should come with a warning, not of 'the God is watching you' kind, but a reminder that if Christians use the freedom that God offers liberally and even with some abandon, then it should be utterly transforming — on the buses, in the tube, and right through our communities.

Father, help me to use the freedom that You give in ways that share freedom and don't create negativity but make a positive difference. In Jesus' name, Amen.

BROADCAST WEDNESDAY 22 JULY 2009

July 23

Peter Townley

Trafford Park in Manchester, where I had a parish, was once a thriving industrial estate and known as the machine shop of Europe.

In its heyday, with tens of thousands of workers there, at night there was a queue of buses literally a mile long waiting to take them home.

Even Henry Ford had a factory there once on First Avenue in the Park.

Now making millions of cars worldwide each year, they have come a long way since July 1903, when Ford in Detroit sold his first car to a doctor in Chicago.

As the Ford factory in Detroit was expanding, Reinhold Niebuhr came to that industrial city to be a pastor. He was a bright young man, and caring for the people there taught him to connect what it is to be human with life in a changing world.

Writing in his diary in 1925 about a visit to a car factory, he said: 'The men seemed weary … and toil is slavery. They simply work to make a living. Their sweat and their dull pain are part of the price paid for the fine cars we all run. And most of us run the cars without knowing what price is being paid for them.'

Later, when he was a Professor at Union Theological Seminary in New York, Niebuhr would sit in the chapel and read the newspaper. For him that was prayer. His understanding of God and people was very much rooted in the messiness of the world. It was there that he wrote the prayer for which he is particularly remembered:

'God, grant me the serenity to accept the things I cannot change, courage to change the things I can, and wisdom to know the difference.' Amen.

BROADCAST TUESDAY 23 JULY 2013

July 24

Michael Piret

Have you ever had the kind of day when you wake up feeling quite easy inside, peaceful and happy, but then, a few seconds later, a shadow descends? You've just remembered something that happened the day before — maybe a mistake, a blunder you made, a regret, some injury that was done to your happiness or sense of security. If only those words hadn't been said. If only that hadn't *happened*. If only you'd done things differently, spoken more wisely, said nothing at all. If only you could go back and undo it.

I once knew a wise elderly bishop who used to say that the two most useless words in the English language are 'if only'. Useless because, after all, they so often refer to things that are now beyond our power to change, things about which we can do nothing. The real question — no matter what happened yesterday — is today's question. Now what? Where do we go from here?

In the Gospels Jesus says we shouldn't waste our energy worrying about tomorrow. That's a rule we can also apply to yesterday. Just as we can leave tomorrow to worry about itself, we can likewise leave yesterday to worry about itself. That means letting go of self-reproach and regret — leaving behind the chains and shackles of past events, so we can live in the present, meeting the challenges of today freshly, with all our strength.

God, help us remember that today is the day You have given us to shape — not yesterday. Set us free from the shadow of past mistakes and old regrets, help us move forward, trusting in Your promise to make all things new. Amen.

BROADCAST SATURDAY 24 JULY 2010

July 25

Peter Townley

Today is the Feast of St James the Great.

He's always been special to me, because I was baptised at St James the Great in Collyhurst in Manchester one snowy December afternoon. For many others he's important because his remains are in the Cathedral at Santiago de Compostela, which is now, more than ever, a popular pilgrimage destination.

St James is well known for two stories in the Gospels. The first is that of James and his brother John's anxious mother and her wish that her two sons are given the best seats in the Kingdom of God. Jesus firmly reminds her that the Christian life is about service rather than status.

The other is his mountain-top experience with John and Peter of seeing Jesus transfigured.

Reading those stories through the eyes of St James turns our world-view upside down so that we see God and each other in a new way.

This dramatically happened to Charles Raven (1885–1964), a great theologian in his day, who was something of a mystic. One of his life-changing experiences happened as he passed a chip shop in Liverpool.

He talked of God meeting him in splendour there. 'I was coming home,' he said, 'and passed some shawl-clad women gathered round a dingy shop. The proprietor, in his shirt sleeves, was dispensing packets of fish and chips wrapped in a newspaper. The place was lit by naphtha flares, and misty with the steam of cooking ... And again of a sudden the glory; and God fulfilling his eternal task and giving to his children their daily bread.'

Father, help us to understand You in a new way and to see Your glory today in everyday things. Amen.

BROADCAST THURSDAY 25 JULY 2013

July 26

❧

Andrea Rea

There is a body of research somewhere that says that the sleep in which we dream is the best, most restful and productive sleep one can have. Some mornings when I have to rise early, I have to confess a desire to be testing that theory, but am prepared to acknowledge that when I wake up and can remember good dreams, I do feel more rested.

A very large dog I had as a pet years ago, a wolfhound called Celt, used to sleep on a rug in the house and dream of running. You could tell, because his feet would start moving, synchronized as if racing to the other end of the field, running for the joy of it. In his prime he was a wonderful companion. Later in life, arthritis slowed him down and kept him indoors, but he would still run in his sleep. In his dreams Celt was as fit and well as a puppy, and when he died I consoled myself with the thought that he was now in a big field in heaven, running to his heart's content.

Certainly, it's good to have dreams, the kind we experience in sleep, and the sort we have about the future and our potential in life and work. It's important, though, to understand the difference between the two, because there's a danger of living your life wishing for things you haven't achieved and ignoring the gifts you do have. Happiness is only real if you know that you're happy.

The folk singer and activist Si Khan wrote, 'it's not the fights you dreamed of, but those you really fought, it's not what you've been given, it's what you do with what you've got.'

Dear God of our dreams and of all that we do and leave undone, give us the wisdom to value our gifts and achievements as well as our dreams. Help us to run at our own pace, even as we dream of winning the race and reaching the other side of every field. Amen.

BROADCAST THURSDAY 26 JULY 2007

July 27

Michael Piret

One of CS Lewis's friends tells a story of how Lewis, on an Oxford street outside a pub, was asked for money by a man who was down on his luck; and Lewis gave him some. As they were walking away, Lewis's friend said, 'Why did you do that? He'll just go and spend it on drink.' There was no contesting the point, no way of telling whether the man would spend the money on drink or not. Lewis just said, 'I know if I keep it ... I will.'

That answer should come as a challenge to us. *Whatever* weakness or selfishness *we* may be prone to, why are we so quick to condemn, in others, things we unthinkingly excuse in ourselves? Maybe it's one of our ways of trying to feel superior. In the Gospels, Jesus has a word for people who do this. He calls them hypocrites. 'Why do you look at the speck of dust in your brother's eye,' he asks, 'with never a thought for the plank in your own?' Sometimes we have a special genius for condemning the very traits we have ourselves, things we may not *like* about ourselves – because they're so much easier to confront when we see them in another person. It's as if we think attacking our faults, in someone else, lets us off the hook, so we don't have to do anything about them within ourselves.

God, free us, today, from eagerness to sit in judgement on others; or at least make us aware of our hypocrisy when we do it – and change our hearts. Help us see how much we have in common with those we are prone to criticize. And teach us how deeply we share, with them, the need for Your mercy and healing. Amen.

BROADCAST TUESDAY 27 JULY 2010

July 28

Clair Jaquiss

A family fortnight by the sea. We always intended to leave at the crack of dawn – but we hardly ever left before half past ten. The car was finally packed up and we squeezed in between the cases, our favourite pillows, the windbreak and the hundreds of other things that parents seemed to think were essential. And yes, there was the standard 'Are we nearly there yet?', comfort breaks at motorway services, glacier mints, stops when people were feeling carsick, and occasionally moments when we had to extricate ourselves from cricket bats and beach bags so our not very powerful car could get up a steep hill. Then there was the picnic lunch with its well-squished white bread egg sandwiches – a delicacy I still relish – and a whole tomato, smelling of the greenhouse. You had to bite into it over the grass, so the juice didn't drip anywhere important. And as this was before the days of yogurt pots, there were small tins of baby chocolate puddings, opened with a can opener that left a lethal jagged edge but never seemed to be a problem.

We felt as if we had all our worldly goods with us. We were safe and self-contained. But we know not all family trips bring joy. Refugee family journeys begin in fear or out of necessity – perhaps because of war or violence or destruction. Then, packing up the safety of home has a very different feel to it. The flight of the refugee is a journey of desperation but perhaps also a sign of hope. One world is destroyed but there is a faith that things can be better.

Lord, we pray for those who journey into an unknown future today – especially those who are afraid or who feel alone. Comfort them in their need and help us to build a world founded on love, where peace and security bring hope for the future of all Your children. Amen.

BROADCAST TUESDAY 28 JULY 2009

July 29

Edwin Counsell

This anniversary of the death of anti-slavery campaigner William Wilberforce in 1833 marks the passing of a man whose influence can be seen in the equality and dignity that many of us take for granted in our society today. His memorial in Westminster Abbey marks both his influence and his faith, yet, ironically, Wilberforce died just three days after hearing that the Act that abolished slavery in most of the British Empire was guaranteed passage through Parliament.

It seems incredible that a civilized society could tolerate the barbaric abuse and indignity of the slave ships, and the wretched legacy of that sad chapter of human history. Yet it took the tremendous determination and commitment of Wilberforce, his comrades and countless other individuals, taking a stance against a tide of convention and declaring that the colour of our skin or the features of our faces, just like our attitudes or our values, simply mark out our uniqueness as a part of God's creation, made as we are in his image and likeness.

Wilberforce's legacy goes further, however, as he committed his energies to improving the education and healthcare of the poorest and most vulnerable children of his day, to increase their life chances. Driven by a faith that saw all of these things as forms of slavery to poverty or social convention, Wilberforce believed in and sought to build a society where all might be liberated.

Yet it's a sobering thought that, despite the legacy that his name inspires, human trafficking and child poverty still haunt many parts of the world today, even touching our own society; and while many battles to secure basic rights and freedoms have been won, the war to recognize the dignity of all goes on.

So Lord, in our world with its contrasts of poverty and plenty, freedom and slavery, give each one of us a lively conscience, and the courage to see through the conventions of our world, to find the truth, liberty, justice and freedom that is Your will for everyone today. Amen.

BROADCAST MONDAY 29 JULY 2013

July 30

Patrick Thomas

Right on the edge of what was once called 'Christendom' is the medieval monastery of Makaravank. It stands high in the hills on the border of Christian Armenia looking across toward Muslim Azerbaijan, and I decided to go there during a recent visit to the country.

The road to the monastery would have challenged the doughtiest rally driver. But it presented no problem to the proud owner of a local taxi. As he miraculously manoeuvred his little car along the impossible track, the sun glinted on the roofs of an Azeri village across the border.

Amazingly, we reached Makaravank unscathed. I went into the church to admire its fascinating carvings and then emerged again into the sunlight.

The normally chatty young driver was standing in sad silence in front of a modern *khatchkar* – a traditional Armenian cross-stone. He quietly explained that it had been put there as a memorial to the farmers of the area, killed defending their land in border clashes. Some of them were people that he had known.

The monument had droplets carved on it: the tears of the bereaved or the drops of blood of those who had been killed. To me they also seemed to be the blood and tears of Christ himself. Christ's blood was shed to break down the barriers between us and our neighbours and humankind and God. Perhaps his tears were for the way in which religion can so easily become an ethnic and tribal badge that strengthens barriers and inflicts wounds, rather than being a source of healing, unifying love.

May the God of Abraham, Isaac and Jacob, the creator of us all, help us work in love to break down prejudice, fear and misunderstanding, and to heal the wounds inflicted by ethnic, cultural and religious divisions. Amen.

BROADCAST WEDNESDAY 30 JULY 2008

July 31

Edwin Counsell

High summer seems to be the invitation to dust off the tent in the attic and go camping. The tent is a stock item for those attending music festivals and for many people camping is the preferred choice of summer holiday.

On this day in 1907, a very different sort of camp was held for the first time. Robert Baden-Powell set up the Brownsea Island Scout Camp at Poole Harbour in Dorset — and the Scouting movement was born. He took a group of lads, some from the local community and others from top public schools, and showed them they could work together, encourage one another and have fun.

And it was out of this first 'experiment' that Baden-Powell wrote the definitive guidebook for the movement, called *Scouting for Boys*, which outlined life skills and personal values, while warning of the perils of drunkenness, gambling and swearing, not to mention the wiles of the opposite sex!

These days, Scouting embraces young people regardless of gender as well as background, and it's come a long way from the time when Baden-Powell's instructions were confined only to boys.

The current Chief Scout is Bear Grylls, who many people know from his exploits on TV. He was once asked what he loved about Scouting, and his response was some words his dad had said to him when he was young: 'Follow your dreams and look after your friends.'

In an age when we celebrate the cult of the individual so often and invariably prize personal attainment, it's encouraging to celebrate a movement that looks to develop the very best of the gifts that any of us possess — and find ways of using those gifts in the service of others.

So today, Lord, give us minds that are filled with possibilities, hearts that are open to every prompting of Your Spirit, and lives that embrace one another in Your name. Amen.

BROADCAST WEDNESDAY 31 JULY 2013

August 1

Marjory MacLean

When August arrives, that means, in many parts of the country, the season of shows: county shows, agricultural shows, Highland shows. Thousands of people gather in Scottish villages, round great English country houses, and in fields all over Britain.

The stars of the shows are not the people, but extraordinary animals, the biggest, fittest, cleanest(!), strongest and most valuable ideal specimens. There are bulls other bulls must aspire to be, ewes scrubbed up as if for Crufts, pigs in perfect proportion. Providence, through the processes of nature, has virtually done it all, with just a little help from the humans who bred the stock, provided the feed, and in some cases wielded the brush and comb.

Throughout the Bible and especially in the Psalms, ordinary people with just a little imagination stand back from time to time in awe, allowing their minds to be crowded with the astonishing number and diversity of the places and plants and creatures and people that God has made. Each has its own design and perfection, even the ones that would win no prizes in the County Show. When we pause and think, and count and lose count and appreciate it all, people of faith suddenly get a new, deeper sense of their place as much-loved figures in a world redeemed by the one who created it.

'O Lord, our Sovereign, how majestic is Your name in all the earth!' Whenever we stop to consider the world, animals, birds, fish, people and the whole created planet, may we be humbled afresh to acknowledge that our own lives are of Your making, our futures are in Your hands, and our well-being is close to Your heart, through the love of Jesus Christ, perfect man and truly God, Amen.

BROADCAST SATURDAY 1 AUGUST 2009

August 2

Edwin Counsell

It's never nice to be called a fool. It often means that others are laughing at us, rather than with us, and anyone who's dismissed as a fool is typecast as easily led or manipulated and, invariably, becomes the butt of someone else's joke.

Today is the Feast of St Basil of Moscow, who gives his name to the iconic cathedral in that city, with the decorated domes and pinnacles that give it the look of an exotic cake! How ironic that the grandeur of the church that bears his name sits in such stark contrast to Basil's life of humility and poverty in the service of the poor and underprivileged.

Back in the fifteenth century, his peers called him a fool for bucking the trend, and challenging his society to remember the needs of others as much as their own needs and, crucially, to do so in the name of Jesus Christ.

Basil's reputation for foolishness didn't stop there. On one notable occasion he apparently chastised Ivan the Terrible for his violence toward others, and for not paying attention in church! The effect on the famous despot must have been startling, though, because Ivan was amongst the mourners who carried Basil's coffin to the cemetery, after he died in 1552.

In a world where many of us worry constantly about the opinions of others and how we might be perceived, it's sometimes no bad thing to hold a line that's different from those around us. Speaking out when we believe things are unfair, or just plain wrong, might make us foolish in the eyes of some, but it can at times be the right thing to do.

So, Lord, as we remember Basil, the 'fool for Christ', may we face up to the opportunities and challenges of our lives and, in so doing, may we have courage to recognize all that is right, and act upon it, even when to do so seems utter foolishness; and may we know that folly to be the wisdom that flows from Your grace and the gifts of Your Spirit. Amen.

BROADCAST FRIDAY 2 AUGUST 2013

August 3

Michael Mumisa

So often, news reports of violence across the world focus on the part religion plays in conflict. Such reports always directly impact upon all our lives and the relationship of our communities here at home. Some people are quick to conclude that religions or their scriptures are the root causes of the violence we witness in our world today. And yet others feel that religious reflection and an ethical reading of religious texts are in fact solutions to the challenges we face today.

There's an ancient Islamic story that goes like this:

A Jewish funeral procession once passed before the Prophet Muhammad. As a sign of respect, the Prophet stood up. His Companions asked him, 'Why did you stand up for a Jewish funeral?' The Prophet replied, 'Is he not a human being with a soul?'

There is also an African proverb that goes:

'If you close your eyes because of the bad people around you, you will not see the good people passing by.'

We have all come across many more people of faith, and those of no particular faith, who are inspired by their beliefs and convictions to work together for the betterment of their communities.

We pray for peace in the words of the Prophet:

'O Lord! Cause love between our hearts, and improve our mutual relations, and guide us to the paths of peace and security; taking us out of darkness and guided toward the Light of peace. O Lord! You are peace, and all peace is from You; and all peace returns to You. O master of power and glory.' Amin.

BROADCAST WEDNESDAY 3 AUGUST 2011

August 4

Gordon Graham

Edinburgh has a long history of cultural eminence. Once known as the Athens of the North because of the number of brilliant thinkers and writers who lived here, today it's equally famous for the Edinburgh International Festival held in August each year.

Actually, there are several festivals all taking place at the same time. For many years, the official festival has been accompanied by an unofficial 'Fringe' that adds over 1,000 performances. Further festivals devoted to books, films and TV have sprung up alongside. The combined effect is to fill this beautiful city with an extraordinary concentration and variety of artists, writers and performers from every part of the globe – from world-famous orchestras to student musicians, from grand opera to street theatre, from long-established masterpieces to the most experimental art.

In such a huge number of events devoted to the arts, mixed in with the memorable and inspirational we are bound to find things that are trivial and offensive. Some people deny this. They believe that art is a law unto itself and the artist can do no wrong. Anyone who thinks otherwise is regarded as censorious, or worse, sanctimonious. But the truth is that in one respect art is on a par with science. Science has unlocked the secrets of the universe. It has also given us the nuclear bomb. Similarly, artistic skill can be used to enrich our experience, and it can be used to glorify the abominable. In fact, it's testimony to the importance of art that it's *not* a realm in which anything goes. It's the most powerful medium human imagination has, and it can be used well – or badly.

Almighty God, in the gift of the arts You have given us a wonderful means of creation, expression and joy. Give us also grace to use that gift so that we may always enrich our lives and the lives of others by reflecting Your glory. Amen.

BROADCAST SATURDAY 4 AUGUST 2007

August 5

Michael Mumisa

When I was a teenager receiving my daily religious education in the Koranic school or Madrasa, as many other Muslim children continue to do, I witnessed the eruption of anger and violence against the publication of Salman Rushdie's *The Satanic Verses*. Suddenly, we were looking at news images of angry, bearded Muslims burning *The Satanic Verses* while shouting 'Allahu Akbar!' — 'God is the greatest!'

I remember a fellow pupil asking our Madrasa teacher, 'Sir, did we not learn that it's prohibited by Islam to burn a book regardless of its content?'

'Yes, but this particular book you should burn!' the *mu'allim* answered back!

His response was an example of how within our different religious traditions we have always witnessed how religious scriptures can easily be manipulated and interpreted to sanction and justify acts that many of us would consider reprehensible. That's true whether it is the burning of books, the promotion of racist ideas, or the marginalization of women. Yet at the same time, religious texts can also be read and interpreted in ways that challenge such practices and habits.

Ali Ibn Abi Talib, a cousin and companion of the Prophet Muhammad, would always say, 'The Qur'an is a text between two covers. It has no tongue and it therefore needs interpreters, and interpreters are human.'

The human temptation to manipulate religious texts to suit our ideological views is always great. Muslims are instructed to pray saying:

'Our Lord! Impose not on us that which we have not the strength to bear, grant us forgiveness and have mercy on us. You are our Protector. Help us against those who do injustice.' Amin. (Qur'an 2.286)

BROADCAST FRIDAY 5 AUGUST 2011

August 6

Marjory MacLean

Today is the anniversary of the birth in 1881 of Alexander Fleming, the Scot who invented penicillin and transformed medical care and disease reduction from his work in a London laboratory. During service in the First World War, he noticed how many deaths were caused by the inadequacy of antiseptics. And it's a story often told, of his lab left untidy during his summer holiday in August 1928, and the unexpected discovery on his return of what came to be called penicillin. In the following generation, many fatal diseases became treatable, some incurable conditions became curable, unthinkably dangerous surgery became possible, and so medical science gained much of its modern promise and hope. To Fleming's brilliant eye, a patch of mould held vast potential to change so much, while the rest of us would have missed it.

Today is the Feast Day of the Transfiguration in many parts of the Church worldwide, when the story is retold of Jesus on top of a mountain, appearing to his disciples in dazzling glory, showing them signs of extraordinary things to come in his life and death and in the world after his rising from death. There the promises and the hope were unmistakable, for us all to know and grasp and celebrate and rely on. We don't need to be brilliant, to be experts in science or theology, to be seized by the picture of dazzling light and promise this story paints in our minds.

Praise to You, our Lord, from everything on the earth. Praise to You, our Maker, from the sun and moon, the creatures of land and sea, the elements and weather, the hills and woods and moors, and from people great and ordinary. Praise to You, our God, Amen.

BROADCAST THURSDAY 6 AUGUST 2009

August 7

Shaunaka Rishi Das

One day, as I sat in my office, I received a call from the Chaplain of the hospital. She asked me to help with a Hindu girl refusing to take her medicine. I agreed to help but was mildly annoyed with this girl imposing on my day — most likely looking for attention.

I was greeted by a consultant and two doctors who sat me down and explained their anxiety. The girl, Neeta, had arrived in this country three months previously, and a month later was in hospital with a drug-resistant form of TB. The drugs they were using had terrible side effects, including psychotic episodes. Neeta now refused to take the medicines, preferring to die and invoking Hinduism as her rationale.

I was decked out in mask and apron to visit Neeta, an intelligent and attractive young girl, who greeted me by saying, 'If you want me to take the medicine, leave now.' So I asked what *she* wanted and listened.

As it turned, out she had no family in the UK and was isolated for these months with only strangers in masks for company, in tremendous pain, with medicine that seemed worse than the disease, and foreign food. I began to understand her desire to die, and yes, she did want attention, and she needed it.

We had friends visit her, bringing her favourite home-cooked food; an Ayurvedic physician who was able to relieve the side effects of her drugs; and a yogi friend who helped her practise very calming meditation. Thanks to this and the excellent medical care, Neeta recovered fully.

Dear Lord, I don't want to feel lonely and unloved and I turn to You expecting Your attention. It is then so sad that I begrudge others who turn to me for attention. Help me to always be available to love. Hare Krishna.

BROADCAST TUESDAY 7 AUGUST 2012

August 8

George Craig

I'm pretty sure that most children have heroes. I certainly did. Mine was the singing cowboy, Roy Rogers – fearless, always on the side of good, biffing the bad guys and generally fulfilling at least this small boy's fantasies. The only downside was that for some years I used to run slightly sideways – because that's how you ride an imaginary horse.

When you grow up you discover that heroism is a bit more complex than that. There are remarkable people who are willing to put their lives on the line day by day. Many of us have very good reason to be grateful to them: look at firemen or the armed forces. And pretty well every natural or man-made disaster seems to throw up ordinary people who will put themselves on the line for others.

But there are other kinds of hero. This is the anniversary of the release from captivity in 1991 of John McCarthy, who was held hostage in Lebanon for more than five years. It's impossible to imagine how his captivity must have felt: the utter powerlessness, the isolation, the sheer hopelessness of it. The way he coped with it looks pretty heroic to me. But captivity comes in many forms.

I think of my friend Ann, who suddenly found herself disabled mentally and physically by a condition she could do nothing about: taken hostage by disease. But she and her husband just took a deep breath and set about making the most of what they could do – never wasting time regretting what they couldn't.

All over this country there are people like that just starting another day. And their resolution, their spirit, their refusal to be defined and diminished by their misfortunes is an example to the rest of us. But it is also a challenge to us to move beyond admiration and find ways in which we can offer real support and help – if they will allow us the privilege of giving it.

Father, we lift up to You the unsung heroes whose extraordinary refusal to be overcome by despair is an inspiration and a challenge to us all. Amen.

BROADCAST SATURDAY 8 AUGUST 2009

August 9

Noel Battye

This afternoon I will be taking part in a wedding in the south of France. When Fergus and Melissa first asked me to conduct the ceremony, I was so pleased because it brought me back 50 years to my schooldays and a poem that I had first learned in French. My memory of it was of a very old man regretting the fact his very advanced years meant that, sadly, he would never see Carcasonne.

On hearing this, the groom's mother did a search of the internet and came up with two copies, one in French, one in English – this poem which begins with the lines, and wait for it, 'I am very very old. I am now sixty years old…' Sobering or what? 'Very very old,' indeed! Is that how I should perceive myself now that her majesty has begun to augment my salary? Or maybe I should go with the line that old is not what it used to be and that 60 is the new 40, in which case 45 doesn't feel too bad. Or should I, as the preacher suggested, subtract the number of decades I have already used, in full or in part, from my allotted span of seven or eight.

Certainly, the odd reminder of mortality does no harm, especially if, like the builder of new barns, it reminds us that nothing is forever, since some day, all too soon, others will claim what is mine and take it as their own. Equally, it puts other things into perspective, reminding me that very few things justify any continuing animosities.

Either way, I like the line of Emily Dickinson on one of my cards last birthday: 'we turn not older with the years, but newer every day.'

Lord, we thank You for this fresh new day
Which now opens up before us.
Bless the opportunities it will bring
And help us to use them for Your glory.
Amen.

BROADCAST SATURDAY 9 AUGUST 2008

August 10

Gordon Graham

In the heart of the city of Edinburgh stands a memorial to one of Scotland's greatest literary figures – Sir Walter Scott. Towering above the gardens in Prince's Street, it commemorates the life and work of a man whose 'Waverley' novels won truly international acclaim and sold hundreds of thousands of copies in many different languages, long before airlines and the internet created the global village we live in today.

It's natural that Scott's contemporary admirers should have sought some impressive way of commemorating him. Yet the monument they built for him is striking only for its size, and the best thing about it is the view from the top. The scale is not so much grand as grandiose, its heaviness in specially sharp contrast at this time of year to the life and the vitality of the festival of arts going on round about it.

But in a way, their mistake lay in thinking that *anything* so tangible could properly commemorate an artist. Art is essentially immaterial, a mental and emotional construct made of sounds and images and meanings. These things are intangible. But they are not fleeting. They are brought into existence again and again by the readers, players, actors, dancers and audiences who are the living tradition made manifest in arts festivals.

In this sense, art is spiritual, and that is why no monument in stone can adequately capture the legacy of the artist, whose bequest is always to the living spirit of art. What the Scott Monument's soaring pinnacles might do, however, is serve as a visual metaphor, one that points us to the source from which all things spiritual take their life.

Almighty God, the Spirit of beauty, truth and grace, grant us today the faith that knows our hearts are restless till they rest in You. Amen.

BROADCAST FRIDAY 10 AUGUST 2007

August 11

Noel Battye

Enid Blyton was born on this day in 1897. Nowadays there are those who would tell me that she was not as child-friendly as she appeared and that the writer who introduced generations of children to the joys of Noddy and Toytown, to the castles and rivers of adventure, and that Famous Five who included Timmy the Dog, was in fact guilty of corrupting and brainwashing children of the middle classes for many decades of the last century.

She always felt a bit dated to me, but I didn't understand the subliminal brainwashing that was going on or recognize the racism that was being nurtured in me as I sided with Noddy against his enemies. Never for a moment did I suspect just what might have been going on in that little house which Noddy shared with Big Ears, nor did it occur to me that George, who was what they called 'just a girl', was in fact the first of the powerful feminists. I should have realized all this years ago of course – when I was a student back in 1970, librarians were banning Billy Bunter in case he made me Fattist and undid all of the good work done earlier by the benevolent Friar Tuck.

So how did no one warn me of all these things at the time? Or could it possibly be that all of these interpretations tell me more about the people who made them than the characters they chose to analyse?

Remind me, O Lord,
As you did the hypocrites who sat in judgment,
That each time I point the finger away from myself,
Three other fingers point back directly at myself.
Amen.

BROADCAST MONDAY 11 AUGUST 2008

August 12

Michael Mumisa

In 1999 the General Assembly of the United Nations declared 12 August an International Youth Day. The theme for this year's International Youth Day is 'Dialogue and Mutual Understanding'.

There has been a lot of talk in recent years about how to avoid a potential 'clash of civilizations'. It has been suggested by many that part of the solution to the growing dangers of misperceptions between people of different cultures is to promote what a learned colleague in interfaith work, the chief Rabbi Jonathan Sacks, calls 'the dignity of difference'.

Young people have not been immune to these developments. In a few cases, we have seen those opposed to such dialogue attempting to use young people as foot soldiers for their cause. At the same time, it has been reassuring to see the majority of young people in our schools and on our university campuses campaigning tirelessly for better understanding between the different cultures. Many of them do so not because of any belief in a God who rewards good and punishes evil, but simply because of their belief in the dignity of our common humanity. I am reminded of the work of the fourteenth-century Muslim philosopher Abu Ishaq al-Shatibi. He understood that individuals and groups from different cultures are shaped by different historical experiences. But we share certain values which can be negotiated through dialogue and mutual understanding. Such values, he explained, are not unique to those who believe in a God.

Lord, grant us the wisdom to value the differences in our cultures, races and ideas. We ask You to forgive us our shortcomings. Amin.

BROADCAST THURSDAY 12 AUGUST 2010

August 13

Musharraf Hussain

In the name of God, the most merciful, the most kind.

When travelling on the London Underground during the rush hour I am always fascinated by the multitude of faces – an ocean of humanity: white, brown, black, pink, round faces, long ones, and yet all beautiful in their own way. Undoubtedly, the human face is an artistic achievement: the icon of God's creation. The face is the mirror of the mind. On this quite compact but complex shape an amazing array of feelings can be expressed: joy, excitement, ecstasy, sadness, sorrow, bereavement, disgust, annoyance, love. There is always a special variation of presence in each one. Each face is unique: no two are exactly the same.

A world lies hidden behind each face. Momentary looks can lead to a gaze of recognition, or of questioning as strangers pass each other – or even to a conversation. In some faces the vulnerability of the person within is obvious – an inner turbulence finding its way to the surface. Then there's the human face that carries mystery – perhaps where the private inner world projects outward. It might only be a smile that calls for understanding and compassion from you or me. That smile from the inner world of the individual can bring such joyous illumination!

The Prophet of Islam taught, 'Meet people with a cheerful face and display good character.' And he also said, 'a smile is charity.'

O Loving God, open our hearts and minds so that we may do good that will bring smiles to the faces of others. Amin.

BROADCAST MONDAY 13 AUGUST 2007

August 14

George Craig

I have two favourite museums. Both are in France: the Strawberry museum
in Brittany and the Mushroom museum in the Loire. I have to admit that I've
never actually been into either of them. It's not that I have anything against
strawberries or mushrooms — quite the contrary. It's just that I have some
difficulty believing there could actually be enough interesting stuff in them to
justify the entrance fee. But someone clearly thought that a fruit and a fungus
were well worth the effort.

I visit enough of my contemporaries' homes to know that most of them, like
mine, are rapidly turning into grandchildren museums. Every available surface
has framed photos of children at every stage of their development to date.
Digital photography has a lot to answer for.

And we find it difficult to understand why it is that not everyone seems to
share our enthusiasm. Visitors are polite, of course, but they have a hunted look
when they see your hand reaching for the latest frame or, worse still, the album.

Christians are supposed to believe in a God who is utterly devoted to every
one of His children. But our own enthusiasm for them runs some way behind
His. Asked to love and care about one another, we tend to be very picky about
just whom and how much we love. And our ideas of God's love tend to be based
on our own version of it rather than His. We find all sorts of reasons to qualify
and limit our love for others and project that attitude onto Him.

Maybe one day I'll go to the mushroom or the strawberry museum. I may
be pleasantly surprised by just how interesting they are. And maybe one day I'll
be willing to take the risk of accepting the reality of God's amazing love for me
and for everyone else and, understanding it, be able truly to share it.

*Father, who so loved the world that You gave Your Son for us — open our hearts and
minds to see and value one another as You see and value us. Amen.*

BROADCAST FRIDAY 14 AUGUST 2009

August 15

Richard Hill

Good morning. On this day in 1998 I watched the news with horror as events unfolded. Carnage: 220 people injured, 29 killed in the bombing of Omagh.

We had all thought the dark days were over, but in an instant we were plunged into one of the darkest moments of our recent past.

My brother, a plastic surgeon who had come to visit me, had his own perspective. He said, 'I'd better ring the hospital and go back.'

He subsequently worked round the clock for days with teams of surgeons and nurses, trying to save and rebuild lives. There wasn't any end to the shift for those medical professionals.

At an international conference years later he was speaking about dealing with this kind of trauma. When he finished his presentation he told me that there was none of the customary applause, just silence.

His professional colleagues had seen a whole world of trauma in their own contexts, but his description of what and who he had to deal with following the Omagh bombing was met with stunned silence.

I'm sure if we ever get to hear of the work of medical professionals in hospitals and clinics in Afghanistan or Syria we might respond with horrified, awe-filled silence too.

Jesus said: 'Blessed are the merciful, for they will be shown mercy ... Blessed are the peace-makers, for they will be called children of God.'

Today I might dare to add: blessed are the healers for whom doing the job is often their only reward.

Father, thank You for those who stand alongside us in our darkest moments to ease our pain. Bring us Your healing, rekindle hope. Amen

BROADCAST FRIDAY 15 AUGUST 2008

August 16

🌼

Musharraf Hussain

In the name of God, the most merciful, the most kind.

This is an exciting time of year for children as they enjoy the summer break after the anxiety of exams. The traditionalists among us insist that children learn the three Rs, reading, writing and arithmetic. But adults could also volunteer to learn a different three Rs: Reduce, Reuse and Recycle – just as challenging for the grown-ups as learning to read and write is for our kids.

As we grow economically rich and our spending power increases, so does the consumption of world resources. At one time we thought natural resources were infinite and unlimited. But as the coalfields are abandoned, oil begins to dry up and forests diminish, the reality has finally dawned that natural resources are indeed limited – a realization heightened by the fear of global warming and the dreaded ozone hole.

It's one thing to be terrified by the next impending disaster, but quite another to take an action. Can we actually control our desires to buy those new clothes or a new car? I believe there's much to be gained by such personal revolution, especially if it becomes widespread and affects society. The three Rs, Reduce, Reuse and Recycle could be one key to world peace! For an ethic of sharing rather than consuming would lessen our need for control, locally and further afield.

O Gracious Lord, the sustainer and the maintainer of the world, guide us on the straight path, the path of life which pleases You. We need Your mercy to help us live a life of simplicity and even austerity so we may care for the world. Amin.

BROADCAST THURSDAY 16 AUGUST 2007

August 17

Catherine Cowley

In the Sermon on the Mount in Matthew's Gospel, Jesus tells his disciples that they are to be 'a light for the world'. But what sort of light?

There is, for example, the searchlight, whose brightness picks out every detail, leaves nothing hidden, exposes all the dark corners. There are occasions when we are called to be that sort of light, to reveal something in the lives of individuals or of society that must not remain concealed. But those occasions are probably pretty rare. There is something harsh about a searchlight which should make us cautious about using it. In some circumstances it can be a cruel light which bleaches out all shades of colour and blinds the one at whom it is pointed.

There is another sort of light shown us in the line from the well-known hymn by Newman, 'Lead *kindly* light'. Here is a gentle light which illumines, reveals, guides, but does not set out to expose every nook and cranny. It enables the one on whom it is shone to move forward, shows the hazards on the way, but respects the fact that people are vulnerable in all sorts of ways that the bearers of that light can only guess at. It leaves some things still obscure because none of us can bear having everything about us exposed to others and still retain a sense of dignity. God does not force us to know everything about ourselves in one fell swoop, but allows us to grow in our knowledge and understanding. We should do the same for others.

God, may we be a light for the world in ways that are life-giving and respectful, knowing that each one of us is precious in Your sight. Amen.

BROADCAST TUESDAY 17 AUGUST 2010

August 18

Kate Coleman

On 18 August 1964 South Africa was banned from participating in the Tokyo Olympic Games, its tolerance of apartheid being cited as the main reason. On this day in 1992 an unrelated incident led to the Serbian prison camps being condemned, as 'hell on earth'. Both occasions fuelled the imagination of a public, who were angry and frustrated at what amounted to the inhumane treatment and blatant disregard of fellow human beings.

Anger is often depicted as being solely negative and destructive. Angry groups and individuals are portrayed as taking extreme measures to express opposition to a particular policy or course of action. The idea of 'redemptive anger' can therefore be difficult to grasp. Yet there are many who, precisely because they are angered and frustrated by a situation, are, as a result, serving the poor, marginalized and vulnerable of our society. Their anger is channelled constructively, providing the necessary motivation to oppose and expose the injustices of institutions and governments – thereby becoming highly effective advocates.

Paul's letter to the Ephesians identifies anger as a potentially redemptive tool. Individuals and communities are challenged to be angry but not to sin (4.26). Today, 'compassion fatigue' is a very real danger. However, perhaps 'anger fatigue' is another consequence of people finding themselves no longer caring any more. The Bible frequently records how a well-placed frustration can yield positive results. Anger can still fuel a resolve to make a difference. Consequently, a certain amount of 'divine indignation' can prevent, cure or lead to positive action from governments, councils, communities, families and individuals.

So Lord, today, if necessary, help me to be angry but not to sin. Amen.

BROADCAST SATURDAY 18 AUGUST 2007

August 19

Graham Daniels

George Orwell said that 'serious sport has nothing to do with fair play ... it is war minus the shooting'.

The 1964 British two-man bobsleigh team of Robin Dixon and Tony Nash wouldn't agree. They were in contention for the gold medal but after the first of their two runs, they discovered that the main bolt holding their back axle in place had snapped in half and there wasn't enough time to find a replacement.

Their main rival, current world champion Eugenio Monte of Italy, hearing of the Britons' plight, removed the bolt from his own bob after his second run, to have it fitted in the British bob. The Britons won the gold medal.

Robin Dixon pointed out, 'Monte knew that he was sacrificing his chance of an Olympic gold medal.' Monte's own comment on the incident was, 'My action was very normal for a sportsperson. You try to help the other people to have the same conditions that you have.' He still has the mug presented to him by the British team, with its inscription: 'A great sporting gesture.' Monte clearly embodied the Olympic spirit and ideals.

The Bible presents high ideals for those who would follow Christ. In Paul's letter to the Church in Rome he urges that 'in view of God's mercy' they should 'offer their bodies as a living sacrifice, holy and pleasing to God'. He comments that to do so is 'a reasonable act of worship'. It is reasonable in God's eyes to use what we have sacrificially, out of gratitude to him.

Heavenly Father, You have shown us great mercy. Please help us to be sacrificial in our relationship with You and with each other today. Amen.

BROADCAST TUESDAY 19 AUGUST 2008

August 20

Catherine Cowley

Many people spend a surprising amount of their lives anywhere but where they are. We often live in the future, looking forward to good things – that holiday, planning the next move in some personal or work project, thinking about the change that comes from starting a new school year or beginning at university. Perhaps we look forward with dread – an illness, loss of a job, death. Equally, we can live in the past – remembrance, nostalgia, regret. We can be like a jockey on a race horse, either at the starting gate, straining toward the future or constantly looking back over our shoulder to see how far we've come and where the other horses are.

Some of this is necessary and helpful, but it can cause us to overlook what's happening right now – indeed, sometimes we do this precisely to avoid thinking about the present.

St Paul gives a strong corrective to any tendency to overlook the importance of the present moment with his insistence that '*Now* is the favourable time; *this* is the day of salvation.' Now is the time in which we live, today is the day when we are called to respond to God and seek to be open to whatever that response requires. It is in the present moment that God's grace is available to us to live by. We can anticipate or remember all sorts of things, but now is the only time we can act for good in the world.

God of all time, may we be alert to what You are asking us to do now to bring about Your kingdom of peace and justice. Amen.

BROADCAST FRIDAY 20 AUGUST 2010

August 21

Tony Rogers

If you find yourself in Ireland at this time of the year, you'll be too late for the wonderful Oyster Festivals in the Far West, but all over the country you'll find celebrations and competitions of traditional music, singing and dancing, involving young and old alike, and there's no doubt that the *craic* will be great. Now, *craic* is a word that combines the idea of fun, enjoyment and atmosphere, but apparently it's just a Gaelic form of a Northern and Scots English word for news or gossip.

It's strange isn't it, how words that sound as if they belong to one language are actually deeply rooted in another. I remember one of Bill Bryson's books looking at words and phrases that sound typically American, but that came originally from England, and, even more surprisingly, quintessentially English expressions that have in fact come to us from the United States. So we can end up totally confused.

The Bible is full of language that confused people. Jesus spoke to Nicodemus about being born again, and Nicodemus thought that the Lord was talking about returning to his mother's womb, which seemed a pretty crazy notion.

In a few hours time, I'll be on board a plane with a group of sick children and people with learning difficulties. We're going on pilgrimage to Lourdes. Something I've done for the last 30 years. Why? Well, quite simply: in Lourdes I meet people who confound the logical and rational side of me, because whether they're close to death, or struggle to speak or read, they have a wisdom that confounds the wise, an ability to proclaim truths about faith and love that leave me reeling in amazement.

Lord, You put down the mighty from their seat and raise up the lowly and meek. Holy is your name. Amen.

BROADCAST FRIDAY 21 AUGUST 2009

August 22

Kate Coleman

Today, as Kenyans commemorate the death of their founding father, president Jomo Kenyatta, in 1978, issues surrounding the nature and value of his legacy will inevitably be raised.

The issue of legacies was brought home to me while attending the funeral of the father of a close friend. He died suddenly and unexpectedly, while overseas doing what he loved doing best: inspiring, encouraging and releasing mission personnel. What a time to be called home!

One particular part of the Eulogy that day struck a chord with me (possibly because it's also an African proverb):

'If somebody wants to eat, they must have food. If they want to eat during one week, they must fill their storehouse; if they want to eat during one, two, three months, they must cultivate a field; and if they want to eat during ten years, they must plant trees. And if they want to eat during a hundred years, they must plant people.'

The things we leave behind are not necessarily as tangible as bricks and mortar. Instead, legacies can be the result of a wise investment of words, encouragement, challenge and inspiration into the lives of friends and strangers. Legacies are often established through spending time in conversation with a child or with a so-called 'non-important' member of the community. Yet such times are frequently considered 'wasted' or inconsequential.

How people may or may not choose to remember us is somehow less important than the impact we're having on them right now. Are we leaving 'gifts' that look and feel like Jesus in peoples' hearts and minds? Do our gifts have eternal value and are we making our world a better place to live in?

Lord, make me 'God's gift' to my world. Amen!

BROADCAST WEDNESDAY 22 AUGUST 2007

August 23

Martyn Percy

I often admire the patience and composure of church leaders, who when pressed to be assertive and directive on delicate or controversial matters, find the grace and strength to hold back. Some call this weakness, dithering or foolishness. But it seldom is. For such leaders, in practising hesitancy, allow the necessary space to develop that permits discussion and deliberation.

This is, of course, not a bad thing. Christians, like all groups of people, disagree. That's the nature of meeting and belonging together, whether it's in politics or just the local social club. The moral question for Christians is not, '*Why* do we not agree?', (it's inevitable we sometimes won't) but, rather, '*How* do we disagree?'. How do we conduct ourselves? With assertion, power and oppressive authority? Or with dignity, patience and humility?

We too easily confuse unity with uniformity. Yet to belong to the Kingdom of God is not to be an elite member of a club for the like-minded. It is, rather, to be part of a communion that is groping its way to a common mind, but through an enormous range of diverse experiences, outlooks and values. If the Church can model the patience and humility that is needed here, there may be hope for our nations, communities and political parties. Living and learning that unity is a higher and better goal than mere uniformity.

Gracious God, grant us the grace to continue Your work of reconciliation. Forgive us the sins that tear us apart; and give us the courage to overcome our fears and prejudices, and seek the unity that is Your gift and will. Amen.

BROADCAST MONDAY 23 AUGUST 2010

August 24

Joe Aldred

I grew up in relative poverty; our household had just enough to get by. And yet our mother — who brought us up almost single-handedly — instilled in us high ideals and values. She insisted on the cleanliness and neatness of the modest clothes my siblings and I wore. She emphasized the importance of good manners, to everyone. We might have been materially poor, but we were taught that poverty, wealth and the issues of life were not just material and external matters, they were spiritual and internal too.

'Dignity' is the word I have come to understand that best describes what mother taught us. Whatever may have been happening around us, however little or much we had, however those around us may have viewed us, we needed to possess and exemplify a deep sense of self-respect and carry ourselves with a dignified pose.

Nelson Mandela, when serving a life sentence in prison on Robben Island, reflected upon the resolve needed to protect and preserve one's human dignity whilst incarcerated. He said, 'Any man or institution that tries to rob me of my dignity will lose; I will not part with it at any price, or under any pressure.'

O God, we learn from the scriptures that our lives do not consist solely of the things we possess. In the teachings of Jesus, time and again we read of Your love for the poor, the sick, the prisoner, and the outcast from society. We see that our value and dignity are not to be surrendered under difficult circumstances.

O Lord, at times when our personal challenges may cause us to lose sight of the inherent dignity with which You have made each of us, strengthen our inner resolve to remain composed under all conditions. Amen.

BROADCAST SATURDAY 24 AUGUST 2013

August 25

Martyn Percy

According to one bestselling American writer, Anne Lamott, the prayer of the Daily Offices can be simply summarized. Morning prayer, she suggests, can be condensed into a single word: 'whatever'. And Evening prayer needs only two words: 'ah, well...'

Prayer, I suppose, is one of those activities that Christians (indeed, folk of all faiths) engage in, but seldom pause to consider what it is they are doing. The habitual, impromptu and mysterious nature of prayer is part of its fascination. Here we have the language of faith, of desire, of hope, of healing – and even occasionally of justification and indignation. And occasionally the quirky: 'Hail, Mary, full of grace, help me find a parking space,' a prayer that not only rhymes but also seems to work – at least for some.

Several years ago, I was an honorary Chaplain to a professional Rugby Club. I performed all the usual duties. Perhaps inevitably, in all the fracas and fury of a game, the name of God would often be invoked by the supporters. And after a crucial-but-missed-kick, my neighbour might turn to me and say, 'I don't think your boss is helping us much today.' The retort: 'Sorry. But I'm more marketing than sales...'

But prayer is not about success. It is about attuning our hearts and minds to God, no matter what life throws at us. Today, across the world, there will be tragedy and triumph, joy and pain, birth and bereavement. Prayer won't necessarily change these realities but it does change how we face them.

Lord, teach us to pray not for what we want, but for what we need. Not for what we desire, but for what is wise. And not for what we crave, but for what You can create. Amen.

BROADCAST WEDNESDAY 25 AUGUST 2010

August 26

Joe Aldred

I recently underwent cardiology tests to see how my heart was doing. The results were good; I feel a certain reassurance about this aspect of my health at least. In fact, my GP tells me that my heart beats at an almost perfect rate like that of a top athlete. I have no idea how this has come about, but I'm grateful.

This wonderfully sophisticated pump, the human heart, has come to symbolize much that is good and wholesome. We speak of someone 'with a good heart', 'tender-hearted' or 'kind-hearted'. And the Christian scriptures espouse the idea of a cleansed heart. 'Give me a clean heart, O God, and renew my spirit within me,' the Old Testament character David is quoted as praying.

The heart, then, is the centre of all that is important about us: our self-consciousness, our emotions and, importantly, the flow of blood around our bodies. The story is told of someone who was unused to medical examination objecting to a doctor monitoring her heart through a stethoscope, on the grounds that only God should listen to her heart because only God should know what is in her heart.

It is important to keep our heart under surveillance because sometimes it does need urgent attention. And it was on this day in 1994 that the world's first battery-operated, so-called 'bionic' heart was fitted in Britain. Equipped with this new heart support, an unnamed patient with only months to live was given a new lease of life.

O God, renew our hearts physically and spiritually that we may lead healthy lives. Thank You for the growing wisdom of cardiologists, surgeons and the scientific community who can now help many to live better and longer lives than was possible in the past. Amen.

BROADCAST MONDAY 26 AUGUST 2013

August 27

Martyn Percy

You may not know it, but today the Church remembers Monica, the mother of St Augustine of Hippo. She died in AD 387, and is perhaps best remembered for the way in which she mentored her son, who in turn became not only one of the great gifts to the Church, but also to Western civilization. Augustine, perhaps more than any person of his age, did the most to establish faith as a key element in the shaping of public life.

Saints come in all shapes and sizes. Granted, it is easy to become humorous with hagiology – the study of saints. There are saints for travellers, sore throats, children, pets and television. Their benefaction leaves nothing untouched. Yet to focus on their patronage misses their point. Saints serve a far more serious purpose in life, and we ignore their function at our peril.

But why remember Monica? I think one answer might be that for everyone who performs and achieves on the world stage, there are many more who are unsung heroes, working hard behind the scenes. Normally, someone like Monica would hardly merit a footnote in history. Yet it is only through the patience and love she showed that Augustine gained the courage and wisdom to become the kind of person and leader the world needed at the time. Sometimes when we look behind the great leaders and saints who dominate the foreground, we can see some evidence of an even greater work of love and service in the background. The invitation is to look with care, and see beyond the immediate.

Almighty God, grant us the grace, wisdom and courage to follow Your saints in faith and hope and love. May our lives reflect Your greater light, and so illuminate Your world with all virtue, godliness and truth. Amen.

BROADCAST FRIDAY 27 AUGUST 2010

August 28

Michael Mumisa

There has been a lot of talk in recent years about the compatibility or otherwise of religion or religious doctrines with a multi-cultural society. The responses from some members of our religious communities to the challenges presented by a pluralist society in which the diversity in religious beliefs, philosophical views and lifestyles is celebrated has made others question whether such members only voice their support for diversity when it suits them.

What is more important to me as a person of faith? Is it to live in a society in which a set of religious beliefs and all aspects of social morality are defined, fixed, and enforced on citizens, or a society in which all members are free to safeguard their beliefs and values? How do I reconcile the reality of living in a pluralist society with the fact that Islam, like Christianity, is a missionary faith which expects me to share my faith with others, or even actively convert them? Whenever I reflect on these questions, I am consoled by these words from the Qur'an: 'Whosoever will, let him believe, and whosoever will, let him disbelieve' (8.29); and 'Let there be no compulsion in religion!' (2. 256).

In fact the Qur'an recognizes the great variety in the human family: 'O mankind, truly we have created you male and female, and have made you nations and tribes that ye may recognize one another.' (Qur'an 49.13).

'Our Lord! Forgive us our sins as well as those of our brethren who preceded us in faith and let not our hearts entertain any unworthy thoughts or feelings against anyone. Our Lord! You are indeed full of kindness and Most Merciful. Amin. (Qur'an 59.10)

BROADCAST FRIDAY 28 AUGUST 2009

August 29

Bert Tosh

Around this time of year, I take myself off for a few days to a monastery. My daughter describes my annual visit as a chance to get my head cleared — and that's not far from the truth.

I started going at a very low point in my life. My marriage was painfully coming to an end — and I found prayer almost impossible. But the calm, unhurried but purposeful monastic routine somehow spoke to the depths of the soul.

The Community sings Vespers every day in Latin. Now, my Latin is limited, to put it kindly, yet as I made the effort of listening to the singing and following the translation at the same time, the words started to speak in a totally new and fresh way. Allied to that was the discovery that my mood, my spirits matched those of the psalmists — particularly when they were in distress.

I learned that the Psalms were there to be prayed. Now, you might be forgiven for thinking I was something of a slow learner, for I certainly wasn't unfamiliar with the Psalms. I had read them and sung them and written sermons based on them. But in the quiet of the Abbey Church, I found that the Psalms weren't just for singing the praises of God, even less for quarrying for sermon material: they were there for praying.

I discovered in a new way that the Book of Psalms contains the whole range of human experience. The great defender of Christian orthodoxy in the fourth century, St Athanasius, said that the Psalter is 'a book that includes the whole life of man, all conditions of the mind and all movements of thought.' And I, and countless others, are grateful!

Lord, we thank You for the Psalms, for their great range of thought and feeling and for their help as we pray, through Jesus Christ, our Lord. Amen.

BROADCAST SATURDAY 29 AUGUST 2009

August 30

George Craig

Most of us have more than one identity. This isn't deliberate pretence, it's just that different people know different things about us and expect different things of us and our relationship is affected by that.

I spend a lot of time with my two-and-a-half-year-old grandson – much of it just wandering round the garden poking things with sticks; we both enjoy doing that. An interesting part of this relationship is that I don't think he has any idea that I might be an adult. I just am part of his life. He can't miss that fact that I am surprisingly tall, but otherwise he seems to see me as just another kid.

Communicating in this sort of relationship is a bit of a challenge. Like so many of us, I have spent years watching what I say and how I say it – to achieve the right effect and put myself in a good light. Saying exactly what I feel in fairly simple language is quite a complicated new skill to learn.

But I think it's well worth the effort. I have been amazed by the extent to which taking the risk of being as direct and open as a child can open real communications with other adults. When people find that we aren't trying to be clever or make an impression, they often feel able to open up in return; and conversation, instead of being a kind of contest, can become a real encounter.

I have met so many people over the years who have been held back in their prayer life because they believe that to talk to God they need to have special words – a particular kind of technical language. And at times all of us can find prayer a bit of a struggle. But I take comfort from the fact that the Bible says so powerfully that we each should become as a child: surely that has to be most true when we are speaking to our heavenly Father.

Father, I'm sorry that we so often feel the need to pretend when we talk to You. Help us to remember when we pray that You are the one person with whom we can really take the risk of childlike honesty. Amen.

BROADCAST THURSDAY 30 AUGUST 2007

August 31

Edward Kessler

Although Descartes thought that animals lacked souls – and you could do with them as you wished – the Bible tells us the opposite: 'The righteous person knows the soul of his animal,' says the Book of Proverbs.

But neither is the Bible sentimental. In the ancient world there were cultures that regarded certain animals as sacred. Reading Schopenhauer, one almost gets the impression that he cared more for animals than for human beings. Judaism does not go down either of these two roads. But it does regard animals as sensitive beings. They may not speak, but they do feel.

So in Deuteronomy we read: 'Do not muzzle an ox when it is treading grain. Do not plough with an ox and donkey together.'

Here is avoidance of cruelty in action: the ox is stronger than a donkey. Expecting the donkey to do the work of an ox is unfair.

The ancient Israelites were commanded to create an ideal society, and within this moral ecology, respect for animals has a significant place. Animals, too, are part of God's creation. They have their own integrity in the scheme of things. What is more – as we are now discovering – they are far closer to human beings than philosophers like Descartes thought.

What is being rediscovered today by science was known to us long ago because the great heroes of the Bible – Abraham, Moses, David – were shepherds. They lived their formative years watching over and caring for animals. That was their first tutorial in leadership, and they knew that this was one way of understanding God. As the Psalmist said, 'The Lord is my shepherd.'

Thank You, Lord, for teaching us that we must treat animals, as well as humans, with compassion and mercy. Amen.

BROADCAST SATURDAY 31 AUGUST 2013

September 1

Michael Ford

Monks are no strangers to getting up early; so, when I was staying at the Benedictine abbey of Montserrat, high up in the mountains of north-eastern Spain, I decided I just had to get over my sleep addiction and join them.

But while the singing of plainchant was heavenly, it was the sight of the rising sun one morning that really overwhelmed my senses. I remember standing on a parapet, spellbound, as a shimmering golden ball ascended between the peaks. It was a sight of extraordinary beauty and its impact that morning has never deserted me. There was a real sense of awe and mystery as the eternal broke into the rhythms of the earthly day. No wonder St Ambrose once reflected: 'Do you not know, my friend, that you owe the first fruits of your heart and voice to God? Run therefore to meet the rising sun so that, when the day dawns, it may find you ready.'

We need to be prepared to face the dawn. It's a time of hope and promise, the opening up of a new horizon. But for some of us the morning can be an anxious time as the light begins to break in on the stark realities of our own lives. Reassurance isn't always on the cards. As the kidnapped BBC journalist Alan Johnston said after his captivity in Gaza: 'I learned that, in Hotel Jihad, all the dawns were false.'

So whatever situation we find ourselves in at the start of a new day and a new month, may these words from the Canticle of Zechariah, also known as the Benedictus, become our own monastic prayer:

'In the tender compassion of our God, the dawn from on high shall break upon us, to shine on those who dwell in darkness and the shadow of death, and to guide our feet on the road to peace.' Amen.

BROADCAST SATURDAY 1 SEPTEMBER 2007

September 2

Michael Mumisa

Muslims are expected to perform five regular daily prayers known in Arabic as *Salah*. Before offering the compulsory daily prayers, a Muslim is also expected to perform ablution — washing the face, hands and feet. What has also been at the heart of this ancient religious practice is the teaching that wasting water is a grave sin in Islam.

It is reported that Muhammad once warned one of his Companions against using more water than necessary when performing ablution before prayers. His Companion replied: 'O messenger of God! Can there be wastefulness while performing the ablution for a religious act?' To which Muhammad responded: 'Yes, even if you perform your ablution on the banks of a rushing river.'

He went on to warn his followers: 'If without any good reason a person kills a sparrow or even a creature lesser than that, it will come to God on the day of judgement saying: "O Lord! So and so killed me for no purpose!"' (al-Nasa'i). 'He who cuts a tree without justification, God will send him to the hell fire' (Tirmidhi).

We often witness a lot of wastefulness and, at times, extravagance during our religious festivals. Should religious piety be a justification for such actions?

When young Muslim boys and girls attend the daily *madrasa* evening school across the country, they are made to memorize large parts of the Qur'an and some of them go on to memorise the whole Qur'an. There are more than 6,000 verses in the Qur'an, of which 750 deal directly with the relationship between living organisms and their environment. The reader of such verses is constantly reminded to maintain the balance and proportion that exist in our environment.

'We pray that our own hands do not become the cause of our own destruction.' Amin. *(Qur'an 2.195)*

BROADCAST TUESDAY 2 SEPTEMBER 2008

September 3

Janet Wootton

On this day in 1803, a daughter, Prudence Crandall, was born to a Quaker couple in Rhode Island, USA. The family moved to Connecticut, and Prudence, with her sister, purchased the Canterbury Female Boarding School.

A year after the purchase, the daughter of a local farmer applied to join the school to train as a teacher. She was black, and at that time this was thought to render her unfit for such ambitions.

Prudence admitted Sarah Harris to the school in 1832. There was an outcry from local white residents, who started to remove their daughters from the school, forcing its closure.

Prudence wrote later, 'I said in my heart, here are my convictions. What shall I do? Shall I be inactive and permit prejudice, the mother of all abominations, to remain undisturbed? ... I contemplated for a while the manner in which I might best serve the people of colour. As wealth was not mine, I saw no other means of benefiting them, than by imparting to those of my own sex that were anxious to learn, all the instruction I might be able to give, however small the amount.'

So she reopened the school for black students only.

This caused uproar. The State passed a 'Black Law', under which the town withheld all amenities from the school, and eventually Prudence Crandall was imprisoned. Sarah Harris later became a prominent abolitionist. Prudence is now State Heroine of Connecticut.

God forgive us when we allow prejudice to remain undisturbed. May we, like Prudence, offer all we can in the service of others, and, like Sarah, campaign against wrong. Amen.

BROADCAST MONDAY 3 SEPTEMBER 2012

September 4

Edward Kessler

Imagine a critic, or even a child, asking: 'How do you solve the problem that has led people to kill one another in the name of God since the birth of human civilization? At the end of the day, religions all claim to be true. They conflict. Therefore they cannot all be true. At most, one is. If Christianity is true, Judaism is false. If Islam is true, both Christianity and Judaism are false. It follows that these religions are bound to conflict whenever their devotees take their truth claims seriously.'

'I, for my part,' my critic continues, 'take this as sufficient evidence that all are false. For how could the God of all humanity command his followers to deny the full and equal humanity of those who conceive Him differently? I would rather live with the uncertainty of doubt than the certainty of faith, for it is that very certainty that leads people, convinced of their righteousness, to commit unspeakable crimes.'

Whilst I may be convinced of the truth of my faith, others believe with equal fervour that their faith, not mine, is true. How can we live peaceably together while at the same time honouring the commitments of our respective faiths?

But, I would suggest, there is a profound error in thinking that if my faith is true and conflicts with yours, then yours is false. Surely, if I and my fellow believers have a relationship with God, that does not entail that you do not? I have my stories, rituals, memories, prayers, celebrations, laws and customs; you have yours. That is what makes me, me; and you, you. It is what differentiates cultures, heritages, civilizations and religions.

Lord, may we learn that the truth of one faith does not entail the falsity of the other. Amen.

BROADCAST WEDNESDAY 4 SEPTEMBER 2013

September 5

Stephen Shipley

There are certain significant news events that make such an impression that you never forget the exact moment you first learnt about them. In some cases these events touch the lives of millions, even change the course of history. The accident that killed Diana Princess of Wales was one, but there was another death that occurred that same week that I shall always remember. I was in a broadcasting van, transmitting the Requiem Mass for Princess Diana from Westminster Cathedral, when the phone rang and we were told that Mother Teresa had died. She'll be for ever associated, of course, with the Missionaries of Charity that she founded in India, and it was for her humanitarian work that she was awarded the Nobel Peace Prize in 1979 . But some time after her death, a number of letters were published, written by Mother Teresa in the 1950s and 1960s, revealing the troubling and at times painful conflicts she sometimes had with her faith. 'I am told God lives in me,' she wrote, 'and yet the reality of darkness and coldness and emptiness is so great that nothing touches my soul.'

I must admit I found it reassuring when Church officials said the letters strengthen Mother Teresa's case for sainthood – the struggle with her own spirituality and purpose showing her humanity. 'You can't be a saint without having suffered,' said one of them. 'God sometimes wants to unite the soul very closely to himself. Even Jesus on the Cross felt he was abandoned.' It's a hard concept to grasp but it's one that must be faced.

So Lord, if we or anyone we know is in a dark place this morning, we pray that we may cling with faith to the promise that You will never let us go. Amen.

BROADCAST SATURDAY 5 SEPTEMBER 2009

September 6

Edward Kessler

The Bible is not just history — what happened sometime else to someone else — but memory, what happened to our ancestors and therefore, insofar as we carry on their story, to us. The Bible speaks not of moral truths in the abstract but of commands — which is to say, truths addressed to us, calling for our response.

Its meaning is found not in theological system but in stories; not in nature but in narrative — the stories we tell ourselves about who we are, where we came from, what is our place in the universe, and what, therefore, we are called on to do. That is why the Bible is written in the form of narrative. Unlike philosophy, narrative celebrates the concrete, not the abstract.

Narratives, as Jonathan Sacks points out, contain multiple points of view. They are open — essentially, not accidentally — to more than one interpretation, more than one level of interpretation.

What is true of texts is true of relationships because they are multi-faceted in a way physical facts are not. I either am or am not black-haired, short-sighted, bespectacled. But I am, simultaneously, a child of my parents, the father of my children, the husband of my wife. The truth of one does not entail the falsity of others.

An acknowledgement of the multiplicity of narratives and relationships, interpretations and covenants, is fundamentally opposed to a narrative of displacement. One of the lessons of the Biblical narratives is that, despite our differences, the validity of one story does not exclude another.

Lord, help us read the Bible — and view the world - from more than one point of view. Amen.

BROADCAST FRIDAY 6 SEPTEMBER 2013

September 7

Nicholas Buxton

In any kind of group or community, mutual discipline of one sort or another is what enables people who may otherwise have little in common to work together or live alongside each other in relative harmony. Contrary to what is commonly supposed, discipline does not restrict our freedom, but is the very thing that makes the variety of our life together possible. Interestingly, I think the problem here is not that we don't understand the need for discipline – we have no trouble with discipline when it concerns something we want to do or want someone to do for us. It's rather that we don't understand the nature of freedom.

Freedom is not simply to be equated with freedom of choice. True freedom is defined by what limits it. Improvising jazz musicians might sound wonderfully and creatively chaotic, yet they are playing within the constraints and discipline of mutually understood musical conventions. Paradoxically then, discipline is actually the basis of freedom, or in this case is what marks the difference between music and an unpleasant cacophony.

Still, for many people, discipline is a word that tends to conjure up negative connotations of punishment and repression. But we should remember that the word 'discipline' is related to discipleship, and in ordinary usage it can also refer to a skill or training. All discipline has a simple rationality: the sacrifice of present enjoyment for the sake of a greater reward in the future. Anyone who has studied for an examination, gone on a diet or trained in order to get fit will already be familiar with the basic principle.

So we pray for God's blessing upon the tasks of the day that lie ahead of us, for perseverance and commitment – especially regarding those things we may be reluctant to do – and for the discipline that enables us to live and work together in harmony. Amen.

BROADCAST WEDNESDAY 7 SEPTEMBER 2011

September 8

Mark Wakelin

One of the signs of ageing not mentioned in the cosmetics adverts is to sense that everything's going downhill. A man wrote, 'We live in a decaying age. Young people no longer respect their parents. They are rude and impatient. They frequently inhabit pubs and have no self-control.' This was not written in a newspaper today but is from an inscription on a 6,000-year-old Egyptian tomb.

I've found that I too tend to become an angry, grumpy old man when faced with the new; or so my children warn me. I hurumph at music, fashion, exam results, changing standards. The decline seems so real. Perhaps every generation, as it gets older, suspects that the world's going to pot and it makes us so angry! Grumpy old men and women swap stories that reinforce their sense of 'the world's decline', and we feel the impotence and fear of not being able to do anything about it.

We've had some truly sad stories about young people in the press recently. How tragic to read of such violence, sometimes fuelled by drunkenness or a desperate need to belong. It's easy to feel that this is a new reality, but in the main it isn't. Reality is far more complex. If young people had in fact been getting worse for 6,000 years, then we would be in an even worse state than we are!

The truth is that so much of the new is filled with creativity, hope and life, and the young people of our nation are by and large hard-working, moral, caring, creative and extraordinary human beings; a real credit to their ever more elderly parents and grandparents.

Lord God, creator of all things new, help me to see the world more as You see it; to 'rejoice in the good', and to think upon 'whatsoever is lovely and of good report'. Amen.

BROADCAST SATURDAY 8 SEPTEMBER 2007

September 9

Nicholas James

Some years ago my brother and his wife moved to Australia. When he told us he was going, I wondered what the move would mean to him — a fresh start obviously, as far away as it was possible to go but in a country where everyone spoke English and where many ties with Britain still remained. I also realized Australia was changing, finding its own identity and forging new links with its Pacific neighbours.

What I hadn't realized was the power of the land itself or how its 'aboriginal' identity would touch my brother. His letters home and emails soon revealed descriptive powers we'd never glimpsed before. He seemed to be finding a new capacity for empathy, and with it came a reaching out to something far beyond the modern towns and beaches.

Of course, he went to see the famous stone formation called Uluru. One of the great natural wonders of the world. For some it still retains its later name, 'Ayers Rock', but its aboriginal name links it with the forces of creation.

As our world emerged, those first Australians believed, there was a time called Dreamtime, which produced the features of the land and gave them spiritual meaning. It was a time of heroes too, who still provide a standard for our lives. 'As it was done in Dreamtime,' the saying goes, 'so it must be done today.'

Something deep inside us always wants to find connections with our ancestors — as the present craze for family research reminds us. Of course, we must continue to emerge and grow, but we can never fully cut the ties that bind us to the past or fully understand ourselves if we ignore them.

Father, teach us respect for those who shared Your world before us and show us how to learn from them. Give us courage and humility in the way that we go forward. Help us always to recognize Your presence in our world. Amen.

BROADCAST TUESDAY 9 SEPTEMBER 2008

September 10

John McLuckie

During this week I'm exploring Jesus' teaching on how to live well by drawing on examples from nature, especially the birds of the air and the lilies of the field. One of our characteristic responses to the natural world is wonder, and today's anniversary of the switching on of the Large Hadron Collider in 2008 is a reminder of the wonders we encounter in both the immensity and the minuteness, the power and the fragility of the universe around us. That extraordinary, huge machine under the ground gave us the possibility of going right back to the origins of life itself.

It's hard to explain this sense of wonder, and it's probably best not to try! But we do know that the experience of amazement can lead to other things: it can give us a sense of our smallness, but in a way that makes us feel truly connected to all that is, it can fill us with an inexplicable elation, and it can lead to a sense of gratitude. For those who have a religious faith, this gratitude is directed toward the One who is the giver of the gift of life, but for all of us, gratitude is a disposition that changes our outlook on the world. The habit of thankfulness orients our life outward, beyond our smaller concerns, toward other people and the concerns of the world that touch us all.

God of all creation,
We look in wonder at the world around us
And this wonder brings us joy at the mystery of life itself.
May our wonder turn to gratitude
And may our gratitude lift us from all that wearies us
And renew us in our commitment to everything that lives.
Through Jesus Christ our Lord.
Amen.

BROADCAST TUESDAY 10 SEPTEMBER 2013

September 11

Mark Wakelin

It's still a fresh memory for the world: the destruction of the Twin Towers on this day in 2001, the appalling sight of the passenger jets ploughing into the skyscrapers. My elder daughter was staying with us at the time and she burst into tears and ran from the room as we watched the extended news. It was not that we had any particular connection with the unfolding news story – it was simply so appalling. What else could anyone do? How do you react when terrorism strikes? I personally can't imagine what it would be like to be bereaved in this way – it is in a very literal sense for me 'too awful to contemplate'. Our hearts go out to those who today will particularly feel their loss and sadness. Our response as a nation to this terrible event was to stand shoulder to shoulder as war was declared on terrorism by the United States.

The preacher and leader Martin Luther King advised people who faced brutality to 'love their enemies'. He quoted the words of Jesus from 2,000 years previously. King suggested that love was not an 'affectionate emotion' – how could you feel that? he asked – but rather 'a creative redemptive good will'. I wonder today what 'a creative redemptive good will' would look like? What creative options have we? What good will can we imagine offering? If expressing our proper anger with the obvious response of violence hasn't actually worked, what else might?

Lord God, You brought order out of chaos through love, help us to find effective ways to heal the deep hurts in our world. Amen.

BROADCAST TUESDAY 11 SEPTEMBER 2007

September 12

John McLuckie

The teaching of Jesus often uses the simple insights of the natural world around us to bring us closer to an appreciation of life itself. In his lovely parables of the birds of the air and the lilies of the field which I've been exploring this week, he draws attention to the beauty of a flower which is achieved without toil. This is in stark contrast to the injustice that sometimes lies behind our human creations.

I remember holding in my hands a beautiful jewelled bishop's mitre which was decorated with a gem that had been prised from the statue of a Hindu god by a zealous Victorian missionary. A thing of beauty was achieved through the subjection of a people and the desecration of their faith. We can also think of the true human cost of many of our cheap, fashionable clothes.

By contrast, our appreciation of the beauty in the simplicity of a flower is an encounter with beauty without injustice. But this appreciation also brings us face to face with our capacity to subject the natural world to our selfish desires. When we appreciate the integrity of that flower, we are also confronted by our ability to treat it as an expendable commodity. Perhaps St Francis got it right when he insisted that the created thing of beauty we see before us is not, in fact, an object, but a brother or sister in creation.

God of all creation,
Teach us to find beauty without injustice,
To challenge the exploitation of all parts of Your creation,
And to see a brother or sister
Whenever we come face to face with everything that lives.
Through Jesus Christ our Lord.
Amen.

BROADCAST THURSDAY 12 SEPTEMBER 2013

September 13

Mark Wakelin

Being angry as a child was frowned upon; but just trying to be calm and not show what you're really feeling pushes it all down inside. I think this is probably why I still tend to have the unattractive habits of passive aggression that anyone who has ever been on an assertiveness course will recognize. 'See how much you've hurt me!' is our battle cry! I would imagine that I'm not alone, that anyone that has been taught not to be angry is good at disguising the fact that they are and at the same time making sure other people feel got at! You can usually tell when it's happening to you: you feel all the sting and hurt of having being told off, but you're not quite sure why. As if from a sniper, the shot of anger has come from a hidden place. It's harder to know when you're doing the sniping, though: expressing anger you've hidden from yourself. I associate it with feeling righteous, of believing yourself to be 'in the right', but often I find that I'm not being that at all: just cross and not wanting to admit it.

On the other hand, uncontrolled anger isn't good either. I came across a web page run by a national newspaper that encouraged readers to get really angry about things. The journalist started something off by reporting on a news story in as provocative way as possible, and then sat back and watched the pack of readers tear into each other. Anger is dangerous and, as a way of making sense of difficult situations, it's not helpful. But it's also part of being human, it's what we rightly feel in the face of injustice and evil, and it's not what you feel so much that matters, as what you do with the feeling.

Lord God, You are slow to anger and full of kindness. Help me to be honest about what I feel today and use my anger in helpful ways. Amen.

BROADCAST THURSDAY 13 SEPTEMBER 2007

September 14

Alison Twaddle

Recently I've been undergoing treatment, which has meant taking several weeks off work. During that time I've been sustained by the huge number of messages of support from friends and colleagues, and it has been good to rest on their faith when my own has been weak and questioning.

A few weeks ago, on a day when I had been feeling particularly low, I had a visit from an elderly neighbour a couple of streets away. Cathy is a widow of 82, who has faced a series of difficult health issues herself over the years, and who gets about, slowly and painfully, with the help of one of those wheeled push walkers. She had come round to bring me a small flower arrangement of heathers and roses from her garden and a packet of fruit pastilles.

This small act of kindness, representing considerable effort on her part, gave me a new perspective on my day. I still felt physically drained, but my low spirits were lifted by her example. That someone with enough to worry about and plenty to bear in her own life – at a time when perhaps she might feel others should be caring for her in her final years – should take time to care for me, moved me deeply. We shouldn't underestimate what we are doing for others when we reach out with a kind gesture or word that shows we are thinking about their situation and caring for them when they are facing challenges.

Help us today to make our prayer active in the lives of others.

Show us, Lord,
Where we can speak the word,
Hold out the hand,
Listen for the cry,
And be Your witness
To our neighbour.
Amen.

BROADCAST MONDAY 14 SEPTEMBER 2009

September 15

Joe Aldred

When the Old Testament prophet Habakkuk wondered how to communicate God's message, he was instructed to 'write down the revelation and make it plain on tablets so that whoever reads it may run with it'. We've moved on from writing on tablets, but our impulse to share our news with those around us has not diminished. And what better news to share than that which is germane to our lived experiences: our defeats and victories, good deeds received and given. Much of this will not make the wider media, but can be of immense value to our neighbours.

Our multi-media age, with its printed and electronic information, means we are surrounded by wall-to-wall news. We're told approximately fifteen million newspapers are sold each day in Britain, with the *biggest* of them, *The Sun*, which first appeared on this day in 1964, selling over two and a half million copies each day. But we don't have to be passive recipients: we can be active participants in this news age.

I was, therefore, encouraged by an article by the General Director of the Evangelical Alliance, Steve Clifford, that called on readers to tell their little stories of changed lives, small acts of kindness and generosity alongside the ones that appear in wider media. Steve argues that small, local stories are as important as big ones. Indeed, it is as we share our real-life stories of lived faith that the world gets to read and be affected by them.

Creator God, amidst the hustle and bustle of life, amidst the growing volume of news media, may we be encouraged to share our stories of what we have seen and experienced so that those who read or hear them may be inspired to share their stories too. Amen.

BROADCAST SATURDAY 15 SEPTEMBER 2012

September 16

Janet Wootton

A few years ago, I was at meetings in South Africa, and took the opportunity to go on a tour through a gold mine in Johannesburg. This was partly personal, as a childhood friend of mine had gone to South Africa to make his career in gold mining, and died there in his early adult years. As a tourist, of course, I was not exposed to the dangers and the harsh conditions, but I wanted to pay my respects to my friend.

I hold no romantic ideas about mining. I grew up in West Yorkshire and later in the Midlands, surrounded in those days by pitheads and slag heaps, and stories of tragedy. Mining has always been a dangerous occupation. Accidents happen a long way from safety, and dangers such as fire or flood develop unexpectedly and travel fast.

Additionally, it is often those who have the least opportunity or choice in life that end up working in so difficult and hazardous an environment, with the consequence that safety measures are sometimes neglected.

On this day, as recently as 1986, fire and toxic fumes swept through the gold mine at Kinross in the Eastern Transvaal, killing more than 170 men, mostly black, unskilled labourers, working at depths of up to 12,000 feet, in one of the worst disasters in mining history.

God of the deep places of the earth, we hold before You the memory of all those who have died in work-related disasters. We pray for people who will go to work in hazardous occupations today, and for all who have the health and safety of others in their care. Amen.

BROADCAST MONDAY 16 SEPTEMBER 2013

September 17

Tim Bartlett

It's a long time since I've been on a roller coaster. As I get older, I seem to be less inclined to seek out frightening experiences. Enough of them arrive in the normal course of a day without paying for extra ones at the fairground. This summer was different, though. My nine-year-old niece had suddenly discovered the thrills of adrenalin. This little bundle of joy, who had only a year before cried at the very thought of getting onto something so fast and furious, was now pleading with her sedentary uncle to join her on the roller coaster.

Eventually I conceded, though not without negotiating her commitment to doing a few odd jobs for her parents as part of the deal. As I took my place on the front seat beside her, I took one look around the snarling twists and turns that lay before us and quickly closed my eyes. I was petrified. In the words of St Paul, I 'prayed without ceasing' as we soared up and down and then turned upside down several times in the space of a minute. As others cheered and screamed with excitement, I just prayed that it would all be over as quickly as possible. And then, just as we glided to a halt at the end of the track, I heard those terrible words so familiar to all parents of children having fun: 'Let's do it again! We have to do it again!' And so we did – again, and again, and again. Four times in all.

The strange thing was that each time we set out, it all seemed less frightening, certainly more bearable and even a little fun.

None of us knows what we are going to have to face today. What is certain is that there will be at least a few unexpected twists and turns. There are few for whom life does not feel like a roller coaster at times.

Lord, as I face whatever comes to me today, give me the ability to face it with courage. May one of the benefits of getting older be that I become wiser and less afraid of the twists and turns of life. Give me calm amidst the storms, and peace in all things. Amen.

BROADCAST MONDAY 17 SEPTEMBER 2007

September 18

Joe Aldred

The history of colonialism in the Caribbean has imbued it with a rich human heritage drawn from around the world. This is typified by the Jamaican national motto: 'out of many, one people.' This cultural polyglotism remains an object lesson in the complexity of our world as God may have intended it, even if its coming together was somewhat problematically based on slavery and indentured labour.

The continent of Africa underwent a similar process of indigenization. And I recall well how it was that the world looked on aghast as the then Ugandan President Idi Amin expelled Asians *en masse*, some of whom found refuge in this country. The first arrivals in the UK happened on this day, 18 September, in 1970.

Whatever the political justification of the President's actions, victims of his ejection found themselves stateless or in foreign lands with little more than the clothes on their backs and whatever they had in terms of inner virtue.

Jesus taught that a person's life does not consist of the things they possess, and this rings truest when one has lost all one's material possessions. How interesting then to look at the Ugandan Asian community in Britain today, who have dug deep into their inner strength and ingenuity to fashion successful lives as business people and much more, proving that out of evil can come good.

Creator God, in whatever circumstance we find ourselves, including when we may have contributed to our own difficulties, may we remember always that we need not surrender and give up as victims of our circumstances. Amen.

BROADCAST TUESDAY 18 SEPTEMBER 2012

September 19

Claire Campbell Smith

I was reading recently about the funeral of Dr Thomas Barnardo, the Victorian philanthropist who died on 19 September 1905. Some 1,500 boys from the various homes that he'd founded followed the funeral cortège through London's East End. They were joined by immense crowds who thronged the streets to pay their respects.

Not all of Barnardo's methods of trying to help destitute children had gone without criticism. But the thing that struck me about him was that he didn't simply wait for children to appear on the doorstep of one of his homes – he regularly went out into the slums at night to *find* those who were sleeping rough so he could give them shelter. At a time when some saw poverty as shameful, the result of laziness or vice, Barnardo focused on the children's need, whatever their background. The sign outside one of his homes read: 'No destitute child ever refused admission.'

Jesus told the story of a man who prepares a great wedding feast. But when those on the original invitation list make up all sorts of excuses not to come, he says to his servants, 'Go out quickly into the streets and alleys of the town and bring in the poor, the crippled, the blind and the lame' – in other words, those who were on society's list of rejects. Jesus is painting a great picture of the inclusiveness of God's kingdom, where *anyone* who accepts the invitation to enter is welcomed, whatever their status in the world's eyes. What's more, just as in the story of the prodigal son, God doesn't just sit back and do nothing – he sets out to meet people in whatever state they're in, and to bring them into his care.

Help me, Lord, to be more like You, to draw a circle that includes rather than excludes. Open my eyes that they may see the deepest needs of people. And give me the compassion and the courage to respond. Amen.

BROADCAST FRIDAY 19 SEPTEMBER 2008

September 20

Dónal McKeown

Not long ago I visited a new church in Belfast. It was built in the inner city to replace an older and crumbling place of worship. It is a bright building. There is lots of coloured glass and a polychrome floor. Many people doubted that it should be constructed: it would cost money, numbers attending are not large in the area. So why burden a parish community with a fancy new building? Wouldn't a plain one have done?

But as I left the church, and walked out into the city street, it suddenly struck me just how important it is for there to be places of quiet and beauty in our world. City streets are functional. Clothes, cars and gadgets are meant to be transitory, out of date almost as soon as we have them. I believe that drabness numbs the spirit and constant noise chills the heart. The human species is capable of great and wonderful things. But if we tell them that nothing is good or beautiful or true, my fear is that our spirits will shrivel in starvation. We do not live on bread alone.

I pray that today I will make space so that I can glimpse at least one beautiful thing. It might be a view or a word of encouragement, it could be a meal or a flower or it might even be just watching the beautiful game. For if we cannot see beauty in other people or places, we will find it hard to believe in the beauty that lies hidden in the heart of each of us.

Lord of glory,
My words wither away in singing of Your beauty;
My music breaks apart before Your grandeur;
And to re-echo Your love,
I find myself without melody.
Take my silence as a song of joy.
Amen.

BROADCAST SATURDAY 20 SEPTEMBER 2008

September 21

Janet Wootton

A few years ago I was at a funeral in a remote rural part of Eastern Kenya, where I was visiting Pentecostal churches.

People came from all around to be with the stricken family. The surrounding fields were full of people sitting silently, or chatting, showing the care they felt for their neighbours by their presence. They would stay for several days.

As evening fell, I heard women's voices in the distance, but getting closer. Eventually the women appeared, dancing and weaving their way through the trees that surrounded the village compound.

Each carried a gift on her head — a full water carrier, a bunch of plantain, a sack of flour. These were provisions for the bereaved family, so that they had no need to worry about food and drink during their time of grief.

As the women danced, they sang: '*Sina sichilile siama ni si chaano*' — 'Tell me, why are the women gathering here?'

And the answer, given in the song, was '*wiantzi wa Tavita*' — 'the joy of Tabitha'. That's what brings the women together.

Tabitha was a woman in the Bible, in the days of the early Church. The story is told in the Book of Acts. When she died, the other women and children were distraught, because she had made clothes for the poor. They wept so much that Peter the Apostle stretched out his hand and raised her to life, restoring her to the people who loved her.

Loving God, grant us **wiantzi wa Tavita***, the joy of all the women and men who make sure there is food to eat, water to drink and clothes to wear, when things go wrong. Amen.*

BROADCAST MONDAY 21 SEPTEMBER 2009

September 22

Dónal McKeown

Today I'm thinking of one of my aunts. She is a woman of great strength and she has needed that to see her through difficult times. Of course, life is difficult. Though my father used to say, 'If all the crosses in the world were piled together and you could take your pick, you'd probably choose the one you have.' For some, the crosses seem to be too much — but for most people, they develop character muscles in places where the rest of us don't even have places. It takes a broad back to be human. But we have only the choice of living or lying down.

Just a couple of months ago, my aunt was walking down an urban residential road alone, probably a little unsteadily, and she fell. It was a nasty tumble — but she wasn't lying long before a car stopped and a husband and wife got out to help her. They brought her home and sent for the doctor. The next day they came round to the house and checked to see she was all right. She hadn't seen them before and hasn't seen them since. But she talks often of the good people who brighten up a dark day. She remembers the kindness even more than the cut face and the cracked ribs. A miserable day became a memorable one.

I know that the world can be dangerous and we feel safer inside our own little space. But today I simply ask for the strength to see who needs a smile and a helping hand. It can be remarkably easy to make someone's cross seem lighter. We will all come across many people who feel that they are lying at the roadside and that nobody cares.

> Lord,
> Often my hands remain closed
> To protect my happiness,
> And yet You tell me that my happiness is in opening them to You,
> Present in my brother and sister.
> Help us to serve one another in Your name. Amen.

BROADCAST MONDAY 22 SEPTEMBER 2008

September 23

Janet Wootton

A few years ago, I gave up being minister of a church, which had been my life for nearly 25 years, and took on a role in training. It was an interesting life change, and quite challenging.

For one thing, I wasn't used to sitting in church, with someone else leading the service – it was both lovely and unnerving. I remember the first communion service I attended in my new life. In the congregational tradition, we don't go forward to receive communion from a priest, but stay in our seats, where the bread and wine are brought to us.

The wine is in tiny cups, about the size of shot glasses. As I took the cup and held it, I had a sudden flash of memory, completely tactile – it was my hands that were doing the remembering, not my mind.

It was because the glass felt different in some way. I couldn't work out what was wrong, but gradually realized that it was because my hands are bigger, clumsier and more arthritic than they were when I used to take communion as a teenager. The little glass no longer fitted into my interlocked fingers as it had done years ago.

But my hands are also stronger than they were, and more skilled. A momentary regret was overcome by recognition of change. These are my hands now. This is who I am now. I no longer have the same vivid and dramatic faith that I had as a teenager either. My relationship with God is more complex, perhaps stronger, certainly more shaped by experience, pain, purpose, disappointment, joy.

God of our youth and our ageing, we give thanks for faith that endures, or perhaps returns after fading. We give thanks for the changing pattern of our life's walk with You. Amen.

BROADCAST FRIDAY 23 SEPTEMBER 2011

September 24

Jonathan Wittenberg

Two of the most important phrases in any language are 'Thank you' and 'I'm sorry'. All our relationships depend on the ability to say them and mean them.

No action is too small for a 'thank you'. When we don't give it, we treat others as tools.

None of us is too important to say 'sorry'. We should say it to our children when we're wrong: it shows humanity – and humility.

If apologizing is hard, forgiving is even harder. I don't believe in 'forgiven and forgotten'. The mind doesn't work like that; we remember plenty of things we wish we didn't. Equally, there are many matters in any human life, and in history, that mustn't be forgotten. Forgetfulness condemns us to repetition, of our worst mistakes and greatest atrocities.

At the heart of forgiveness is the ability to let go of anger and bitterness. That's why, as Judaism teaches, we can only forgive wrongs done to ourselves. Otherwise, forgiveness is a meaningless word.

That still leaves plenty for us to do. We all bear wounds, inflicted by other people or by life itself. Do we nurse thoughts of vengeance? Or do we try to accept and comprehend, or even enter in imagination into the minds of those who hurt us and, without justifying their deeds, ask 'Why?'

I admire those who use their very wounds to create understanding and healing, like those bereaved Israeli and Palestinian parents whose grief has brought them together. They don't forget, or romantically forgive. They listen and strive for peace.

God, give us the courage to make our hurts our teachers.

BROADCAST MONDAY 24 SEPTEMBER 2007

September 25

Jane Livesey

Yesterday I was talking to someone about pilgrimage, and that put me in mind of one of my favourite sayings : 'With patience, perseverance and a bottle of sweet oil, the snail at length reaches Jerusalem.' Patience and perseverance are rather counter-intuitive gifts in a world such as ours where staying for the long haul is very often not really part of the deal. We want it and we want it fast and we want it now. And then we want a new one – even if it isn't broken. But we all know that the journey of our lives does sometimes require that things, and most importantly, relationships, be repaired – and that's where qualities like patience and perseverance come in.

It is also worth pondering on the ingredients of that bottle of sweet oil. It is, presumably, to be used to provide balm for the soul. Perhaps a kind of spiritual arnica. My sweet oil recipe would certainly include the following: my faith in a loving God; the love of family and friends; a dose of attentiveness for all the aspects of the journey, including the beauty of creation; a good slug of forgiveness; some opportunities to both give and receive generosity; and definitely some kind of antidote to self-pity, which would incorporate a robust sense of humour. If the ingredient list would stretch that far, I wouldn't mind some kind of concentrate of the music of JS Bach as well.

So those are the main ingredients of my bottle of sweet oil. I wonder what would be in yours?

Lord, give us patience, perseverance and some drops of sweet oil for the part of the journey that today will bring. Amen.

BROADCAST WEDNESDAY 25 SEPTEMBER 2013

September 26

Edward Kessler

When the Jewish physicist Isadore Rabi won the Nobel Prize, he was asked how he first became interested in science. He explained that his mother made him a scientist without him knowing it. All the other children would come home and their mothers would ask, 'What did you learn at school today?' *His* mother would say, 'Izzy, did you ask a good question?'

Every religion raises questions and offers different answers. For example, there is no single definition of Judaism that is acceptable to all Jews. Some maintain that Judaism is solely a religion; others that it is a culture; still others emphasize nationhood and attachment with the Land of Israel. And just as there is disagreement about the definition of Judaism, so there is rarely a single agreed Jewish view of any topic.

One common rabbinic teaching is to have more than one right answer to a question. The Talmud, one of the most important collections of Jewish writings from the fifth century, sometimes concludes a discussion with the word *teyku* ('let the problem stand'), because the rabbis were unable to choose one from a number of answers to a problem, so they decided it was better to accept that there could be more than one answer than choose the wrong one.

The ability to allow for conflicting positions is a feature of Judaism. We all think that the opposite of truth is falsehood: a Jew might suggest that the opposite of one truth may well be another more profound truth.

God, may we seek to ask good questions and learn to accept that there is more than one answer. Amen.

BROADCAST SATURDAY 26 SEPTEMBER 2009

September 27

Philip Robinson

On this day in 1905, Albert Einstein first published the equation E=mc², part of his theory of relativity.

Einstein's theory changed science, but it couldn't change human nature. In 1946, recognizing the need for a moral dimension to science, Einstein observed, 'The unleashed power of the atom has changed everything save our modes of thinking and we thus drift toward unparalleled catastrophe.'

The news media often reports a new science theory as if it were established fact. Scientists rarely have that level of certainty about their propositions, especially when they are pushing at the boundary of human knowledge. When Einstein published, he did so in a scientific journal rather than a newspaper, so his latest ideas could be validated by experts in the scientific community, not just splashed as headlines across the front page. That is the scientific method.

Unfortunately, most of us just look at headlines, such as those that recently announced a new controversial theory from Stephen Hawking that there was no need for God in the creation of the universe. Just like the Athenians of the first century, as we're told in the Acts of the Apostles in the Bible, we love to debate new ideas, but when it comes to understanding things of real importance, such as the nature of God, the meaning of life and the kind of moral code we need, it would be wise to build on truths that have stood the test of time, not just the latest headlines.

Almighty God, in a puzzling world, full of ideas, give us the wisdom to know what is true and the desire to live in the light of that Truth. Amen.

BROADCAST MONDAY 27 SEPTEMBER 2010

September 28

Simon Doogan

My wife's daily train journey to work in Belfast passes the yard of a military or police depot of some kind, where for the past five years she has been trying to identify a large pile of rectangular Perspex boards. I made the trip with her recently for the very first time and there they were: rack upon rack of these man-sized, plastic artefacts. To my eye, they were instantly recognizable as riot shields but then, unlike my wife, I grew up in Northern Ireland.

On a personal, even spiritual level, our view of the world is something most of us probably feel we can inform and change. The world's view of us, and where we come from, may be another matter. On this day in 1985 a woman called Cherry Groce was accidentally shot and seriously injured by armed police officers on an early morning house search in Brixton, south London.

The community violence that exploded that night has became part of the social narrative of twentieth-century Britain.

If the phrase 'race riot' remains synonymous with certain parts of some English cities, then what has become known here as the 'recreational riot' would seem to be Belfast's contribution to the civil unrest lexicon.

Though clearly, wherever people take to the streets in lawless anger, the last thing on their minds is what the watching world will think of them and how long that unfortunate association will continue to linger.

Father God, whose Son Jesus Christ was condemned by the baying of a mob, we hold before You today those places where unease runs dangerously high, and where all we can do is pray that, in time, opportunity and optimism may take the place of dejection and despair. Amen.

BROADCAST SATURDAY 28 SEPTEMBER 2013

September 29

Edward Kessler

The word 'dialogue' and the nature of dialogue activity are often misunderstood and ill defined, both in the negotiations of daily life and in discussions that take place between people of different faiths. A casual conversation may add up to no more than a loose restatement of entrenched positions. This is sometimes claimed to be dialogue, as is simple communication between people of different faiths, perhaps by phone, email or Facebook.

However, dialogue, which is derived from Greek and literally means 'through words', is not simply synonymous with 'communication' or 'assertion'. For dialogue to take place, there must be a genuine hearing of 'the other'. In so many contexts, dialogue can be very important, even a matter of life and death.

In the religious context, dialogue consists of a personal meeting of two people and involves a reciprocal exposing of the full religious consciousness of the one with the 'Other'. This means that dialogue speaks *to* the Other with a full respect of what the Other is and has to say: dialogue consists of a *genuine* encounter so that we may understand the Other as the Other understands him or herself.

Dialogue therefore involves a respect that takes the Other as seriously as one demands to be taken oneself. This is an immensely difficult and costly exercise. We find it all too easy to relate to others in a casual way, perhaps lacking sincerity or concentration on the reality of the Other.

This is not an original idea, for the Biblical prophets were experts in the personal encounter. The prophet Isaiah powerfully commends the Children of Israel to enter into a personal relationship with God, stating, 'come now let us reason together' (Isaiah 1.18).

Lord, may we learn to engage in dialogue and gain real understanding in our encounter with one another. Amen.

BROADCAST TUESDAY 29 SEPTEMBER 2009

September 30

Simon Doogan

My introduction to the late James Dean who died on this day in 1955 was at university, nearly 40 years after his death. His posters must have graced thousands of student walls. You probably visualize him as I do: a dishevelled picture of twenty-something attitude, smouldering like the cigarette he always seemed ready to flick, still burning, somewhere down near your feet. For such a brooding, static presence the irony was that his life ended at such high speed.

For road racing enthusiast Dean, it was a head-on collision in a sports car as he drove to attend a race meeting, and in so many situations that end in grief for young people, speed, and the craving for it, would seem to be a recurring theme. I have to say, as the epitome of bad boy cool, James Dean was never a big icon for me. But little did I think in those carefree student days that in my working life as a clergyman I would end up drawing alongside a number of families who know that there is nothing romantic about a life frozen in time by tragedy.

More than once I've wondered, is the youthful urge for ever faster experiences something instinctive? Certainly there are times when it feels like a rite of passage young people simply have to go through. And for those who love them, well, it's a matter of holding their breath, crossing their fingers and, frequently, saying their prayers:

Lord, we thank You for the energy and impatience of youth but in today's go-faster world we remember those for whom life is simply one rush after another: guard them, protect them, and still the hearts of the ones on the sidelines left to watch and to wait. Amen.

October 1

Neil Gardner

The other day I realized something that simply hadn't occurred to me before. I was reading a book of Lenten reflections written by a clergyman based in Christchurch, New Zealand, and it struck me that, in New Zealand, Lent and Easter coincide with autumn. Up here in the Northern hemisphere Easter is so readily and obviously associated with spring, with all its budding signs and symbols of new life and fresh hope, that I find it hard to imagine celebrating it against another backdrop altogether. Not least in the 'season of mists and mellow fruitfulness', as Keats famously described autumn. With the arrival of the month of October, that season is undoubtedly upon us once again. Yet even as the autumn leaves fade and fall, and the daylight and the temperature with them, God's care remains constant over all creation, all around the world and all through the year. As Thomas Chisholm's popular hymn puts it so beautifully:

> Summer and winter, and seedtime and harvest,
> Sun, moon and stars in their courses above,
> Join with all nature in manifold witness
> To Thy great faithfulness, mercy and love.

These words were inspired by the Book of Lamentations, where it's written, 'The Lord's love is surely not exhausted, nor has his compassion failed; they are new every morning, so great is his constancy.'

Lord God, we thank You for the rhythm of the seasons and for Your unfaltering care and compassion. Open our eyes to see the signs and symbols of Your great faithfulness, mercy and love all around us, new every morning, and guide us and guard us this new day, this new month, for Jesus' sake. Amen.

BROADCAST SATURDAY 1 OCTOBER 2011

October 2

David Chillingworth

It's not good to wake up in hospital. I remember that sudden dreadful jolt, realizing where I was – bright lights, curtains and busyness. Another long day stretching out ahead of me. So this morning I think about people starting the day as patients in hospital or ill at home.

I used to be a Hospital Chaplain. I liked to visit quite late at night when things were quieter. People do a lot of thinking in hospital – you are out of your familiar place and routine. You don't have the freedom to walk away and you have time to fill. The chart at the end of the bed tells one story – temperature, blood pressure, bowels and the rest. But it can't record all the pondering that people do – about life and relationships and family. Nor can it record the struggle to understand what their illness means – why has this happened to me? Sometimes they choose to tell a chaplain – usually a complete stranger – about it. To be with people at a moment in their lives when their defences are down and they are very open is a great and sometimes scary privilege.

But my memory of being a patient is that, no matter how crowded the hospital is with staff, patients and visitors, it is lonely. You're there – with much more thinking time than usual. There is a sort of pretence that everything is routine – like routine surgery. But it's not routine if it's you. You think about meaning and faith, the existence of God and the hope of healing.

At the start of the day …
We remember people for whom today brings challenge,
People who will have surgery,
People awaiting the results of tests.
Father, comfort the lonely, be with the lost and
Bring healing to all who seek Your aid.
Amen.

BROADCAST TUESDAY 2 OCTOBER 2007

October 3

Mary Stallard

In many churches at this time of year, we sing about how we're ploughing the fields and scattering good seed on the land. For townies like me it's sometimes been hard to relate to traditional harvest hymns, but this year they do reflect something that more of us seem to be engaging with: environmental concern, tighter budgets and a desire to connect with where food comes from have led many of us to spend more time in the garden.

Our family have had some moderate success trying to grow things ourselves. Our back yard was a challenge to plant; it's very bare so we bought wooden troughs, which we filled with our own compost and bedding plants. As the weeks passed, we were glad to see the growth of beautiful, delicate flowers. Amongst them, though, a number of enormous potato plants sprung up. There must have been some old spuds or peelings in our compost that took root and developed. As the flowers have faded, we've discovered we have an unexpected crop of potatoes giving us food for reflection as well as for our stomachs.

The world faces enormous issues relating to development and fair sharing of crops and resources. Many people are anxious about climate change and our global future.

Celebrating harvest provides space to bring these worries to God and to commit to living more responsibly; it also reminds us of God's engagement with creation. One of the ancient books of wisdom in the Bible describes how God has blessed the world with rich potential, creating 'a time and a season for everything, a time for planting and a time for harvesting', telling us that God has not abandoned us, but still cares for all of creation.

God of hope and harvest, hear our prayers for the world as well as our thanks for all You give us each day. Help us to use Your gifts wisely and open our eyes and hearts to notice the growth and goodness that You generously provide. Amen.

BROADCAST SATURDAY 3 OCTOBER 2009

October 4

Simon Doogan

At 125 miles per hour, British Rail's first High Speed Train Service began life today in 1976.

The first scheduled journey was from London to Bristol and arrived three minutes early — I'm guessing, to the relief of all concerned.

I don't share the weakness of some clergy for all things train-related, but my wife travels to work that way and on those occasions when things don't move quite as fast as they're supposed to, I share her frustration. No amount of Quiet Carriages or Wi-fi internet connection will ever make up for the feeling that time spent getting from A to B is time wasted.

Now, I may not persuade many regular intercity rail passengers that idle moments on their journey are actually heaven-sent opportunities to be still and to know that God is God. Besides, if prayer becomes something we only squeeze in as and when we can, the same inevitably becomes true of God Himself. The fact is, if we're honest, as more and more is available to us more and more quickly, no form of public or private transport will prove as rapid or as reliable as we would like it to. So far as most of us are concerned, whoever made time simply didn't make enough of it, at least not for the things that we think are important.

Lord, as the world flashes by through our windows today,
And as we long already to have arrived at our final destinations,
Teach us the lesson that in Your holy gift
There is time sufficient for all that truly matters.
Amen.

BROADCAST THURSDAY 4 OCTOBER 2012

October 5

George Craig

There are many things that we commonly use – from domestic appliances to hi-tech devices – but have no real idea whom we have to thank for them. So I doubt whether many of us realize how many English words and phrases that we use every day were actually coined by a man who was burnt at the stake nearly 500 years ago. That man was William Tyndale.

He was a gifted linguist, and the driving passion of his life was to produce an English translation of the Bible. Up to that point the Bible was available only in Latin, Greek and Hebrew. Tyndale believed it should be available for anyone, and particularly ordinary people, to read. But to do that he needed a form of English that would be generally understood. So he simplified the grammar and invented a vocabulary of phrases that survives to this day: 'signs of the times', 'the land of the living' and 'go the extra mile' – all first used by him and still used by people who may never have read the Bible, still less heard of Tyndale.

Religion and politics are often a toxic mix, and so it was in Tyndale's day. The powers that be (another of his phrases) didn't want the Bible translated at that point. So they hounded him all over Europe and eventually executed him as a heretic. Ironically, within four years of his death, the very people who had persecuted him were arranging for the publication of an English Bible. Henry the Eighth's Great Bible, together with the King James Version 80 years later, were mainly based on the work of William Tyndale.

So his achievement lives on in his work. His Bible has been a source of inspiration to generations of Christians but his wider legacy is an enriched language that continues to benefit from his genius wherever English is spoken.

Thank You, Father, for people like William Tyndale, whose commitment to their mission gives positive results they never dreamed of. Amen.

BROADCAST SATURDAY 5 OCTOBER 2013

October 6

Martyn Atkins

Whereas I while away my all-too-rare evenings at home watching sport on TV, Helen, my wife, maintains regular contact with our large circle of friends and family by what she calls 'her telephone ministry'.

Then, at the end of the evening, over a cuppa, she relays the news to me, though in truth she doesn't always need to. The gist of the conversation is made clear by overhearing her regular comments: 'oh, how terrible', 'that is fantastic', 'we'll be praying for you'.

A few evenings ago I was struck by how different two conversations were, one coming quickly after the other.

The first was with someone who was clearly in great spirits. She had a new job and a new love in her life, and was positively bubbling with excitement. She'd hardly slept the night before, just longing for the morning to come.

The other caller was in a very different mood. He has dementia and his wife looks after him. Things are very difficult and they're not going to get better. They won't sleep so well either, I expect, but for very different reasons than our happy friend. They won't look forward to the new day.

The scriptures urge us to 'Rejoice with those who rejoice, and weep with those who weep, and so fulfil the law of Christ,' which is why it is right to regard certain telephone conversations as a Christian ministry.

Lord, Your new day arrives, but we are in very different circumstances as we receive it. Bless those of us for whom this day is an eagerly awaited gift, and those of us for whom it is a daunting challenge. Amen.

BROADCAST MONDAY 6 OCTOBER 2008

October 7

George Craig

Probably one of the best-known Christians in the world is Archbishop Emeritus Desmond Tutu, whose birthday is today. Alongside that of Nelson Mandela, his name will forever be associated with the fight against apartheid and the peaceful transition to the new South Africa. It made him an internationally recognized figure, winner of the Nobel Peace Prize and many other awards.

While widely respected, Desmond Tutu can at times be seen by some people – and certainly by some of the world's leaders – as a controversial figure and not always an easy friend.

I know that I am not alone in needing friends who will take the risk of telling me what they honestly think. The same, surely, can be said of those who are our leaders. So often, we can be tempted to justify bad things in the short term on the basis that they are a price worth paying for some greater good. But we all sometimes need to hear uncomfortable truths about the real impact of our actions, so our consciences can be stirred and our behaviours challenged.

It seems to me that, in taking on this role, Desmond Tutu is in a long line of individuals, many of them motivated by a religious conviction, who have tried to live out their faith by standing up fearlessly against what they saw as injustice.

And whether they were anti-slavery campaigners, prison reformers or social activists, they were almost invariably criticized as naïve, meddlesome idealists, who didn't understand the harsh realities of life. Yet we often have good reason now to be very grateful for their courage and persistence.

It's sometimes called 'speaking truth to power', and it can be a hard and lonely thing to do. Those of us who may not have the courage to do it – even if we have the opportunity – can still be grateful for those who can and will.

Father, thank You for the courage and commitment of those who speak out against injustice. May we be encouraged by their bravery to follow their example. Amen.

BROADCAST MONDAY 7 OCTOBER 2013

October 8

Tina Beattie

'Season of mists and mellow fruitfulness...' So begins John Keats's famous poem 'To Autumn'. This is the season when nature ripens and the buzzing activity of summer gradually subsides into winter's dreaming stillness. Yet in our consumerist culture we have no time to reflect on the changing seasons. No sooner are the summer sports over than the shops are thrusting Christmas upon us and we're plunged into another frenzy of activity. We no longer celebrate seasons of feasting and fasting, as our religious ancestors did.

For many families today, the early arrival of Christmas creates an extra burden of anxiety. How can they afford Christmas, when they can barely afford to live from day to day? Maybe the economic uncertainty is an opportunity for us to take back what we've lost — what the commodification of time has stolen from us. The story of Christmas is, after all, the story of the most freely given gifts of all — the gift of life, and the gift of love. It takes time to nurture and appreciate those gifts. Our ability to give and receive love, to live life fully, requires an unhurried commitment to being rather than doing.

So let's resist the frenzy of the shopping malls for a few more weeks. Let's rediscover the tranquil beauty of this season of mellow fruitfulness. As the ancient sage reminds us, 'To everything there is a season, and a time to every purpose under the heaven.'

May we have the wisdom to discern the seasons and purposes of our lives, and the grace to live them well in the time that is given to us. Amen.

BROADCAST MONDAY 8 OCTOBER 2012

October 9

George Craig

Judging by the number of TV programmes on the subject, the properties we own and the houses we live in are close to a national obsession. And our houses − if these programmes are to be believed − make an important statement about what sort of people we are … or would like to be.

Which is maybe why recently, in the Black Forest in southern Germany, one of the things that most powerfully struck me was the sheer size of the older farm buildings: huge cathedral-like structures which seem to grow out of the hillsides with spectacular roofs: huge single sweeps of wooden shingles outside and vast open spaces inside. Under these single roofs are barns, animal sheds, workshops, dairies, living quarters for the farmer and all sorts of other spaces.

Which prompted me to wonder: what were these buildings saying about the people that built them? What vision of themselves drove farmers to put up structures like that instead of the kind of houses and barns that you tend to find elsewhere? And the simple answer is that the buildings are not about the farmers − they are about the land. The trees in the Black Forest are so huge that it actually makes more sense to use them as they are than it would to cut them up to make smaller buildings. They are just perfect for making these gigantic structures. There are actually many other practical advantages for the farmers in getting everything under one roof, but without the trees to start with it would be pretty difficult to achieve. The people there just went with nature and used what was to hand.

In a world where so many of us seem anxious to create monuments to ourselves or our money, it's refreshing to see what magnificent results happen when humble people just make solid practical use of what they're given.

Father, open our eyes to the gifts with which You surround us, make us inventive in grasping them and grateful for the opportunity. Amen.

BROADCAST WEDNESDAY 9 OCTOBER 2013

October 10

Peter Smith

Emotions are wonderful things, but very difficult sometimes to keep in check. Deeply felt responses to people or events can enhance our own lives and those of others, but if they are uncontrolled and inappropriately expressed they can wreak havoc!

When I was Rector at a seminary, I remember, to my shame, once losing my temper with a student, who to my mind was being particularly obstructive and arrogant. I got more and more angry, and suddenly that anger burst out as I told him in no uncertain terms what I thought of him. He was utterly devastated and his face went white. Later, I felt thoroughly ashamed at having lost control of myself and my feelings. It was a classic example of intemperate behaviour, which reduced me to responding in a totally childish way. It not only diminished me in the eyes of the student concerned, but also diminished my own sense of self-worth.

As we confront different situations in our lives, we can often be involved in trying to keep our emotions well-ordered and under control. If we deny or suppress them, we are diminished. If we allow them to enslave us, and become driven by our desires and compulsions, we do damage to ourselves and harm others. Uncontrolled emotionalism can so easily deaden our moral sensitivity to our own behaviour, which ultimately debases us, and causes damage to those around us.

The virtue of temperance helps us strive towards a stability as we order our emotions and respond in a mature way when issues move us deeply. Temperance helps us to shape our behaviour into a proper balance of reason and passion.

Lord, help us to appreciate the wonder and power of our emotions and never allow them to cause harm to others. Amen.

BROADCAST WEDNESDAY 10 OCTOBER 2007

October 11

David Arnott

I watched a programme recently about Herb Alpert of the Tijuana Brass.
I found it interesting to learn about the life of the man behind the trumpet,
but what I find most interesting was his revelation that there was a time when
he was quite unable to play the trumpet. The gift had deserted him and the
trumpet lay for months where he had put it down. Fortunately for him and
for his fans, he worked hard to re-find the gift, and it came back.

Life is rarely a straight line. It's always full of bumps and bends. One day
everything comes so easily, while the next we feel we are lost in a wilderness.
It's easy to feel hard done by, and life can be very unfair – bad things do happen
to good people. Some theologians tell us there is justice in the world, but it's
divine justice – and one day all will be revealed. At the moment we just see
through a glass darkly, and in the meantime we have to get on with life. I suppose
the question is, how can we make the most of life, even through the dark times?

Herb Alpert eventually realized that if he were going to play his trumpet
again, he had to work hard to nurture the gift he'd been given. But these arid,
dry spells of life can also give us the opportunity to take stock. They allow us to
examine our priorities in life and not take what we have been given for granted.

Lord, open my eyes today so that I may see my world afresh and not take anything or
anybody for granted. Amen.

BROADCAST MONDAY 11 OCTOBER 2010

October 12

Tina Beattie

What's your favourite word? Mine is 'serendipity'. It's a word that reminds us that life is what happens when we're busy making other plans. In modern society we have an obsessive desire to be in control of our lives and to forecast the future. We don't want to leave anything to chance. Yet the world has been changed more dramatically by serendipity than by human planning.

The word 'serendipity' comes from Serendip, which was the old name for Sri Lanka. Horace Walpole made it up from a children's story called *The Three Princes of Serendip*, who, as they travelled, 'were always making discoveries by accident or sagacity, of things they were not in quest of'.

Today marks a serendipitous event which changed the course of history. On 12 October 1492, Christopher Columbus landed on an island in what is now The Bahamas, believing that he had arrived in Asia. This was indeed the beginning of a new world. For Europeans, it ushered in a new world of empire, power and domination. For the indigenous peoples, it was the beginning of a new world of exploitation, enslavement and misery.

Our lives are serendipitous, and the sense of a future that is outside our control can be very frightening. Yet the prophet Jeremiah tells us that God's plans for us are for peace and not evil, and for a future full of hope.

Dear God, help us today to trust You in all that we do, and to remember the words of St Paul, that 'neither the present nor the future, nor any powers, neither height nor depth, nor anything else in all creation, will be able to separate us from the love of God that is in Christ Jesus our Lord.' Amen.

BROADCAST FRIDAY 12 OCTOBER 2012

October 13

Betty Matear

If you're like me, every morning you make your way to the bathroom and without much thought turn on the tap or shower.

In my years living and working in the Caribbean, particularly in Haiti, I learned to be thankful for water.

Hot water, heated on the roof of my Jamaican home, while not a power shower, was a luxury. In some places cold water running off the guttering into the shower was a luxury. Elsewhere, water had to be carried a fair distance. Every drop was a luxury. It's amazing how far you can make water go when every drop is precious!

There's an old ditty: 'Cleanliness is next to Godliness, soap and water is divine.' We may smile at this, but there is a kind of deep cleanliness of mind and spirit that reaches into our lives, and into our personalities, which can become polluted and choked with the dust of human striving.

In the searing heat of what you might call 'revival meetings', my Caribbean family would sing, 'Send down the rain, send down the rain, send down the Gospel rain.'

This prayer asked God to shower us with blessings that could be found nowhere else and to cleanse our lives. A Divine Power Shower!

When you turn on the tap this morning and thank God for running water, you might also pray that God will pour out His blessing on you.

Lord, You can make us clean in thought, word and deed. Help us to experience not just the drops and dregs of Your provision but the full measure. Help us also to give a little kindness, if nothing more than a cup of water to someone who is thirsty. Amen.

BROADCAST MONDAY 13 OCTOBER 2008

October 14

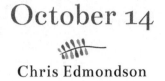

Chris Edmondson

Managing change is something all of us as human beings are called to do. But change, especially when it is not chosen, is not an easy process to live with.

On this day in 1969, the people of the United Kingdom literally found change in their pockets, in the form of the 50p coin, which came into circulation to replace the old ten shilling note. I was a second-year university student at the time, and remember the less than enthusiastic response, especially from shopkeepers, to the third decimal coin to be introduced into the British currency. The change to total decimalization, in 1971, was an even greater shock waiting to happen, but in the meantime why produce this strange septagonal coin, the only one of its kind in the world?

I guess we rarely, if ever, give the switch to the 50p piece much thought now. For those born since 1969, it's just an accepted part of our currency. But change continues to be challenging. At least in some areas of our lives we appreciate familiarity.

That may be why some of the people who heard Jesus speaking about the need for change, in terms of a re-ordering of priorities, a re-orientation of their lives, found it hard to take, because change always comes at some cost. Yet in that instance, then as now, short-term pain definitely leads to long-term gain.

In a world of change and uncertainty, thank You, Lord, that You are unchanging. Today, help us to welcome those changes that need to happen within us, and to deal with those other changes we find hard to cope with, in Your strength. Amen

BROADCAST WEDNESDAY 14 OCTOBER 2009

October 15

Noel Battye

My local harvest festival takes place tomorrow. Whether it's the later reaping of crops here or the canny Ulster-Scots nature, harvest thanksgiving services in Northern Ireland tend to be later than anywhere else — but they're often worth waiting for.

The traditional little church in which I last served always laid such emphasis on a profusion of fruit and vegetables that the place sometimes looked more like Covent Garden market than a suburban church.

It was very different from my previous place, built in the 1960s and modelled on an aircraft hangar at a time when trendy clergy were encouraged to roll out bales of local textiles at harvest or even the odd model of the *Titanic* in deference to the local shipyard workers. Since then, passing trends in society have left their own mark on the services. One year it is industry, the next the environment, and in-between world poverty has come and gone, and come again.

Indeed, I can remember once persuading the floral artists to decorate just one side of the church while leaving the other side completely bare as a stark reminder of the have-nots in our world. Human labour, environment, world hunger — all major issues and each deserving of a place in every believer's calendar of prayer. But even more than these, we all need to hear over and over again those lovely words in St Matthew about the God who provides for the flowers of the field and the birds of the air, who bids each of us to live and to enjoy just one day at a time and so to still the turmoil of endless discontent within, as we learn once more to pray.

'Give us this day our daily bread' — just enough to get us through today
And for tomorrow and its needs
But only as and when it comes.
Amen.

BROADCAST SATURDAY 15 OCTOBER 2011

October 16

Chris Edmondson

If your work involves any contact with people, you will know that we have to understand something about motivation to be effective. Why do people act and react the way they do? Throughout history, great minds have suggested different answers to that question. Coincidentally, three such minds were psychologists who had their roots in the same country – Austria.

Sigmund Freud suggested that behaviour is motivated by the desire to avoid pain and experience pleasure. Adolf Adler believed that the desire for power and prestige is what motivates us. Victor Frankl believed that it is the desire for purpose and permanence that explains why we do what we do. As a survivor of the Nazi death camps, Frankl learned that people's search for meaning is the root of human motivation. People can live with minimal food and comfort, but they can't live without hope.

The truth is, each of these views is partially right. As human beings, we have physical, psychological and spiritual dimensions. Our physical side understandably hopes for a safe workplace and a secure income. Our psychological side wants to be valued for who we are, as well as what we do. And our spiritual side requires there to be some meaning and purpose to what we do.

When these values are integrated in our lives, as St. Irenaeus put it 'the glory of God is seen in a human being, fully alive'.

Lord, guide us today in all our contacts and connections with others, that we may learn to see them as You do, and that their potential in all its aspects may be fully realized. Amen.

BROADCAST FRIDAY 16 OCTOBER 2009

October 17

Musharraf Hussain

In George Orwell's *Animal Farm*, one of the main characters, Major, a pig, leads the animals against man. Major's main tool is to sow seeds of suspicion in the minds of the animals, so much that they begin to regard all two-legged creatures as their enemies. Anyone who has read Orwell's novel, perhaps as a school set book, will recall how this most famous satirical allegory of Soviet Totalitarianism describes a process in which the leadership of the pigs turns from friendship to oppression of other animals.

Trust is eroded in Orwell's story with very good reason. But how tragic it is when situations develop without good reason. Doubt and suspicion are enemies of friendship. I can recall several embarrassing incidents personally where friendship has turned into enmity and trust into cynicism. We believe someone may be plotting against us – perhaps indulging in a little playful office politics, for example. Such situations are exacerbated when we feel we're 'on a different wavelength'.

The prophet of Islam predicted that a time would come when people sitting next to one another will not trust each other. 'Avoid anything that puts doubts in your mind and move towards that which builds trust,' he advised. Of course, communication and openness can go a long way to heal such situations, at both a personal and a community level, but it does need good will and a willingness to take risks, from both sides. Sometimes we're called to exercise that trust as an act of will, to bring health and wholeness to ourselves and our communities.

O benevolent Lord, we put our trust in You and seek Your protection in every situation, from evil motives, thoughts, doubts and superstitions that veil the heart from seeing truth. Amin.

BROADCAST WEDNESDAY 17 OCTOBER 2007

October 18

Joe Aldred

The Soviets glimpsed for the first time beneath the clouds of the planet Venus on this day in 1967. In recent years it has become commonplace for probes and powerful Earth-based telescopes to peer ever deeper into space. We know more about the universe today than ever in the history of mankind. And the more I see of the sheer vastness, complexity and beauty of the cosmos, the more in awe I am of the designer, creator and sustainer of what is being discovered. For me, these grand discoveries serve to remind us of how fallible and vulnerable human beings are in the cosmos, even as they demonstrate the immense power of our enquiring minds. Understanding how the universe functions does nothing to diminish the wonder of these huge spherical objects hurtling through space and time, obeying the laws of gravity and, in the case of our own planet, sustaining life.

When I reflect upon these celestial matters, I feel small by comparison, yet grateful that I am, by God's will, part of something bigger. Right here on planet Earth, there are signs of the divine presence and of realities beyond my own private world. Those of us who work with people whose lives have been shattered by tragedies are well aware of both the struggles and the transformations that can co-exist. Discovering previously undiscovered worlds around us in so many different contexts and arenas can be every bit as challenging as discovering what's beneath the cloud cover around Venus.

Almighty God, as we search deeper and deeper into new worlds near and far, help us that our discoveries draw us closer to You and to those around us. Amen.

BROADCAST MONDAY 18 OCTOBER 2010

October 19

Musharraf Hussain

Standing on the top deck of a cruise ship is the patriarch of the Eastern Orthodox Church, a Buddhist monk from Korea, a Roman Catholic cardinal and representatives of most of the major world religions. As a Muslim representative, I felt it a great honour to be invited to this 'silent prayer to save the planet'. It was part of a conference of religious leaders and scientists from all over the world. The backdrop was the stunning scenery of icebergs stretching endlessly into the distance – they were surreal in their majesty and beauty. Yet what we were witnessing was so very real. The icebergs in Greenland are, we were assured, melting – apparently a clear sign of global warming. What came out of the conference held at Ilulissat was an 'Icefjord Commitment', a statement by the religious leaders who had gathered on the deck that morning:

> 'Amidst the wisdom and majesty of water, ice and sunlight, we have
>   each prayed within the realm of our own traditions.
> Now we stand side by side in acknowledgment of our responsibility
>   toward God's Creation …
> We commit ourselves to the simplest acts of love, compassion and
>   gratitude toward the vast web of life …
> We make this pledge before the whole of creation.'

But silent prayer, no matter how powerful, cannot save the planet by itself. It will only happen if all humanity works together for this most sacred goal.

O Lord, give our political leaders the will, our scientists the knowledge and understanding, our industrial leaders the tenacity and perseverance, and our spiritual leaders the wisdom, to work together for the good of all humanity and the well-being of this wonderful planet Earth. Amin.

BROADCAST FRIDAY 19 OCTOBER 2007

October 20

Joe Aldred

As a child growing up in rural Jamaica, shooting birds with my catapult or slingshot was an everyday activity. And yet a few days ago, when a wasp got trapped in my house my instinct to reach for the insect spray was quickly overridden by my counter-instinct to preserve its life. So I got the key, opened the patio door and ushered the defenceless insect out. As it flew away, I have to admit to feeling relieved I hadn't killed it, as it was entirely in my power to do. Maybe I have become soft and sentimental over the years. This, in my view, is nothing to be ashamed of, because the preservation of life, all life, is worth being sentimental about, especially when we consider the threat to life posed by several factors on the planet, particularly human interaction with the environment.

Life is God-ordained, precious and, importantly, interconnected. We're all part of the divine ecosystem. Our task is life's preservation and enhancement, not its destruction. 'Thou shalt not kill' remains a divine order, and whilst this simple statement always needs unpacking, the principle is crystal-clear: 'don't take life lightly; protect it, don't destroy it.' This may seem high-minded and idealistic, and I imagine some responding by reminding me of the many wars, just and unjust, kidnappings, famines and other factors that compromise human well-being in our world. A fatalistic view is that there's nothing we can do. But the scriptures teach that we should do all we can to protect life made in the image of God.

Almighty God, teach us to love the life You have created, our own and that of all others. Amen.

BROADCAST WEDNESDAY 20 OCTOBER 2010

October 21

Shaunaka Rishi Das

A rare adventure loomed, with twenty Irish pilgrims off to India — our destination, Mayapur, West Bengal.

Our first stop in India was Vrindavan, the birthplace of Lord Krishna. It was an immersion in devotion, and often literally so in sacred rivers. Vrindavan is a town of saintly folk, temples and chanting. So we prayed, chanted and prostrated ourselves from morning till night.

And then by plane to Calcutta, train to Krishnanagar, bus to the Ganges (on the roof), boat to Navadvip, then by foot to Mayapur, nestled in the middle of nowhere, yet teeming with pilgrims.

I was soon enjoying the grim delights of dysentery, cramped as I was in a room for six but inhabited by twenty. The night before the celebration of Sri Chaitanya Mahaprabhu, the event we had travelled so far to observe, I went to bed aware that the temple opened at 3am. I awoke at 7am to an empty room.

How had I not heard the clamber of all those Irish chaps arise, bathe and dress? I jumped up, showered, and raced to the temple to find it practically deserted and decorated with tired flower garlands. I rushed outside and asked the first person I saw where everyone was. He told me they were having the feast. 'But it's a fast day!' I cried. He reassured me that that was yesterday. Indeed, I had travelled all the way to Mayapur only to sleep right through the festival day and beyond, over 36 hours.

Lord, I dash around with plans and schemes I think are great, but which sometimes go wrong. And although I have no control over my future, I will take credit for any good result, which actually comes by Your grace. Please help me to wake up. Hare Krishna.

BROADCAST WEDNESDAY 21 OCTOBER 2009

October 22

Michael Mumisa

We have recently been witnessing a growing trend on social networking sites such as Facebook, where well-meaning people send images to their friends with the accompanying message: 'Click "Like" or "Share" if you care about this, and ignore if you don't care!'

These are often images depicting different forms of suffering, injustices or abuse in our modern societies.

Some people feel that this new trend amounts to emotional blackmail, and that we cannot hope to simply click the world's problems away. If we truly care, we should be doing more than just clicking a key on a computer or mobile phone.

Thankfully, there are people who are still committed to speaking out against human suffering and injustices. Fourteen-year-old Malala Yousafzai is a Pakistani girl who was gunned down by the Taliban just because she demanded equal access to education for girls. She was brought to a hospital in the UK.

At her tender age, Malala already stands in a long line of people in history who spoke out for what they believed in. Aisha, the wife of the Prophet of Islam, although much older than Malala, is regarded by many today, both Muslim and non-Muslim, as a woman who was not afraid to express herself.

Aisha is a controversial figure between Sunni and Shi'a Muslims. Whatever one thinks of Aisha's role in Islamic history, her controversy is also due to the fact that she did what people of her time did not expect a woman to do. In that sense, she established a trend for both men and women in subsequent Islamic societies. It is this trend that girls like Malala and others are fighting to keep alive.

O Lord, we pray for the health and safety of all those striving and fighting to make our world a better place to live in. Amin.

BROADCAST MONDAY 22 OCTOBER 2012

October 23

Peter Baker

There are only a limited number of occasions when we may be asked to indicate our religious affiliation. When we are admitted to hospital, or asked to fill in a national government census or, as happened to me the other day, when approached by a market researcher on a street corner.

We may not frequent places of worship on a regular basis or be great supporters of ecclesiastical pomp and ceremony, but when push comes to shove, many of us will scratch something in the box marked religion. Even when the actual box we tick is not 'Christian', 'Jewish', 'Muslim' or 'Hindu' but 'other'!

It seems to me that one of the greatest challenges we face in an increasingly secular culture is to define the meaning of religion. Perhaps it needs to be rescued from the concept of a remote and vague hobby enjoyed by members of an exclusive club, entrance to which is open only to those who like to pray a lot and sing songs while sitting on hard pews.

James's New Testament letter breathes a blast of fresh air into the stereotypes which the word 'religion' can conjure up. He writes:

'If anyone considers himself religious and yet does not keep a tight reign on his tongue, he deceives himself and his religion is worthless. Religion that God our Father accepts as pure and faultless is this: to look after orphans and widows in their distress and to keep oneself from being polluted by the world.'

What I like about that working definition is that it's so unreligious, so down-to-earth, and practical. It concerns the way we communicate with others, the way we look after some of the most vulnerable in our society and how our personal behaviour is shaped by a distinctive code of values.

The religious life, then, is more than the cultivation of the individual self: it has to do with making a difference to other people.

Lord, free us from misconceptions and make us truly religious. Amen.

BROADCAST THURSDAY 23 OCTOBER 2008

October 24

John Cairns

If the weather is half reasonable today, I reckon that many people will be heading for the garden to tackle those late autumn jobs of clearing debris and preparing the ground for next year — work that shows little immediate result but is so vital to the next growing season.

I'm definitely the labourer rather than the gardener in our household, but I've become an avid garden visitor — being lucky enough to be delighted by gardens from Kyoto to Kew and Caithness to Cape Town. One of my favourites is in a leafy suburb of Washington, DC, where, in the 1920s and 30s, the appropriately named Mildred and Robert Bliss created a haven of peace and beauty in the grounds of their house, Dumbarton Oaks.

In autumn 1944, with the Second World War still raging, representatives of China, the Soviet Union, Britain and the United States met in that idyllic spot and through a series of conversations produced a draft of the United Nations Charter. One year later on this date the United Nations Organization was inaugurated also in Washington. Photographs of the conversations at Dumbarton Oaks show the delegates wandering in the gardens, eating on the terraces, admiring the vistas. I like to think that the gardens helped to bring a sense of harmony — an awareness that the world contained beauty and goodness that, to flourish, required peace.

Like this autumn's gardening, that work for peace has not yet come to fruition, to a full flowering — but work has been done that offers hope that more seeds of peace will grow.

Lord, by the work of our hands, the gentleness of our thoughts and the power of our prayers, may seeds of hope grow to peace in hearts and lives. Amen.

BROADCAST SATURDAY 24 OCTOBER 2009

October 25

Stephen Shipley

'This day is called the feast of Crispian: / He that outlives this day, and comes safe home, / Will stand a tiptoe when this day is named, / And rouse him at the name of Crispian.' Thus declared Shakespeare's King Henry V on 25 October 1415, the day of the Battle of Agincourt – and you can probably hear Laurence Olivier's steely voice saying those words with the stirring film music of William Walton in the background. Henry's men gathered round him, the King spoke with a steady courage and God-given certainty – and, as we well know, it turned out to be a day of triumph for the English army. But who was Crispian? Well, in fact there were two people sharing a similar name – Crispin and Crispianus, two shoemakers who lived in the third century. They were known as great preachers, as well as giving their support to the Christian community in Rome. But their witness was considered too dangerous, and tradition says that, after fleeing persecution, they settled in – of all places! – Faversham in Kent and did their leather work at the site of the Swan Inn. To this day the inn bears a commemorative plaque. They then set off on more missionary journeys and, after refusing to reject their faith, they were executed in AD 296. We honour them as the patron saints of shoemakers and saddlers.

Now, it's unlikely that today we'll face the sort of opposition that Crispin and Crispianus had to put up with. Apathy and cynicism are more likely to drag us down. But we can pray for conviction – a belief in the things that matter.

Lord, strengthen us with the promises we trust You have made to us and give us the courage to do Your will. Amen.

BROADCAST MONDAY 25 OCTOBER 2010

October 26

〰〰

Richard Hill

On this day in 1994 Israel and Jordan signed a peace agreement, which ended nearly 50 years of war.

King Hussein of Jordan welcomed it at the time, saying, 'This is our gift to our peoples and the generations to come.'

Prime Minister Rabin called it 'our own peace, the peace of soldiers and the peace of friends'.

The end of war marked the beginning of a new diplomacy that still has some way to go nineteen years on.

There is still tension, trouble and violence. Division and walls persist – but so at least does the dialogue in that part of the world.

Coming as I do from a country where we have ideology and physical walls still dividing my home city of Belfast, I know all too well that signing a peace deal is merely the beginning. All too easily the world news agenda moves on, assuming that the signing of a peace deal concludes things. It doesn't.

It marks the beginning of a new conversation that is not easy, but it has to be better than what preceded it.

If peace is both the absence of conflict and the presence of wholeness, the development of communities at peace with themselves, then the second aspect, wholeness, takes much longer and at times must seem no closer.

Whether it is in the Middle East, contested space in Belfast or the divisions that occur in society, politics or families, building trust can be a tall order.

Jesus said, 'Blessed are the peacemakers.' I think he knew it was difficult.

Lord, help us to see where we have built walls in our hearts that divide us.
Show us how to build trust and wholeness. Amen.

BROADCAST SATURDAY 26 OCTOBER 2013

October 27

Stephen Shipley

'Sing-along-a-Sound-of-Music' isn't going to be everybody's favourite way of spending an evening in the theatre but it's immensely popular and usually draws lots of people. The audience is encouraged to dress up too, so there are always plenty of nuns sitting in the stalls, as well as a smattering of gentlemen sporting lederhosen and, dotted around, a few 'brown paper parcels tied up with string'. Three weeks ago, I admit to indulging in this activity myself — although I didn't don a costume — and I must say I enjoyed it hugely, singing along to the film's soundtrack, waving a sprig of edelweiss and letting off my party popper when Maria and Captain von Trapp finally acknowledge their love by the moonlit lake with a kiss. People stamped and cheered in their excitement! But there were some quite profoundly intense moments too during the evening, reinforcing for me just how powerfully songs from musicals can touch people spiritually and speak to their deepest and most intimate feelings and concerns. I was reminded of a clergyman I read about in Ian Bradley's book about the theology of the musical, who for the last four years has sung to his congregation 'A bell is no bell till you ring it' from *The Sound of Music* and then gone on to share with them the grace-centred message of the subsequent song, 'Sixteen going on seventeen', with its lines about the life-changing impact of someone touching your heart, after which nothing is quite the same.

None of us knows exactly what the day ahead holds. We'll meet people and address situations that were planned and expected. But we'll also be surprised by things that we couldn't possibly have foreseen.

Lord, make us ready maybe to recognize You in unforeseen circumstances — and to respond. Amen.

BROADCAST WEDNESDAY 27 OCTOBER 2010

October 28

John Cairns

I have a beautiful carved head of an African girl. I bought it on a visit to Kenya in 1999. On the first day, I went to Nairobi market to see what was on offer — the answer was very nearly anything! Stalls with day-to-day necessities were mixed in with those selling local souvenirs of every description, from soapstone and wood carvings to leather and bead work, with a section selling the most gorgeous flowers. On one stall I saw the carving. I knew it was what I wanted and unerringly so did the vendor. I still had ten days' travel ahead of me — to Uganda to visit the African Children's Choir in Kampala, the Nile pouring out of Lake Victoria and a school of hope built in Idi Amin's killing fields; to Sudan to visit the then rebel-held areas and villages where starvation was rife; then back to Mount Kenya Safari Club for a break.

So I said to the stall-holder, 'I'll come back at the end of the trip and get it.' He gave me a pretty cool look that said everything. Sales hadn't been good. The look said without words, 'Oh sure, I've heard that before!' He was the picture of disbelief.

The trip proved as exciting as I had anticipated — full of overwhelming and at times heart-rending experiences, indelibly printed on my mind. The words of children, rebel soldiers and politicians, starving village leaders, pastors struggling to keep hope alive in desperate situations, all resound in my head. But none more so than the stall-holder's reaction, when I re-appeared on the last day to buy my carved head. 'You came back,' he said, before I had even said a word. He had remembered me. My return mattered.

Lord, help us remember that you might make us important to someone today. Amen.

BROADCAST WEDNESDAY 28 OCTOBER 2009

October 29

Stephen Shipley

There's no doubt that Seville is one of the most exuberant and colourful places in Spain – the home of celebrated figures of literature and history. The legendary Don Juan set out from the city to conquer the hearts of women across all Europe, while Christopher Columbus sailed from a port close by to discover a new world. Prosper Mérimée's Carmen, who couldn't make her mind up between the officer Don José and the bullfighter Escamillo, was a worker in Seville's old tobacco factory. And by the way, this factory serves today as part of the university – a piece of knowledge that might give you a glimpse into the Andalusian talent for improvisation!

But it's the huge Gothic cathedral – the largest in Europe – that I want to take us into this morning. One day I crept into the vast building myself for the early devotions. The crimson-cassocked priests stood in the choir stalls chanting the psalms. They then processed to the chancel in front of the enormous golden altar reredos carved in the fifteenth century out of walnut, laburnum and chestnut. To be able to kneel and gaze at this fantastic creation as the light gradually revealed more and more of its detail was a profound experience – 44 sculptured panels telling vividly the life of Jesus: the story of how God gave himself to the world. Then the main doors opened and more and more people flooded into the cathedral – mainly tourist parties clutching cameras, but their faces were obviously affected by the glory around them. It wasn't difficult to utter a prayer for them and for us today:

Lord, you came as one of us to stand with us in the struggles of life. Encourage and strengthen us that, whatever our circumstances today, through you we may know God's will. Amen.

BROADCAST FRIDAY 29 OCTOBER 2010

October 30

Richard Hill

On this day in 1957 the UK government outlined plans to reform the House of Lords to admit the first women peers.

I'm amazed that it took so long – nearly 30 years after all women over 21 were given the vote, nearly 40 years after the first woman was elected as an MP.

I enjoyed a visit to Tate Britain's 'Art under Attack' exhibition. Much of it featured the iconoclasm of the Reformation, but there was also a wonderful section on how the Suffragette movement attacked art as a way of raising their concern that women did not have the vote.

There were examples of attacks on galleries in 1913 in Manchester, and paintings slashed at the Royal Academy in 1914. Alongside the art were wonderful archive descriptions of the protests and police surveillance photography of some of the militant Suffragettes who took part. They rightly challenged what many regarded as the orthodoxy of their day.

Jesus challenged the politics of gender in his day. Asked by religious leaders what to do with a woman caught in adultery, we are told that he paused to draw in the dirt before answering, 'Let whoever is without sin cast the first stone.'

I'd love to know what he drew or wrote – we aren't told. I'd like to think that it was something as subversive as his answer: 'neither do I condemn you, go and sin no more.'

We don't often think of the radical nature of Jesus' message. St Paul summarizes it beautifully for me when he says, 'There is neither Jew nor Gentile, neither slave nor free, nor is there male and female, for you are all one in Christ Jesus.'

Even prayers can be subversive.

Lord, how easily we have judged and condemned with our thoughts and words. As we have been forgiven, so teach us to forgive. Amen.

BROADCAST WEDNESDAY 30 OCTOBER 2013

October 31

George Pitcher

Today is All Hallow's Eve and tonight Hallowe'en parties will be held all over the country, with pumpkins hollowed out to make jack-o'-lanterns, aerosol cobwebs and dancing skeletons. When our children were young, there was a tradition that Daddy had to submerge his whole head in the apple-bobbin' bowl and emerge with an apple in his mouth. Our daughter made herself into a great witch, with blackened teeth and reddened eyes, though her little brothers always claimed she was much scarier the rest of the year.

I have encountered Christians, especially when I was training for the priesthood, who criticized me for celebrating Hallowe'en. At best, they said, I was honouring the pagan festival of Samhain, at worst, they claimed, I was letting the Devil in. I think that's muddle-headed for a number of reasons. First, they seemed to be conjuring up the very superstitions that they said their faith denied. Second, there's plenty of sound evidence that children learn about right and wrong, life and death, light and dark and the moral choices to be made between them through safe role-play. And, third, ridicule is a very powerful weapon against evil. 'Laugh at the Devil and he will flee from you' is a dictum that can be attributed to St Paul, Martin Luther and Karl Barth. Hallowe'en doesn't celebrate Satan, it satirizes him – and, in doing so, puts the evil that humans can do when they turn away from the fount of all goodness firmly in its place.

So, while we hope no trick-or-treating gets out of hand tonight, let's pray that all families' parties are full of the kind of harmless fun that gives thanks for the great gifts of love and laughter, which drive away all darkness from human hearts. Amen.

BROADCAST MONDAY 31 OCTOBER 2011

November 1

Michael Piret

George Eliot begins her great book *Middlemarch* by writing about Teresa of Avila – a famous Spanish mystic, saint and Doctor of the Church, who lived in the 16th century. Teresa, she writes, was a passionate idealist in search of an epic life. And one of the main points of Eliot's novel is that most people do not *have* epic lives. We have very ordinary ones, often an untidy jumble of mistakes, hindrances and missed opportunities – ending in obscurity.

That's how it is for the heroine of *Middlemarch*, Dorothea Brooke. She has the passionate idealism of a St Teresa; but this ordinary world we live in frustrates her epic dreams. The energy of her life must, instead, be used up in ways that 'have no great name on the earth', and mainly go unnoticed. Never mind, says Eliot. The growth of goodness in the world depends hugely on the work of those whose deeds are quiet and completely 'unhistoric'. Her book closes with these words: 'That things are not so ill with you and me as they might have been, is half owing to the number who lived faithfully a hidden life, and rest in unvisited tombs.'

Today, 1 November, is All Saints' Day. Maybe we should have a tomb of the unknown saint, as we have for the unknown soldier.

Help us, God, to celebrate not only the saints whose holy lives have made them famous. Keep us mindful of the obscure and forgotten people, who have not lived epic lives, but have poured themselves out for others in quiet, ordinary ways, that have 'no great name' in the world. Thank You for their labours and example. And help us to continue their work. Amen.

BROADCAST SATURDAY 1 NOVEMBER 2008

November 2

George Pitcher

When *Lady Chatterley's Lover* by DH Lawrence was first published in Britain, its graphic description of sexual liaisons between a married woman of means and the family gamekeeper outraged the establishment. Its UK publisher, Penguin Books, was put on trial under obscenity laws and, famously, the prosecution counsel marked the old, paternalistic world that was coming to its end when he asked the jury: 'Is it a book you would wish your wife or servants to read?'

Clearly the answer to that question was Yes, because Penguin was acquitted on this very day in 1960, and *Lady Chatterley's Lover* went on to sell two million copies within a year, outstripping even sales of The Bible.

Looking back, it's difficult to see what all the fuss was about. Some will say that's because explicit sex has become commonplace in our society and that's a shame. But we do tend to take offence quite easily as a society.

Jesus' ministry is characterized by a refusal to be offended by people's actions or the condition he finds them in. He welcomes adulterers, lepers, prostitutes, hated Roman collaborators, and all who were considered unclean by reason of race or ill-health. The mad, bad and dangerous to know.

OK, he tells some of them to 'sin no more', and we often glean from that that we must hate the sin and love the sinner. But he goes further than that — to him the sin is irrelevant in seeing the person, made in God's image and loved completely, despite what afflicts them.

So, Lord, we pray that we might, like You, be a little less offended by those around us of whom we disapprove, and rather more willing to see the people whom God loves, rather than the people who offend us. Amen.

BROADCAST WEDNESDAY 2 NOVEMBER 2011

November 3

~

Roger Hutchings

The other day I was passing through a town called Trèbes in the south of France. In the church there you can see medieval paintings which are said to be unique and very important. Well, I say you can see them, but that's not strictly true. The church has a high nave, and the windows don't let in too much light. The paintings are at least 60 feet (or I suppose 18 metres) above the ground. They're on wooden corbels just beneath the ceiling. On a bright day, you can just make out that there are indeed paintings there, and with some concentration you might be able to work out that they are human faces. The only way to discover more – unless you happen to have a very long ladder handy – is to look at a display of photographs in a side aisle, where some of the saints these faces belong to are named.

I wondered aloud why on Earth such invisible works of art were ever put there. 'Perhaps,' said my companion, 'they're for God!' Which, of course, was a wise comment. It's like the amazing carvings that are invisible on the roof of a great cathedral. Artworks like these were made to the glory of God, by men and women who knew perfectly well that almost nobody would see them. We can't easily enter the minds of such painters and sculptors, but it seems certain that they worked to offer their talent to God – even if they were also paid for what they created!

There's a verse in the Bible that says that God knows what is done in secret.

Lord of creation, we seek to offer our talents, and the labour of this day – at home or in a place of work – to You. May our offering be worthy of Your greatness and of Your love for us. Amen.

BROADCAST TUESDAY 3 NOVEMBER 2009

November 4

Shaunaka Rishi Das

The Hindu celebration of Diwali, which falls between mid-October and mid-November, is hosted in homes, temples, community centres and even whole streets up and down the UK. Well, having said 'Hindu', it is also celebrated by Jains, Sikhs, Buddhists, Muslims and Christians in India, and is a public holiday in countries as far-flung as Nepal, Thailand, Bali and Singapore.

It has become an important event in the Houses of Parliament, and is becoming as popular as the Gunpowder Plot celebrations, with its splendid fireworks and lamps, and may be more meaningful for this country as well.

At Guy Fawkes we celebrate the defeat of the jihadists of the day. In Diwali we join with another tradition to renew our commitment to *dharma*, to doing things that will nurture our relationships, our community and our environment. Both use light as a symbol, through bonfires and through placing rows of lamps in our windows, and both appeal to our sense of right, and of what is best for our society.

The rows of lamps are to light the path of Lord Rama and his wife Sita, who are returning to their kingdom after years of exile, adventure and struggle. Rama has just defeated Ravana, the scallywag who stole his wife, and who represents our tendency to take rather than give. Rama personifies *dharma*, and acts, at great personal expense, even to the extent of losing his wife, for the benefit and betterment of others.

Dear Lord Rama, in this 21st-century world our national celebrations and stories are changing, developing — and we celebrate many. Pray guide our thoughts so that our sense of public good is based on non-violence, and what is best for our society is recognized in the dharma of our actions. Hare Krishna.

BROADCAST MONDAY 4 NOVEMBER 2013

November 5

Sam Wells

Gunpowder, treason and plot. Or, as we call them today, fireworks.

In the 19th century the balance of the English religious imagination was kept by the celebration of two annual festivals. On 30 January, the feast of Charles I, king and martyr, people rejoiced that England never became narrowly Protestant. Today, on 5 November, the day of Guy Fawkes's foiled gunpowder plot, people gave thanks that England was never overrun by Roman Catholics.

The celebration of 30 January is now rare; and the festivities around November 5 have blended with Hallowe'en. The British state has succeeded in domesticating Catholicism and privatizing Protestantism so they both seem equally harmless. But that doesn't mean religious bigotry has disappeared.

In the last 400 years, people of faith have struggled to hold religious convictions deeply and at the same time to recognize the right of others to believe differently. In 1605 they were perhaps better than we are at the first. They held convictions deeply, even to the extent of going to war. Doing so gave religion a bad name, from which it's never fully recovered. Today we are perhaps better than our forebears at the second. We applaud individual rights and freedoms, but we've rather lost the appetite for profound religious convictions. The challenge is to be equally proficient at both.

God of glory, give us the gift of faith, hope and love; but with them bring grace that allows others to believe differently or not at all. And make this Guy Fawkes Day a day of mercy, peace and understanding. Amen.

BROADCAST MONDAY 5 NOVEMBER 2012

November 6

Shaunaka Rishi Das

One evening my young brother arrived home, walked into the kitchen, stood for just a moment, and my mother announced that he had been smoking.

She berated him for being so irresponsible, whereupon my father said, 'You can't give out to him.' There was genuine shock and the whole family was now at attention. Never before had my mother been so questioned. 'What do you mean?' she demanded. To which my father told a story about Gandhi. One day, he said, a woman took her child to Gandhi and told the Mahatma that her son ate too much sugar, and could he get him to stop? Gandhi asked her to return in three days. Three days later the mother and son returned and Gandhi told the child to always listen to his mother and not to eat sugar if she asked this of him. The child nodded and his mother politely asked why she had had to come back after three days.

Gandhi told her that three days ago he also ate sugar. My father – and I don't know where he got this stuff from – had very succinctly explained the principle of guru in Indian tradition, in fact the principle of the highest kind of guru, the *acharya*. Guru simply means teacher but *acharya* means 'one who teaches by example'.

He then explained to my mother that, as she smoked 40 cigarettes a day, she could not chastise my brother for smoking. But, worse for my brother, he could have chastised her, as he did not smoke. It was a very important lesson in my life, and wonderfully taught.

Dear Lord, thank You for my teachers whose personal example and sacrifice have made spiritual life real for me, worth the effort, and whose virtues encourage me every day to get up, dress up, and show up for service. Hare Krishna.

BROADCAST WEDNESDAY 6 NOVEMBER 2013

November 7

Michael Piret

I was in my early twenties when I made my first visit to a monastery, for a two- or three-day retreat. Getting the train to Kalamazoo – a real city, in Western Michigan – I made my way to St Gregory's Abbey, a community of Anglican Benedictines, at a place called Three Rivers. Their guest accommodation has since improved, I understand, but in those days it was spartan. You got what you needed; nothing more. An individual cell with a sliding door, an upright chair, a small desk, a bed. The visitors' cells were squeezed into a corrugated metal Quonset Hut – an old war-time structure like a Nissen Hut. Each had the luxury of its own window.

After the Guest-master had shown me my cell and left me, I remember thinking it strange to see that my window had no curtains or blinds. I had no clear idea, yet, of the community timetable. Matins at four in the morning, the next service at six ... and so on, through the day. Compline, their bedtime service, was at seven-thirty in the evening. So, broadly speaking, when the sun was up, so were the monks. When it was dark, they went to bed. Curtains would have been of very limited use.

In a setting like that, we quickly realize how disconnected our own lives have become from the ordinary patterns and wholesome logic of nature: day and night, light and darkness, time to work and time to rest.

God of peace, help us, in the midst of a whirlwind of activity, sometimes to be different. In this new day, show us how to regain our balance, if only in one small way, so we can order our lives more naturally. Amen.

BROADCAST FRIDAY 7 NOVEMBER 2008

November 8

Anna Magnusson

In a box of old family photographs there's a tiny, dog-eared one of my uncle, taken sometime in the late summer of 1944. Although it's black-and-white, you can see how sunburnt he is. His hair is dark and glossy, and he looks strong, and fit and swarthy.

You could never tell that he'd been a prisoner of war in Italy for more than eighteen months of the war. Neglected and virtually starved by the Italian guards, he eventually escaped. He roamed the foothills of the Apennines, desperately searching for food and shelter, until a peasant family took him in. For the next nine months he worked on the farm. He learned Italian, dodged the German patrols and lived with the family like a son until the Allies liberated Europe.

At 11 o'clock on the Sunday nearest Armistice Day, the crowds at the Cenotaph in London will fall silent; people in churches will stand quietly; the poppies will have rained down at the Albert Hall, and we all will hold our breath for reasons we can't quite explain, our remembering will be numberless. But each memory will have a name, and a story.

My uncle's 88 now. He went back to Italy with his new wife after the war was over, to say thank you. The two families wrote and visited for years afterwards and are still in touch. My uncle also wrote a book about this brave, ordinary family who risked their lives to give him shelter, food and friendship. He remembered them and named them. Their name was Pelotti. And the dedication of his book is our prayer this morning:

I was a-hungered and ye gave me meat:
I was thirsty and ye gave me drink:
I was a stranger and ye took me in.
Amen.

BROADCAST SATURDAY 8 NOVEMBER 2008

November 9

Dónal McKeown

I went to secondary school for the first time about three weeks after the Berlin Wall was erected. Mind you, that particular fact wasn't on my mind as I began my first lessons in German. However, during the course of many visits to that country over nearly 30 years, I worked on the common assumption that the so-called Iron Curtain — and its bizarre division of Berlin — were just part of the normal run of things. Immutable powers had divided Europe into camps and we had to accept that fact. The nightmare does not want us to dream.

But then, on this day in 1989, brave, crazy dreamers marched and the walls came tumbling down. Within a decade of the fall of the Wall, we had tragedy in the former Yugoslavia — but also saw the end of apartheid in South Africa and the Belfast Agreement.

We all have to live with the realities of life — but what we take to be normal can sometimes blind us to latent possibilities. It takes the vision of some to help others believe that change and growth are possible.

Many will rise this morning, worried about work and finances, burdens and bills. Some will have major decisions to make. We may be partially prisoners of our personal and communal past — but we are also capable of being audacious architects of our future. That future will belong to those who dare to dream of healing, community, laughter and love. To dream of anything less is to do an injustice to ourselves and our potential.

Lord,
Today is full of challenges and possibilities.
Help me to believe that we are all capable of great little things.
And in that belief, help me to chip away at the harsh cold walls
That disfigure the face of humankind which was made in Your image and likeness.
Amen.

BROADCAST TUESDAY 9 NOVEMBER 2010

November 10

Anna Magnusson

The climber WH Murray wrote an autobiography called *The Evidence of Things Not Seen: A Mountaineer's Tale*. It's a marvellous title which takes climbing in high places beyond physical challenge, to the realm of imagination and beauty and spirit.

Someone once said to me that the exhilaration and contentment she felt after a day on the hills was that she 'brought the day home' with her. All the air and light and beauty, all the sounds and thoughts and moments — all brought back in red cheeks and aching legs, and a full heart. She carried the high places back down again, and they remained part of her. What she experienced on the hills gave her perspective in her everyday living.

Remembrance is carrying the past with us, bringing it home. What else are we doing when we stand in silence around the village war memorial; or when the names of the dead of 9/11 are read out, one by one, hour after hour; or when we tell each other about the people and events of yesterday, and of long ago, and why they were important. Remembrance is not just a collection of memories: it's the careful carrying with us of those parts of our past to which we give value and meaning. That is the kind of remembering that shapes us, and gives us perspective. We bring it down from the hills, and into the valley where we live.

When my niece was fifteen she went on a school trip to the First World War battlefields. I asked her what the experience had been like. She said, simply, 'I'll never forget it.'

Lord, we thank you for Your love in Jesus Christ which persists in life and in death. Amen.

BROADCAST MONDAY 10 NOVEMBER 2008

November 11

Dónal McKeown

One dark and damp 11 November when I was seven, my grandfather died suddenly. I was too young to understand much about what was happening. But I still vividly remember my first meeting with what happens when a living smiling body becomes a corpse. Just before the coffin was closed, when everybody was saying their final goodbye to a decent man, I was lifted up so that I could kiss my granddad's forehead. And since then I have never been frightened of death and dying.

On this day many countries in Europe mark the end of the horrific First World War. It was an appalling conflict with death on an unimaginable scale. And each year presents us with a challenge about how we remember the millions of individuals who were devoured by that and subsequent conflicts.

Now, forgetting is not an option. But we can choose to use the rubble of the past either as a weapon to throw at each other, or as the foundation for a new place where we can celebrate or be silent together.

On this Remembrance Day, we might remember all those who have been plucked from the tree of life, in whatever way. If we can tell stories that enable us to somehow grieve for the past with all its pain and brutality, and then let it go, then both we and it can rest in peace.

Lord, You are the source of life and its destination.
You offer meaning to both living and dying
And teach us that death has no ultimate power over us.
Help us to love life in all its forms, so that we can find peace,
Whenever and however death and bereavement knock at our door.
Amen.

BROADCAST THURSDAY 11 NOVEMBER 2010

November 12

David Anderson

There is an inscription on the wall at the Scottish National War Memorial in Edinburgh Castle. It goes: 'The whole earth is a tomb of heroes, and their story is not graven in stone over their clay, but abides everywhere, without visible symbol, woven into the stuff of other men's lives.'

If we are going to move on successfully, then we have to remember and be inspired by every little act of integrity, compassion, courage or sacrifice by those who have gone before. It matters. In this week of remembrance we give our thanks to God for those who have given their all-seeking to be peacemakers, seeking to bring peace with justice in some difficult and dangerous places. We remember the faces, the names, the characters that they were, people we knew and with whom we drank life to the lees. We remember too those left to grieve their loss and those grieving the scars and the wounds that are life-changing, visible or invisible.

Edmund Burke, political philosopher, reminds us that 'All that is necessary for the triumph of evil is for good men to do nothing.' Ours is the privilege to stand with and to remember those good men and women, who need not be ashamed in the halls of their fathers.

Lord God, as life moves on, let us not forget those gone before and what they have done. Help us to choose consciously to live a life that matters, to try and make a difference for the peace of Your Kingdom. Enable us to be good and faithful servants to Your truth, working to the fullness of life and of living. Amen.

BROADCAST TUESDAY 12 NOVEMBER 2013

November 13

~

Anna Magnusson

Some years ago we sat my mother down and recorded her life story. Well, of course, not her entire life, but we recorded and transcribed her talking about her childhood and family, life during the war, school, becoming a journalist, the scoops she had, meeting my father, having children – all the stories we'd heard in bits and pieces over the years, and wanted to have on record to keep for ever.

I'm glad we did, because memory is fragile. It can fade and wither and drop away, like November leaves. And be blown far away into the gloom of a winter's afternoon. It's easy to take words for granted, until they slip through our fingers like goldfish. It's natural to think that the familiar landscape of memory will always be there, showing us where we've been and allowing us to see where we're going. Until the scene changes, a mist closes in and we can't recognize where we are any more.

So now we have my mother's stories and her precious memories, the ones she's shared with us over the years, and we're keeping them safe for her. They're not gone; they're somewhere, still – it's just that they're harder and harder for her to find. But when one *is* found, suddenly, gloriously, it's like the woman who swept her room and found the precious coin. Small and glinting in the darkest corner. A name and a face. Or a whole poem learned a lifetime before at school. Or a funny story. Or just the one word that was lost.

God, who makes all broken things whole, and restores to us what is lost in ways that are both hard and beautiful, grant us light in our living and strength in our journey. Amen.

BROADCAST THURSDAY 13 NOVEMBER 2008

November 14

Judy Merry

I visited a children's hospice recently — not to see the children who have limited life expectancy, but to look at the work of a group that tries to help their brothers and sisters. When you think about a hospice for children, you immediately think of a child who will almost certainly not reach adulthood. But perhaps we don't give much thought to the other children in the family.

It doesn't take much imagination to realize that the parents often concentrate on the needs of the ill child. But life is very tough for their brothers and sisters.

For instance, I hadn't thought about how difficult it is to get a wheelchair onto a beach — so a simple visit to the seaside is rarely possible. That's why the hospice took the children there for a day out. One little brother was asked what was the best part of the day. It wasn't being able to paddle in the sea or looking for crabs in rock pools. It was — in his words — 'having Mum to myself'.

Children get a great deal of criticism these days — and I don't think I'd have blamed these particular children if they'd shown a great deal of resentment at the limitations which circumstances had put on their lives. But when I talked to them, what struck me was the way they put the needs of others before their own.

They know they can't have the attention from their parents that other children get. One teenager said he didn't talk to his family about his worries, because he didn't want to upset them — and a nine-year-old boy didn't seem to resent his brother at all. He said, 'I really love him,' and spoke passionately about how angry he got if anyone stared at his brother or called him names.

Jesus implied that we have a great deal to learn from young children. They have little status — and yet they often behave better than the adults around them.

Lord, give us the humility to admit that children can often teach us the way to live. Help us to see the needs of others and know that there are times when someone else's needs must come before our own. Amen.

BROADCAST MONDAY 14 NOVEMBER 2011

November 15

Nigel McCulloch

For several years I was a member of the Gypsy Lore Society. As a parish priest I sometimes took services for Romany families. Hundreds would turn up for christenings — many having travelled huge distances to be there.

It's sometimes overlooked that Gypsies were systematically exterminated by the Nazis in the Holocaust — victims, like others, of a warped ideology that believed in a perfect race free from blemish. Thank God such evil was removed from Europe. Indeed, whatever may be thought about the bureaucracy of Brussels, the European Union has brought peace to a continent that had become a mayhem of murder.

But what we haven't solved is how to cope with the vast worldwide increase in refugees and, in particular, those who are seeking asylum. In Manchester I frequently meet asylum seekers whose desperate stories are heart-rending. Of course, it's a big and genuinely complex problem for a small country like ours — but those who try to help asylum seekers get deeply frustrated by what seems, sometimes, to be the inability or unwillingness of authorities to listen.

In the Old Testament scriptures, which Jesus knew so well, there is actually only one occasion when we are commanded to love our neighbour; but there are 37 occasions when we are commanded to love the stranger. Jesus' point in the Good Samaritan story was that the stranger *is* our neighbour.

God, make us wide enough to receive all who need human love and fellowship; and narrow enough to shut out all envy, pride and strife. Amen.

BROADCAST THURSDAY 15 NOVEMBER 2007

November 16

Jeremy Morris

It's astonishing how often we seem to meet people who know people we know. I once met a couple, quite by chance, in a bar in Estonia who were next-door neighbours to one of my students back here in England. There was an extraordinary sense of growing, mutual surprise as we narrowed down our horizons from places to names, until we found out how close we were.

I never cease to be surprised at how small our world has become. I fly to countries my parents never dreamed they or I would see. It's often said that air travel has made the world a global village. And yet there are billions of us.

We're a networking species. In the distant past, our lives depended on knowing people with whom we could barter goods. Knowing more people was a way of securing more advantage. Now the goods are more complex, the travel longer, the means of communication immensely more sophisticated. But in the end, it still all depends on the basic human desire to connect.

The world shrinks, but our sociability stays much the same. The world over, people like to get together and talk, to tell stories, to laugh, and perhaps to sing or dance, and certainly to eat and drink together. There's something immensely reassuring about that.

God made us, not to be wrapped up in ourselves, but involved with each other – making friends, loving others, delighting in the richness of humanity. We should celebrate this God-given desire to enjoy the company of others. It's one of the most attractive sides of the portrait of Jesus the Gospels give us – a man who loved company.

Bless those we meet today, Lord, and guide us in all our doings with them, so that we may see in them the same image You made in us, and learn to understand and love them as You have loved us. Amen.

BROADCAST TUESDAY 16 NOVEMBER 2010

November 17

Martyn Atkins

I know exactly where I was on this day in 1984. I was in a maternity hospital with my wife, and after a few fraught hours we were joined by our second son – a wonderful experience.

I remember visiting a church member who'd been in hospital several days, awaiting the birth of her first baby. I arrived a couple of hours after she had given birth and just as her husband, called from his work, burst into the room. I will never forget this tattooed, built-like-a-tank builder holding his daughter, the size of his hand, with tears rolling down his face.

The birth of children and arrival of grandchildren are two key points when people arrive at church. They come for many reasons, but key among them are a sense of privilege and gratitude. And responsibility.

There is much in the news these days about children, our care of them, the level of our provision for them as a society, and sadly, sometimes our scandalous lack of care and protection of them.

We periodically hear of the cost of having children – tens of thousands of pounds a year. And, though the information causes an intake of breath, such data always seems to me totally incongruous: I mean, as if you can measure the relationship between parent and child in pounds and pence!

Generous God, who in Jesus comes to us as a child, and died for us on a cross, but who never makes us feel like we cost too much, we pray for those who give birth today, for those who would love to give birth and never will, and for children in danger of all and any kind. Increase in us all the sense of gratitude, privilege and responsibility. Amen.

BROADCAST SATURDAY 17 NOVEMBER 2012

November 18

Frances Finn

You'll have heard it said many times that if you want help with technology, ask a child. Their rapacious brains seem to just devour new information. And their ability to pick things up is unfettered by their quaint habits of the past. I do sometimes think that I'm from a different world than my daughter. I watched her pick up a toy telephone — the type I grew up with, with a swizzle-round dial — and she poked her fingers *onto* the numbers expecting to hear them bleep. And having mastered our tablet at the age of two, she now swipes her hand across the TV screen, expecting the channel to swish to one that's more interesting.

It was on this day in 1963 that the first touch-tone telephones were introduced. A group of companies called The Bell System made them available to customers in parts of Pennsylvania. The push-button keypad is so familiar to us now, it's hard to imagine seeing it for the very first time and thinking how new and alien it looked. To begin with, it was only businesses that saw its appeal. It took another twenty years for homeowners to become convinced.

I wonder whether our willingness to embrace innovation and change diminishes as we get older. I certainly can't match my daughter's appetite for ever more gadgets, gizmos and buttons. Change can sometimes feel uncomfortable — 'better the devil you know', said my grandparents. But there can be no progress without change. We won't find better ways of doing things unless we're prepared to let go of the old, familiar ways. And Jesus called his followers to be agents of change for the good, however uncomfortable that might feel.

Lord, thank You for innovators, for creative minds, and for those who seek progress for good. Help me to be willing to embrace positive change in my family, at work and in worship. Amen.

BROADCAST MONDAY 18 NOVEMBER 2013

November 19

Robin Eames

Memories, visions of the past, faces, events, the sound of voices – memories are a vital part of our make-up as a person. In fact, it has been concluded by those who study such things that memories make us what we are and to a large extent shape the sort of person we will become. There are the happy recollections of precious moments and precious people. There are the memories of childhood. Happy recollections mingle with those of sadness, sorrow and loss. The whole tapestry of human experience goes together to provide us with our memories.

Here in Northern Ireland some of us have been given the job of finding ways this community can come to terms with the years of what we call 'The Troubles'. Now there are people who would say, 'The time has come to move on and to stop going over what happened in the past. Concentrating on memories can only keep old wounds open. A new generation is impatient of dwelling on the past.' But it is never, I believe, as simple as that. Our memories need to be aired, for to suppress or ignore them can do immeasurable damage. So, we're listening to a host of stories and memories. We're hearing about hurt as much as courage and healing. Some people want to cling to the past, others want to move on. But they all want to tell their own story.

All of us have a story to tell – even if it is something we will always keep to ourselves.

Dear God, remind me of the goodness, the kindness and the compassion I have found in my memory of my story. Amen.

BROADCAST MONDAY 19 NOVEMBER 2007

November 20

Frances Finn

It was 6.30 in the evening, and 15 million people watched as a BBC journalist was handbagged into history. There was John Sergeant, clad in his usual grey rain coat, on the steps of the British Embassy in Paris. He told the nation that Margaret Thatcher had failed to win enough support to stay as Conservative party leader and there must be another round of voting. This was *not* something she would come out and comment on, he said confidently. And with the timing of a well-rehearsed pantomime, the door behind him opened. 'Mrs Thatcher is behind you,' said Peter Sissons from the studio. As John turned to look, the Iron Lady tangoed him out of position to address the microphones that had sprung up into shot.

Looking back on those events, the BBC's former chief political correspondent says it was the making of his career. He says he was hardly noticed until his mistake on the evening of this day in 1990. He went on to become a household name.

As someone who's no stranger to making mistakes, I do enjoy hearing stories of success born out of failure. Failures are so rarely tolerated in public life.

I'm thankful that the God I follow is a fan of second chances. The Bible's full of stories of people who are called to do jobs, who mess up, but then go on to do even greater things. Even St Peter lied three times about knowing Jesus. For him, there was not only forgiveness and restoration, but transformation into something better than before. As one church leader puts it, 'God can make a winning hand out of a pair of twos!'

Lord, give me the humility to learn from my bad decisions. Thank You that when we ask You, You give a fresh start after each mistake. Bless our work and make it fruitful, in Jesus' name, Amen.

BROADCAST WEDNESDAY 20 NOVEMBER 2013

November 21

Derek Boden

The VHF radio on my own boat was tuned to the same frequency, so I heard my friend's voice loud and clear: 'Belfast Coastguard, Belfast Coastguard, this is *Eagle Wing*, this is *Eagle Wing*, over.' He was aboard his yacht *Eagle Wing*, which he had named for a special historical reason, and both of us were on the water for it was the day, some years ago now, when the tall ships sailed into Bangor in Northern Ireland.

Their arrival had been eagerly awaited, and a splendid spectacle they made. Looking at them, it was difficult to imagine the voyages they had undertaken. How did they face ocean hazards with no modern technology, how did they cope with food and water shortages, as well as with serious health hazards?

So it's amazing to ponder that on this day in 1620 the *Mayflower* dropped anchor at what we now call Provincetown Harbour on Cape Cod.

And those ships, the *Mayflower* and the original *Eagle Wing*, have a lot in common. While the *Mayflower* carried the Pilgrim Fathers, the *Eagle Wing* was the first immigrant vessel to sail out of Ireland to America. She carried people who felt themselves dispossessed or constrained in their worship or in civil society. Both ships sailed with those who faced the universal and continuing problem of having to struggle against nature and circumstance to forge for themselves a new life in an unknown land.

Almighty God, grant those who today take voyages of discovery to new places or with new people or who newly seek themselves, the courage to begin, Your presence on the journey, and a haven prepared for their arrival. Amen.

BROADCAST FRIDAY 21 NOVEMBER 2008

November 22

Frances Finn

Today the life of a great Christian thinker, and more famously a wonderful storyteller, is remembered around the world. CS Lewis died on this day in 1963, and his imaginative work is as alive now as it was then. *The Silver Chair* has become the fourth book in the *Chronicles of Narnia* series to be adapted for the big screen.

As a theological student I was introduced to his writings about theology and reason. I was taken with this man who was a respected academic, and yet was willing to speak publicly about matters of faith and affairs of the heart. As a student I was nervous about being taken seriously as a thinker, while believing in what some called an imaginary friend. Lewis engaged his heart *and* brain, and in doing so connected others to God. He was gifted in making difficult concepts understandable.

But Lewis knew he could never prove Christianity through reason. And he knew that at the heart of it was love. Love which transcended the empiricism of the day. In his relationship with God and with people, love brought him both joy and pain. He found to his cost that to love requires vulnerability. It may lead to brokenness. He believed the only way of protecting one's heart is to wrap it up and avoid all entanglements. In his book *The Four Loves* he says: 'Lock it up safe in the casket or coffin of your selfishness ... It will not be broken; it will become unbreakable, impenetrable, irredeemable. To love is to be vulnerable.'

Lord, thank You for the life of CS Lewis. Let us dare to be vulnerable. Open our hearts in Jesus' name. Amen.

BROADCAST FRIDAY 22 NOVEMBER 2013

November 23

Peter Baker

Type the word 'happiness' into a search engine and you'll discover thousands of related books in print. I finished one of them recently.

According to the economics professor Richard Layard there's a paradox at the centre of our existence. More is less. Western societies have got richer but not happier. Why this should be is the product of many factors, of course. But put simply, things can't make us happy. So what does?

Well, there's a link, apparently, between well-being and thanksgiving.

As the lines of that old hymn say, 'Count your many blessings, name them one by one, / And it will surprise you what the Lord hath done.'

Taking things with gratitude instead of for granted is an exercise routine with considerable health benefits. It may not be as good for you as a long walk but it promises to take some of the stress out of life, if not exactly remove the pounds!

The Apostle Paul went so far as to suggest that thanksgiving is an antidote to worry. He writes to the church at Philippi. 'Do not be anxious about anything but in everything with prayer and thanksgiving let your requests be made known to God. And the peace of God, which surpasses all understanding, will guard your hearts and minds in Christ Jesus.'

If he is right, a grateful heart generates quite a pay-off. A mind at peace, a spirit at rest – all because of two words: 'thank you'.

Of course, the challenge in such a fast-paced, consumer culture is to stop, reflect and value the small things which cost nothing but mean everything. Many of us are so busy moving from one issue to the next, one project to another, climbing the next hill, that we fail to look back and remember how far we've come and how amazing the journey.

Lord, may I count my blessings and value the things that really matter. Help me to turn my worries into thanks today. Through Christ whose peace keeps me strong. Amen.

BROADCAST MONDAY 23 NOVEMBER 2009

November 24

Karen Smith

Charles Darwin's *On the Origin of Species* is a work largely remembered for its theory of evolution by natural selection. First published on this day in 1859, Darwin's ideas were hotly debated at the time. Yet, while people argued over his theory, Darwin's work highlighted the rich variety and diversity of life within the world. People, animals, plants, birds, flowers, insects, fish, all in a variety of sizes, shapes and colours: there seems to be no limit to the vast assortment of living things.

Confronted by the dissimilarity within the world, human beings have at times gravitated toward likeness. At best, the desire for the security of sameness inspires us to join with people of similar interests to cheer on our football team or unite to work for a charitable cause. At worst, the fear of difference is at the root of the ugliest prejudice, racism and xenophobia. Yet difference and diversity are marks of the richness of life.

The Apostle Paul said that just as the human body has many parts which all work together, so people need each other. 'As it is there are many members but one body,' Paul wrote. 'The eye cannot say to the hand, I have no need of you, nor again the head to the feet, I have no need of you ... on the contrary the members of the body which seem to be weakest are indispensable.'

Paul's words were directed specifically to the Christian Church, though I wonder if the challenge to unity may not be embraced by people everywhere. Imagine what life might be like in a world where we recognized our need for one another and valued all creation.

Lord, help us to open our eyes to see the diversity of people as Your gift. Remove our fear of difference and unite us in Your love which embraces all. Amen.

BROADCAST WEDNESDAY 24 NOVEMBER 2010

November 25

Steve Williams

We don't expect our footballers to be philosophers or our weather forecasters to write poetry. So it comes as something of a shock to discover that one of the world's most influential scientists was taught how to use his mind by one of the world's most famous hymn writers. Without the work of Michael Faraday in the first half of the 19th century, we wouldn't have the electric motor that we understand and use today. His research into electromagnetic fields led the pioneer of nuclear physics, Ernest Rutherford, to say, 'There is no honour too great to pay to his memory.' At its heart was a brilliant mathematical mind – a mind trained by the work of a poet and logical thinker who died on this day in 1748: Isaac Watts.

Isaac Watts is responsible for some of the best-known hymns in the English language. No ceremony of remembrance is quite complete without those words, 'O God, our help in ages past', and no Christian gathering on Good Friday is conducted without a rendition of 'When I Survey the Wondrous Cross'. Yet this poet, pastor and schoolteacher, who lived and worked in Stoke Newington most of his adult life, was also a prolific writer of books about Logic. His textbooks were used for generations – and his work *The Improvement of the Mind* could be found under Michael Faraday's arm as he made his first inquiries into electricity.

Relate both the language of faith and electromagnetic fields to God – and this sheds new light on Isaac Watts's most famous prayer in response to the love of a creator God who stops at nothing for the needs of the world:

> *'Were the whole realm of nature mine,*
> *That were an offering far too small;*
> *Love so amazing, so divine,*
> *Demands my soul, my life, my all.'*

BROADCAST MONDAY 25 NOVEMBER 2013

November 26

Stephen Shipley

The French composer Olivier Messiaen, it's said, was brought up in an atmosphere of poetry and fairytales such as develop enormously a child's imagination. He was also attracted to the supernatural and the spiritual – above all, to the Bible and to music. I was fortunate enough to be able to attend an organ recital of his music in a darkened church in New York. You couldn't have found a starker contrast between the carnival strains of all that was going on in the city streets outside in the run-up to Thanksgiving Day and the foretaste of a different kind of heaven expressed in Messiaen's timeless harmonic progressions. Here was a man whose melodic inspiration is uniquely found not only in ancient plainchant but also in the song of the birds, the supreme musicians of God's creation, whose calls he notated and collected with passionate enthusiasm. What was so revealing, though, was the mixture of old and young people who packed into that still church the afternoon I was there, silent before the recital began, aware only of the rumble of the subway deep below. And then the exotic colours of Messiaen's music were slowly revealed – 'the swords of fire, blue and orange lava flows,' as he described them, 'sudden stars and rainbow's clouds'. They captivated all with ears to hear. Messiaen's music won't appeal to everyone, of course, but a glimpse of heaven in whatever form is something most of us yearn for.

Whatever today holds, Lord, thank You that You have placed heaven in our hearts. Keep that loveliness alive and help us to trust You to bring us and those for whom we pray to the hope of the eternity You set before us. Amen.

BROADCAST WEDNESDAY 26 NOVEMBER 2008

November 27

Alison Twaddle

Later today, I'll be going along to a community singing group I joined when I retired from full-time work last year. I've never been much of a one for hobbies, and I'm no great singer, but the poster attracted me. It read: 'Singing for Fun — no auditions necessary.' It was so undemanding and inclusive that I was emboldened to go along, and I've enjoyed it ever since. A close friend belongs to another, rather grander choir, where auditions are very much required and cause her a great deal of anxiety as the annual test day approaches. There's nothing wrong with the pursuit of excellence, and it's perfectly valid for choirs to hold auditions in order to maintain their high standard of performance. But we can all enjoy singing, whether or not we're destined for Carnegie Hall.

If auditions were to be held for the Christian Church, not many of us would meet the mark. In terms of our life and witness, we're all aware of times when we hit the wrong note, or lose the tune altogether. But we're not disbarred. Others are there to support us; second chances are offered to us; and when we *are* able to act as we should, our contribution is accepted. Each of us has particular gifts to bring to our family, community or workplace, and each of us has a role to play in encouraging others to share their particular talents. The strength of the Church, like the joy of the choir, is in the coming together of all the different parts.

Loving God, forgive us the discord of our ill-considered words, harsh judgements and unforgiving spirits. Thank You for accepting the praise of our voices and the work of our hands as we renew our efforts to do Your will this day. Amen.

BROADCAST TUESDAY 27 NOVEMBER 2012

November 28

Steve Williams

A friend of mine works in a council housing office, taking rent and dealing with enquiries from world-weary tenants. On the day we met, just one of these many encounters stood out in her mind. A face she thought she recognized stood before her and the person said, 'You may remember I came here with a difficult problem last week. Well, thanks to you, it's all sorted – and I just came back because I wanted to say thank you.' And that was all. But my friend said that brief meeting had made her day.

If that's what thanks does for the person on the receiving end, I wonder what it does for the one who gives it. On Thanksgiving Day, the fourth Thursday in November, you won't get any business done in Wall Street. The day's origins lie in giving thanks for the harvest to God – the words of George Washington, 'the beneficent Author of all the good that was, that is, or that will be'. Some Native Americans have compared it with their celebration of *wopila*, thanksgiving that the Great Sioux Nation, for example, has been giving on their land for far longer than the settlers.

Properly done, to give thanks is an act of humility – a recognition that you depend upon someone else to do something you can't do for yourself. To give thanks, you recognize they made your day, and you can make theirs, too.

Almighty and gracious Father,
We give You thanks
For the fruits of the earth in their season
And for the labours of those who harvest them.
Make us, we pray,
Faithful stewards of Your great bounty,
For the provision of our necessities
And the relief of all who are in need. Amen.

BROADCAST THURSDAY 28 NOVEMBER 2013

November 29

Alison Twaddle

My husband has just begun a course of piano lessons, at the age of 62. So far he has been very committed to his programme of practice, and I'm confident that the early evenings will soon be filled with the sound of recognizable tunes, rather than the current repertoire of stumbling scales and exercises. A friend who teaches the flute tells me she has a pupil who is in his 80s – and foreign language classes seem to be filled with eager subscribers of riper years. Never too late to learn, it seems.

The irony is that all of these skills would probably be more easily acquired at a younger age, when the fingers are nimbler and the brain more retentive, but the opportunities on offer in our youth are often squandered. When we're young, the necessary practice and homework are sometimes resented as restrictions on our free time, and we try to get away with the bare minimum of commitment, only to regret it in later, wiser years. 'Youth,' as Shaw said, 'is wasted on the young.' The regrets felt by older people are often to do with time wasted, or chances not taken, and are expressed in terms of 'if only I'd known then what I know now'. But sadly, that's not how it works – we can't re-live the past, with all the advantage of hindsight and experience, but we can transform our regrets into a purposeful future, making every day count, whatever our age.

Loving God, may this day be one lived positively in the light of Your love for each one of us. Where there are choices to be made, grant us wisdom; where we are faced with challenges, make us bold; where we find needs, may we respond with generosity, in the name of Christ our Lord, Amen.

BROADCAST THURSDAY 29 NOVEMBER 2012

November 30

Johnston McKay

Good morning on St Andrew's Day. I've got to know the town of St Andrews on the Fife coast quite well over the past five years or so because our daughter was a student there and still lives nearby. Which is how I heard all about Hamish MacHamish.

Hamish MacHamish is a shaggy ginger cat, with a white mane and green eyes, and he has taken over from William and Kate as St Andrews' most famous resident. For thirteen years, traffic has stopped for Hamish, who invariably uses zebra crossings. Not only has he been adopted by locals and students, tourists quickly get to know about him, and he has over 2,500 friends in social media.

One of the things I find fascinating about Hamish MacHamish is that he knows how far he can go. Sitting near the open door of one of the coffee shops, you can see Hamish approaching. But he stops before the doormat and never crosses it. Call it a feline understanding of the hygiene regulations, or a self-interest which recognizes that going beyond acceptable limits will meet disapproval: whatever the reason, he sits outside until something else attracts his attention.

I can learn from Hamish that a proper concern for the good of other people or their welfare involves not only a commitment to identifying with them and a willingness to be alongside them but also a recognition that there are times and occasions when respect for them requires an appropriate distance. Which is why I think that Jesus was right always to send away those he had helped afterwards, so that distance could prevent over-reliance.

So it is, loving God, that the space You give us is a sign of the love You have for us. Amen.

BROADCAST SATURDAY 30 NOVEMBER 2013

December 1

⁂

Alastair McIntosh

People often ask what spirituality is, and how do you open up to it.

One response comes from a medieval mystic called Richard of Saint Victor. For him, spirituality was less about imposing belief systems on the world and more about an ever-deepening direct perception of reality.

He suggested that we have three eyes. The eye of the flesh reveals the physical world. The eye of reason lets us see sense. And then there's the eye of the soul. That eye is like the other two. If we don't use it, if we don't look … then we won't see. But how is the eye of the soul opened? That's what the spiritual practices of many different paths are about.

I have a morning contemplation that I try to follow when waking up at an early hour. In my mind's eye, I'll slowly scan up and down my body, becoming present to every physical sensation and especially to inner pools of emotion.

I'll then shift attention to the coming day's activity. I'll gently look at what's needing to be done, and see what's most calling out for attention. And sometimes it's at odds with my carefully planned 'to do' list.

Lastly, I'll observe how my life's being held in the greater life of this world, and open out to just a few of the people, organizations and issues that I in turn help to hold.

And perhaps I'll hear the Pakistani neighbour scraping off the ice, starting up his grocer's van and setting off in service to the community.

And I'll silently wish him safety, and respect, and in his Islamic custom,
'As-Salāmu 'Alaykum'.
… and that's about it, really.
But it feels a kind of blessing.
And it feels like being blessed.
Amen.

BROADCAST TUESDAY 1 DECEMBER 2009

December 2

Alison Twaddle

I remember that when I was pregnant, it seemed as though every second woman I saw in the street was in the same condition. Similarly, when I had my first car, a red Renault 4, it seemed as if they were everywhere on our roads like a rash. I guess that's just down to our heightened awareness of those things that are important in our lives at any time, but it's a rather spooky feeling. Having been diagnosed recently with a form of cancer, I've been struck by just how many people I meet are in that same boat. It's not that I actively seek them out, it's just that there's a lot of us around and our paths sometimes naturally cross.

One friend has been living with cancer for many years now, and her example through many remissions and setbacks has been an inspiration. Recently she invited me along to a support centre for cancer patients for a pampering session. For two hours a dozen of us were given skin treatments and make-up tips, and emerged looking good and feeling better. Apart from my friend, I knew no one in the group. We covered a wide age range, and many different life experiences emerged as we chatted over the moisturizer and the eyeshadow. The mood was one of fun and excitement, like children at a party, and at the end of the session we were all sincere in our thanks to those who had provided it.

Loving God, we know that difficulties are part of our human life. Each one of us can expect to experience some pain on our journey, whether that is physical pain through illness, or the pain of disappointment, betrayal or loss. We pray that, today, those who are in particularly dark places will feel the warmth of Your presence; that they will find comfort in knowing that they are not alone in their suffering; and that the light of companionship and compassion from their fellow travellers through this life will break through to bless and to heal. Amen.

BROADCAST FRIDAY 2 DECEMBER 2011

December 3

❧

Noël Vincent

Many people have strong views about prison. That's why we read so much about prisons in newspapers – overcrowding, miscarriages of justice and the fact that there are people in prison who probably shouldn't be: they're not so much criminal as mentally sick, or addicts.

Some people feel prison isn't enough of a punishment – more like a holiday camp – and it's ineffective because the re-offending rate is so high. There were mixed reactions to the news that a working party was being set up to look at prison policy, chaired by a former cabinet minister who was himself jailed for perjury. He came out apparently a reformed character. So the system worked for him. Concern for prisoners is an important, if neglected, priority for Christians, especially at this time of year. It's one of the criteria that defines Christian behaviour: 'When I was ill you came to my help, when I was in prison you visited me,' said Jesus. He didn't mean it literally: it was an illustration of care toward our fellow human beings.

People in prison get there through the judgement of the courts but the word applies to us all – assessing value and quality, we're making judgements every day. Are we making the most of our lives? What would help us bring added value to our environment – at work, in the family or in the community at large?

The ancient Israelites had judges who were leaders of the nation. They administered justice, but they also had the trust of their people and worked for everyone's welfare. Their responsibilities weren't so much to condemn and confine criminals as to define moral quality and enhance people's lives in the community at large.

Lord God, You are our judge and guide. We pray for prisoners, that they may find new direction in their lives, and guide us too that we may be good and faithful servants in all we do. Amen.

BROADCAST MONDAY 3 DECEMBER 2007

December 4

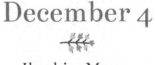

Ibrahim Mogra

My wife and I have just recently returned from the hajj in Makkah, a duty on Muslims at least once in a lifetime. More than two million Muslim pilgrims of every colour of the human race gathered at the hajj. We witnessed the truth of God's declaration in the Qur'an: 'O mankind! We have created you from a single male and female and We have made you into nations and tribes so that you may recognize one another. Indeed the most honoured of you in the sight of God is the one who is most righteous. Indeed God is All-knowing, All-aware.'

Under the desert sun in the plains of Arafat, we remembered the Messenger Muhammad's last sermon (peace be upon him): 'O people, indeed your Lord and Sustainer is One and your ancestor is one. All of you descend from Adam and Adam was made of earth. There is no superiority for an Arab over a non-Arab nor for a non-Arab over an Arab; neither for a white person over a black person nor a black person over a white person except the superiority gained through righteousness. Indeed the noblest of you is the one who is most conscious of God.'

It was truly amazing to see people of every description. Yet here, no one but God was great. Here was proof that every colour is equal before God and before each other. We were all dressed in two pieces of simple white cloth, we prayed at the same time in the same place, ate together, rested together and became dearer to God together. Indeed, there is only one race: the human race.

Dear God, give us the strength to be more righteous, to see all human beings as equals and to respect them all as part of Your family. Amin.

BROADCAST SATURDAY 4 DECEMBER 2010

December 5

Alex Robertson

The church I attend has a fleet of four minibuses, which we use for ferrying people from all over Manchester and Salford. We keep them locked overnight in a compound, but one Monday morning last year we arrived to a scene of devastation: four burnt-out buses reduced to twisted metal shells, the compound floor blackened, and that damp, acrid smell that pervades after a fire is put out. A thief had got in during the night, broken into each bus, and then tried to cover his tracks by burning the vehicles. The sight was overwhelmingly disheartening and dispiriting.

But then something amazing happened. Two days after the incident, a man called our senior pastor. 'I'm at a garage', he announced, 'and I'm buying you two minibuses.' Within a week all four buses had been replaced by better models than we previously had, and a further bus had been promised to us. Hard times often bring out the best in people, and congregation members and friends from outside proved to be the friends we needed in that time of discouragement, and turned the situation around.

I was reminded of the Bible story of Joseph, the boy who was betrayed by his brothers and sold as a slave, but who rose to become prime minister of Egypt, and ended up saving the lives of his family. 'You meant it for evil,' he said to his ashamed brothers, 'but God meant it for good.' In the darkest times, the light of generosity and love shines all the more brightly.

Father, help us not to despair when things are against us, but to trust in Your ability to turn evil to good. Amen.

BROADCAST WEDNESDAY 5 DECEMBER 2012

December 6

❦

Noël Vincent

As Christmas shopping gathers pace it's tempting to ask yourself, 'What's the connection between Christmas in the shops and Christmas in church?' The lights are cheerful and carols are everywhere, but the cards are a chore. OK, the presents and parties lift the spirits, but why do it? The spirit of Scrooge niggles away. To bridge the gap you can send charity cards or give really useful presents. Last year we received a note to say our present was a goat for a village in Africa.

Strangely, a symbolic bridge between secular and sacred manifestations of Christmas is Santa Claus. On the one hand he's commercial, with day trips to Santa-land in the Arctic, wish-lists posted to his toy factory, and entrance fees to visit his grotto. But he's also a link to the spiritual dimension of Christmas. His name is a corruption of St Nicholas – Sanctus Nicholaus – who was Bishop of Myra in the 4th century.

As with many ancient saints, facts about St Nicholas are few and hard to come by, and legends are many. He is revered as the patron saint of sailors because of his travels. We're told he cared deeply about the poor, especially children. Benjamin Britten's cantata, *Saint Nicolas*, tells how the saint restored three little boys to life and rescued three young girls from prostitution. It's his generous care for others, following Christ's teaching, that makes him the Santa prototype.

So St Nicholas, celebrated today by the Church, reminds us of the true nature of Christmas – caring, loving and life-enhancing. It's not about how much cash we spend, it's how much care we show, how much joy we bring to others.

Generous Father, we give thanks for the life of St Nicholas and especially for his generosity to those in need. Help us to give freely and wisely, for the benefit of those we care about. Amen.

BROADCAST THURSDAY 6 DECEMBER 2007

December 7

Alex Robertson

On the way to work the other day I saw a spectacular rainbow. Not unusual in Manchester, of course! But this one, though it was only a fragment, was unusually strong and vivid, every colour shining out brightly against the darkened sky. Of course, I didn't have a camera with me. But even if I had done, the transient nature of the event was such that by the time I'd have got the camera ready, it would have been too late.

As I drove on, I did regret that I couldn't capture the moment, show it to my friends, broadcast it, make it available to everyone. But then I started thinking, Why? Is the experience only worthwhile if we can show it off to others and record it for posterity? Isn't there something beautiful in the fact that it was only there for those few brief seconds, then gone forever? Isn't it precious precisely because it was unrecorded, unrepeatable – a personal, private, intimate moment 'just for me'? Why waste the impact of the present moment by wondering what I could do with it in the future?

The present is full of glories, unique and precious, if we refuse to allow our minds to be distracted and invaded by the future and the past. When Jesus said, 'Don't take thought for tomorrow, because tomorrow will take thought for itself,' he was very much encouraging us to live in that present.

Father, may we have eyes to see, ears to hear and hearts to recognize the moments that You have for us today. Spare us from anxiety and regret, and grant us the ability to live in the joy of the present moment. Amen.

BROADCAST FRIDAY 7 DECEMBER 2012

December 8

Patrick Thomas

Harold the carpenter was the oral historian of our village of Brechfa, in Carmarthenshire, south Wales, like generations of his family before him. The cottage where Dylan Thomas's grandfather was born had vanished long ago. Only Harold could show you where it once stood.

He alone could demonstrate the forgotten implement that charcoal-burners used to strip the bark from trees. And Harold could tell stories about the 1860s as though they had happened yesterday.

Old age, infirmity and illness eventually took their toll, and the carpenter was moved into a nursing home. I visited him there. He'd forgotten his English, as older people sometimes do with their second language, but we'd chat together in Welsh about the distant past.

One day, while I was with him, the matron introduced a woman from the hospital. She had been sent to assess Harold, and asked him a series of questions in a language he no longer understood. When he didn't respond, she turned to the matron and remarked, 'Permanent vegetative state!,' as she scribbled something on her report sheet.

I was too stunned to say anything, but when she'd gone, Harold turned to me with a broad smile, and made an unrepeatable remark in Welsh about his visitor. No doubt she had a heavy schedule and could only spare him a few moments. But with just a little more time and sensitivity, she might have discovered the old man whom I knew, and admired so much.

Lord Jesus, we remember the older members of our society, particularly those who are in hospitals and residential homes, and those from our own families and communities. Give us the patience and imagination to value and respect each individual, so that we may learn from them and share their joys and sorrows. Amen.

BROADCAST SATURDAY 8 DECEMBER 2007

December 9

Ibrahim Mogra

A man once asked the Messenger Muhammad (peace be upon him) for some advice. He said, 'Do not get angry.' The man asked for more advice and Muhammad kept repeating the same advice.

Upon reflection, I have found that many of the things that happen around us which cause us problems are, by and large, as a result of people not being able to control their anger. Perhaps that's why anger management has become a lucrative business for some. Anger is the inferno of the heart, the desire to take revenge and the loss of one's dignity and good manners. Anger encompasses all evil.

If a person wants to be of good character, then they must first learn to control their anger. When a person gets angry, they are not bothered about the foolish and violent way they behave.

Muhammad said, 'The strong person is not the one who defeats his or her opponent in a wrestling match, but the strong person is the one who controls themselves when angry.'

He also said, 'There are three things which if they are found in a person God will give them protection, shower them with His mercy and enter them into His love: the person who when they give to the needy is thankful, and the person who forgives when they have the power to avenge, and the person who controls their anger when angered.'

Dear God, save us from anger. Make us slow to get angry and quick to forgive. Amin.

BROADCAST THURSDAY 9 DECEMBER 2010

December 10

John Holdsworth

At this time of year everyone, from archbishops to politicians, seems anxious to give us their Christmas message. Often these are attempts to point us beyond immediate and petty concerns to greater themes, one of which is usually peace. I've been looking at the different ways that familiar Christmas carols interpret the significance of Christmas, and peace is a central theme there, often connected with a new rule of God. 'Joy to the World', for example, includes the words: 'He rules the world with truth and grace.' 'It came upon a midnight clear' looks forward to an 'age of gold, when peace shall over all the earth its ancient splendours fling'. And one of the most popular of all carols includes the line 'Hail the heaven-born Prince of Peace.'

All of these are allusions to the hopes that we read about in the pages of the Old Testament – hopes that Christians believe Jesus began to fulfil. People then were looking forward to a new age in which there would be a transformation of individuals through a new stress on forgiveness; a transformation of creation itself to make it a more secure setting for human flourishing – a place without pain and suffering, for example; and a transformation of society. To describe this society they used the language of a new kingdom, in which creation would be honoured in a new way, and justice and peace would be established. After the first Easter, Christians interpreted Jesus' ministry in terms of these hopes, and eventually all that was projected back to the stories of his birth.

The popularity of the carols, and the Bible passages that prompted them, bear witness to a longing that persists.

Lord of all our hopes and fears, inspire in us the longing for change, the will to be part of it and the desire to live in a new age. Make all things new, we pray, and begin a new thing in us and in our world. So might all creation demonstrate the glories of Your righteousness and wonders of Your love. Amen.

BROADCAST WEDNESDAY 10 DECEMBER 2008

December 11

Michelle Marken

I am still almost certain I heard the sound of jingle bells wakening me from an excited sleep as a small child, on the night before Christmas. I am convinced I saw Santa Claus quietly leaving my bedroom, a quick shadow disappearing round a door as I sat up in bed. It would have had to be quick, for Santa had to visit seven eager boys and girls in our house.

If my parents had perfected an effective management strategy, each of us might have expected that Santa would only visit the living room where we would have left our stockings suitably labelled and draped over various chairs.

In time management terms, all personnel would have met in one designated spot, business would have been concluded effectively and successful outcomes would surely have been guaranteed.

That is, if there hadn't been the impossible-to-estimate quality of that supreme childish emotion, 'excitement'.

But my parents understood that what goes to make up happiness, as an outcome of excitement, cannot be time-managed, time-bound with smart targets, nor time-poor in terms of personal attention to what the human heart needs.

Indeed, their creation for us of the true magic of Christmas lay in a story of love, the story of a family in need being offered a pretty humble shelter for the night, and the birth of the Christ-child.

Lord, create within us a child's sense of wonderment which allows us to step aside for a moment from the stresses of our lives to hear the inner music of our day. Amen.

BROADCAST SATURDAY 11 DECEMBER 2010

December 12

Ibrahim Mogra

As holidaymakers dash off soon, what about the burglar alarms, post, wheelie bins and, in my case, my tropical fish? But I needn't worry, for God has blessed me with two most wonderful neighbours. I know they would take care of everything.

Muhammad (peace be upon him) said, 'Your neighbour has a right over you. Help him if he asks for help. Lend to him if he needs a loan. Show him concern if he is distressed. Nurse him when ill. Attend his funeral if he dies. Congratulate him if he meets any good. Sympathize with him if any calamity befalls him. Do not block his air by raising your building high without his permission. Do not harass him. Give him a share when you buy fruits, and if you do not give to him, bring what you buy quietly and do not let your children display them to excite the jealousy of his children. Nobody can be a true believer if his neighbours pass the night hungry while he has his stomach full. Nobody can be a true believer unless his neighbours are safe from the harm of his tongue and hands.'

But do we really know our neighbours? We live in the same street, same block of flats, yet we do not know one another. Islam teaches that a neighbour is not only the person next door; fellow students, work colleagues, fellow passengers all are neighbours.

Dear God, awaken the springs of goodness in our hearts and strengthen our society with the bond of love, affection and good neighbourliness. God, grant us Your love, and the love of those whom You love, and the love of those who would bring us closer to Your love, and make Your love dearer to us than cool water on a hot day. Amin.

BROADCAST SATURDAY 12 DECEMBER 2009

December 13

Michelle Marken

A child stood in front of me the other day, actually no longer a child but a young adult, someone I taught several years ago. Where once I wanted her to hang on *my* every word, now she spoke generously to me, the retired teacher, and I appreciated *her* every word, for she wanted to tell me how she was progressing in her A level studies.

I felt drawn back to that classroom, the quickness of each child's response to the challenge of new ideas and their readiness to be creative and open-minded.

Of course, such themes must resonate with real life, and John Steinbeck's novel *The Pearl* caught their imagination with its story of Kino the pearl fisherman and his family. It described how the pearl merchants exploited the poor, uneducated village fishermen, operating a cartel to buy pearls cheaply, regardless of their market value. Pupils, possessing all the honesty of their age, clearly related to those with no voice. When Kino found the perfect pearl and refused to sell it for less than its value as he struggled to buy medicine for his sick child, they understood what Steinbeck writes of as 'the song of the family'.

The pupils' strongly developed sense of right and wrong helped them empathize with Kino, describing those in positions of power who would not help him as being 'without conscience'.

'Conscience' is a strong, vibrant word, and speaks instantly to us all. The poet John O'Donohue writes that 'Words may know the way to reach the dark,' and 'conscience' is one such.

Lord, today let us find a way to reach through that dark and help us to be aware of those around us, demonstrating care and respect for them, made in Your image. Amen.

BROADCAST MONDAY 13 DECEMBER 2010

December 14

⁂

Patrick Thomas

'What I *really* want for Christmas is a teddy bear,' remarked Llinos, my eight-year-old daughter. It wasn't an unreasonable request. After all, as she pointed out, her brothers and her younger sister all had one. The problem was that she made the remark at 7pm on Christmas Eve. Our west Welsh village was thirteen miles from the nearest town — and by then the shops would have been closed anyway.

My mind was soon taken up with another difficulty. Peggy was an eccentric and elderly recluse, whose long-deceased father had once regarded himself as the commanding figure in the community. One of my annual duties was to take her to the candlelit Midnight Mass in the remote mountain church of Llanfihangel Rhos-y-Corn. Peggy, who lived and slept in her armchair, was a considerable size. My car was very small. The road up the mountain was extremely steep. The task was formidable.

Somehow we reached the church. I took the service, and then brought Peggy home. As I carefully helped her out of the car and manoeuvred her toward her front door, she asked: 'Do you know anyone who needs a teddy bear? I ordered one for one of my relatives' children, but it was *far* too big.' When Llinos came down to breakfast next morning, that teddy bear was sitting on her chair.

As we begin to gear up for Christmas, perhaps it's worth remembering that at the heart of it all is an unexpected gift: the surprising generosity and love of the God who gives Himself to us in Jesus Christ.

Heavenly Father, as we get caught up in the pre-Christmas rush with all its pressures and demands, help us to discern Your presence, responding with a generous and open spirit to Your loving kindness. Amen.

BROADCAST FRIDAY 14 DECEMBER 2007

December 15

Anna Magnusson

There are some lines in a short story by Anton Chekov, describing a late winter's afternoon in the country, when everyone is gathered in the house: 'Through the window,' the sentence runs, 'could be seen grey sky and trees wet with rain; since there was nowhere one could go in that kind of weather, there was nothing else to do but tell stories and listen.'

There's something about this time of year, when the darkness eats into more and more of the day and the cold creeps ever closer, that makes storytelling more precious. We need the light of imagination. We need to hear about other worlds which can break through the solidity of winter.

Each December I re-read a story by the Icelandic novelist Gunnar Gunnarsson about a shepherd called Benedikt who, every year around the time of Advent, would pack his kit and make a journey. 'He would take the way to the mountains,' says the story, 'the desolate mountains of Iceland, where at this season of the year nothing was to be found but birds of prey, hard and cruel as winter itself, foxes, and a few scattered sheep, lost and wandering about.' Benedikt's self-imposed task was to search the icy wilderness and bring home the sheep that had been left behind in the autumn round-up.

'When a holy season approaches, men make ready for it,' we learn in the story. This is Benedikt's way. It's a story about survival in the face of a magnificent and dangerous natural world; and it's about hope and love in the midst of darkness. It's a story for Advent.

God, in this winter of waiting, inspire us with the story of the Light of the World who has been promised to us. Amen.

BROADCAST SATURDAY 15 DECEMBER 2007

December 16

Eugene O'Neill

On this day in different years, two marvels of engineering skill were inaugurated at Heathrow airport: in 1955, a huge new terminal; in 1977, a Tube link to central London.

Both feats recalled for me the tradition in Canada for every newly qualified engineer to receive a small iron ring...

It's worn on the little finger of the hand they write with – not as a piece of jewellery, but as a reminder of the obligations they undertake. Tradition maintains that each ring is made from a piece of the Quebec Bridge, which collapsed in 1907 owing to poor design.

And every time a Canadian engineer looks at the iron ring on their writing hand, they are reminded of the impact they can have on the lives of others.

When I surfed the net, I found out that Canadian engineers do receive a ring, but the bit about the collapsed bridge providing its metal is a myth.

However, like all myths, it conveys a deeper truth – about the responsibilities we carry in our daily lives; and about life's fragility.

Maybe our responsibilities don't have the weight of those who wear an engineer's ring, but each of us has the capacity to make a daily impact on others.

At a reunion of school friends recently, we talked of the people who had the greatest influence on us ... and agreed that most of them probably don't know it. Sometimes it's easy to feel that your life makes no difference unless the influence is obvious or public. The truth is: it can – and almost certainly does.

Sustainer of the universe, give each of us, Your masterpieces of creation, a deeper sense of our capacity for good – even though the impact is often invisible to us, wielded without our thinking and in the smallest things. And guide the hands of all who design and build transport and travel today. Amen.

BROADCAST MONDAY 16 DECEMBER 2013

December 17

Joe Aldred

At the heart of the Christmas story is the birth of a baby in a vulnerable situation. Two thousand years ago, Jesus was born to an unmarried mother and a sceptical human father. They were so unprepared for his birth that delivery took place away from home in a stable. Then, under threat from the authorities, the family fled into exile in Egypt to protect the baby's life. The baby's vulnerability would one day give way to physical, intellectual and spiritual growth. His progress is said to have astonished his parents and scholars alike! Christians believe that the baby Jesus was God incarnate. And as a baby, Jesus remains a symbol of both the vulnerability and the redemptive potential of babies everywhere.

Every day in our world, children are born into difficult situations. And yet at birth no one knows a baby's potential, so in theory at least each child is as special as the next. The reality, however, is quite different, depending on whether a child is born in poverty or plenty, in the developing or the developed world. The gap in a child's prospects of surviving and realizing their unique potential is illustrated well by comparing infant mortality rates: in Singapore it's two in a thousand but in Angola it's 180 in a thousand! Meanwhile, individuals and agencies work tirelessly for a better world for vulnerable children and adults alike; and for some it's the story of Jesus that gives hope, even in hopeless situations. It falls to all of us, people of faith and none, to do all we can to make a better world for children everywhere.

O God, help us to protect the well-being of every child born into our world so that each may live to realize its destiny. Amen.

BROADCAST SATURDAY 17 DECEMBER 2011

December 18

Dónal McKeown

I recently saw a striking advertisement for a well-known international charity. The slogan simply said: 'You are what you give.'

That resonated with me on two levels. Firstly, even though the gifts that we give at any time of the year are meant to be for someone else, they also reflect who we are and what we like. We've all been moved by the simplest of presents. A gift is more important for what it says that for what it is.

Secondly, in our Western culture that is so attached to the idea of retail therapy, we risk believing and telling our children that we are what we have. In that context, giving can be seen as a sign of the power of the giver rather than an expression of generosity, sacrifice and love.

But I am more than what I have, or achieve, or feel. I like the wisdom of the monk who noted that 'Abundance is not measured by what flows in, but by what flows over.' The Christian belief system is based on the abundant generosity of God, who shares our human nature that we might share God's divine nature. This is a God who models transcendent freedom through giving, that we might be liberated from the self-centred temptation to seek salvation in acquiring. We are offered healing through the Trinity and not just through the trinket. We are invited to wait in joyful hope and not to be satisfied with jealous having.

For each of the last days of Advent, there is a traditional short prayer called an 'O Antiphon'. The prayer for today is as follows:

O Adonai,
Who appeared to Moses in the fire of the burning bush
And gave him the law on Sinai:
Come and redeem us with Your giving arm.
Amen.

BROADCAST TUESDAY 18 DECEMBER 2012

December 19

Alan Abernethy

I found it strange at first and was surprised that I missed the mess. It's an unusual and difficult moment for parents when their children leave home. Both our children left their various piles around the house and their bedrooms were declared parent-free zones. It wasn't that we weren't welcome or were told to keep out, it was just easier not to comment on the mess as it was *their* mess.

When they both left home to start university life, it was strange not having piles of clothes lying around the house or wet towels covering the bathroom floor. When they come home now, I'm almost glad to see the mess because it's good to have them around and the various clutter is just a part of their presence at home. I've always found something unreal about some of the images used in advertising where the family home is in a state of tidiness and perfection. My experience is certainly more of disorder and untidiness. Of course, one of the things my own mum would remind me of when she heard me frustrated with my children was that I caused her similar irritation.

She would often remind me that life could be difficult and messy, but how we responded to what life threw at us is what really mattered. She had been left with two young children as essentially a single parent. It always amazed me that she remained so positive and full of faith despite the difficulties she had to face.

And my own experience of spending time with many people in pain and difficulty has helped me reflect upon the events of that first Christmas. There was no room in the inn and the baby was laid in a manger. God came into the mess that is ours to be present with us in it.

Lord, whatever mess we are in or whatever mess we find around us, may we know Your presence and help. Amen.

BROADCAST SATURDAY 19 DECEMBER 2009

December 20

Joe Aldred

There is something quite predictable about the world in which we live. Sixty seconds in every minute, 60 minutes in every hour, 24 hours in every day, seven days in every week, twelve months in every year. Spring, summer, autumn and winter come and go with remorseless regularity. We're born, we live and we die. For me, this predictability speaks of the faithfulness of a creating and sustaining God. How different life would be were this monotony turned into the chaos of haphazardness and uncertainty! But between the cracks of this veneer of certitude emerge some wonderful tales of the unexpected that have the power to surprise, shock and entertain us. Life, like any good book, should never be judged simply by its cover.

The story of Christmas is full of surprises. A virgin realizing she was pregnant exclaimed, 'How can this be, seeing I know not a man?' as the King James Version puts it. And expectation is turned on its head when the Son of God is found born in a stable. Shepherds tending their sheep were surprised by the melodies of a heavenly choir singing glory to God in the highest and on earth peace, goodwill to all. And to cap it all, a lad brought up in a carpenter's house starts performing miracles and demonstrating the kind of wisdom he certainly could not have learned from his dad. It was not all plain sailing, though. Some were surprised to see Jesus hanging from a cross; they were even more surprised when he rose from the dead. Life is ever full of surprises.

O God, even as we experience Your faithfulness, may Your ability to surprise us with the unexpected be a happy feature of our daily lives. Amen.

BROADCAST TUESDAY 20 DECEMBER 2011

December 21

Anna Magnusson

I remember as a child that when our favourite great-aunt came to visit, there was one moment we looked forward to most of all. When the table was cleared after the meal, she would pick up her big brown handbag and rummage around it for the loose barleysugars she always carried. She would snap the bag shut with a loud, satisfying click, hand us a sweetie ... and then tell us a story. About how she met her husband when she answered an advert to became his housekeeper. About learning the Charleston in the 1920s. Or, best of all, stories about our mother when she was *our* age, and the naughty things she did.

Every family has its stories. In a few days, families of all kinds will come together over Christmas. We'll re-tell our old stories, happy and sad, and create new ones. The people we've lost will come back to us when we tell *their* story. The hurts we thought we'd forgotten will bite again; we'll laugh at the remembered comic chaos of living. Every moment of every day, the stories of ourselves will multiply, and tell us more about who we are and what our lives mean.

In Luke's Gospel there's this line: 'Mary treasured up all these things and pondered over them' — all the life-changing, frightening, wonderful things that had happened to her. The words people spoke to her, the visitations and dreams, the strangers who told her extraordinary things. So extraordinary, that Mary's story has outlasted the people in it, and the ones who wrote it down for us. As we ponder the wonder of the Incarnation and the Christmas story, it has become *our* story to treasure.

Light of the world, in the darkness of these winter days the story of God-among-us burns bright. We pray that it may live always in our hearts. Amen.

BROADCAST FRIDAY 21 DECEMBER 2007

December 22

⁂

Alan Abernethy

I remember my first primary school nativity play and the woollen dressing gown with the cord belt tied around my waist and the tea towel, both essential for me to play the part of a shepherd. I would really like to have been one of the wise men or kings, but I was grateful I wasn't an angel, as they had to sing and wear wings.

The Christmas story is fantastic for the annual nativity play: there is a part for everyone and simple costumes for all. I attended a nativity play last year in Belfast in an estate on the outskirts of the city that endured much over the many years of violence. The children were 'hyper' and the teachers had that anxious look, wondering what might possibly go wrong. There was not one but two innkeepers who were to not let the travellers in. The first one duly said no, but as Joseph knocked on the imaginary door of the second inn the young boy with an earring in each ear and a very short haircut shouted at the shocked couple to 'get lost'. This was not in the script but he was getting into the story and giving it a local interpretation. The audience duly laughed and the teacher looked embarrassed. The boy was very pleased with himself, and the story moved on to the innkeeper with a stable to spare. The shepherds and the wise men made their entrance, and the performance ended with the song from the entire cast wishing us all a very merry Christmas.

It was a morning that everyone enjoyed. Parents and grandparents were all delighted that their child had been on stage; the teachers were thrilled that things had gone so well; and the children had had fun.

Lord, we pray for all children this week and especially those who will have little to celebrate that they may know the message of that first Christmas of peace on earth and goodwill to all. Amen.

BROADCAST TUESDAY 22 DECEMBER 2009

December 23

Joe Aldred

It has been said profoundly that peace is more than the absence of war. As I speak, there are several wars taking place in our world, with the inevitable consequences of maiming and death. But even in war, people live in hope of real peace, without knowing how to attain it. Their cry echoes Jesus' prayer for the coming of God's kingdom of peace. At the time of his birth, his people were under occupation and therefore in a state of war. The nation looked to a time of liberation and rejoiced at the angelic announcement of 'peace on earth, and good will to all people'. Of course, the person at the centre of that announcement, the baby Jesus, grew to be a controversial figure who was violently put to death. No peace there, it seemed.

But an enduring lesson from the life of Jesus is that peace is easy enough to announce but has to be striven for, and the peace process is often messy, unpredictable and costly. To keep peace, we must first make peace, and in making peace Jesus was unconventional, challenging vested interests, particularly those of the religious and political sorts, and in the end was prepared to lay down his life for a greater cause. It is customary at Christmas time to sing carols that express sentiments of peace; what is needed, however, is a move beyond wishing to a deliberate willingness to pay the price of peace. Christmas reminds us to awaken the messianic gifts in each of us that can bring liberation and peace to the world we live in.

O God, we long for wars to end and Your kingdom of peace to come. We declare it and work for it. Amen.

BROADCAST FRIDAY 23 DECEMBER 2011

December 24

Richard Chartres

It was on Christmas Eve 1968 that astronauts on the *Apollo 8* mission to the moon took photographs of the Earth from outer space. They revealed our planet as sapphire blue and beautiful. The photographs showed what no human being had previously seen. Overnight they became a hopeful symbol of the beauty and fragility of our planet.

One of the *Apollo* crew said, 'The vast loneliness of space is awe-inspiring and it makes you realize just what you have back there on Earth.'

But the symbol of the beautiful and good Earth is balanced by another, more ominous symbol revealed to the post-war generation: the symbol of the mushroom cloud that brought destruction. That stands for the peril that menaces the human race from the misuse of knowledge.

The planet and the cloud; the promise and the peril of human life in this 21st century. Shall we have the wisdom to use our knowledge and our power to alleviate misery to build a civilization of love, or shall we just continue the sad story of warring tribes?

The great struggles in life have an apparent variety but they share in reality a similar underlying pattern. There is always the struggle between love and fear; love and illusion; love and self-protection.

The crew of *Apollo 8* finished their Christmas Eve broadcast with these words: 'Good luck, a Merry Christmas and God bless you all — all of you on the good Earth.'

Eternal God, who came not as our conqueror but as a child full of radiance, draw us like the shepherds and the wise men to the brightness of Your love and fill us with Your light that we may discern the true path which leads to life in all its fullness. Amen.

BROADCAST FRIDAY 24 DECEMBER 2010

December 25

Alan Abernethy

The sight, sounds and smells of Christmas bombard my memory. This is a time of year that has such a rich store of things that make me smile. I can see my granny in her small kitchen making the stuffing for the turkey. I can remember helping my mum fill bottle after bottle with her homemade ginger wine – it certainly helped warm the inners on a cold winter evening, and this was a non-alcoholic wine. On Christmas morning early, at 5.30, our youth group would meet and walk around the neighbourhood singing carols outside the homes of the elderly and infirm. This was followed by a real breakfast, an Ulster fry. There was the fun of Christmas morning and the excitement of presents; the one I remember best is the Northern Ireland football shirt, and unfortunately this is the closest I ever came to wearing one.

Our family gathered in my auntie's house on Christmas Day and my granny insisted we were not allowed to open our presents until after the Queen's speech on television. I remember feeling very envious of my grandfather, who had the patience to watch the joy of others as they opened their presents and when all were opened would slowly and deliberately open his and say thank you to each donor in person. Inevitably, dinner would follow, when we all ate too much and the adults would fall asleep and my uncle Ivor would be heard to say 'Only 365 days to Christmas,' and then he would disappear and do the dishes.

These memories still make me smile, for they are about family, friendship, giving and thinking of others. The babe lying in a manger was announced by a heavenly host declaring good news of peace on earth and goodwill among all people. And there is something about this time of year, and particularly this day of parties and gifts, that helps me capture the spirit of that goodwill.

Lord, may we share the goodwill of Christmas with others all year round and help those whose memories bring lonely pain to find comfort. Amen.

BROADCAST FRIDAY 25 DECEMBER 2009

December 26

Martyn Atkins

A very happy Boxing Day to you all!

When I was growing up, I was always told that Boxing Day was the proper occasion for opening the presents piled in boxes around the Christmas tree. If this was true, our family — like many others, I suspect — broke with that tradition, opening all our presents on Christmas Day. Nowadays we operate a two-stage system, opening the presents from immediate family on Christmas Day and those from friends and relatives from afar on Boxing Day.

But whether opened yesterday or today, Christmas is about gifts given. And one of the traditions I like to remember each Boxing Day is that, originally, gifts were given to the poor. Alms boxes in churches were emptied on this day, and shared with those most in need — as Dickens made clear in *A Christmas Carol*. Today I see that tradition continued by those who inform me that my present this Christmas is a goat given to a needy community, or funding for a micro-project for AIDS victims.

For many, though, 26 December is not so much Boxing Day as St Stephen's Day. Today's the day when 'Good King Wenceslas looked out, on the feast of Stephen'. But the theme of gifts given remains, as Stephen was the first Christian martyr — one who gave the gift of their life for their faith in Christ.

Lord God, on this special day we remember the poor and our deep responsibility to them, we remember those today who give their lives because of their faith in You and their love of others. And we thank You for the most special gift given of all, Jesus Christ, Your Son, who inspires and enables us to be gifts given to others in Your name. Amen.

BROADCAST SATURDAY 26 DECEMBER 2009

December 27

Vincent Nichols

As these days of the Christmas holiday slip by, the end of the year comes ever closer.

That makes us ponder a little, for every year has its regrets as well as its joys and achievements. It's not a bad idea to fashion an overview of the year and take stock of the movement of our lives and relationships.

One image for such an overview is that of an eagle, soaring high above the earth, seeing all, and knowing when and where to swoop.

Despite its being a bird of prey, most churches contain an image of the eagle, often fashioned into a lectern to hold the Bible. After all, it is from the Bible that we can take our overview of life, seeing its patterns and purpose more clearly. And within the books of the Bible there is one that lays special claim to the eagle: the Gospel of St John, whose feast day is today. John appears with an eagle, for his Gospel is the finest of all overviews as he lays out God's purpose in our history. And then he swoops down precisely onto the person of Jesus as the centre of that history and the defining moment in our salvation. John tells us that Jesus is the Eternal Word of God, through whom all things came into being, now born in our flesh and blood. Only the eagle eye of faith can see the truth so clearly!

Lord, help us to look with honesty at our lives. We thank You for all our blessings and we regret, with sorrow, our failures and betrayals. Help us to see Your purpose in the tangle of our lives and turn trustingly to You for Your grace and forgiveness. Amen.

BROADCAST THURSDAY 27 DECEMBER 2012

December 28

Steve Clifford

I'm sure we all have our catalogue of festive disaster stories. My list includes the Christmas decoration fire which could have turned our home into an inferno; the joint of meat which somehow ended up in a suds-filled washing-up bowl; and the forgotten first course which my wife insisted could still be eaten prior to our Christmas pud.

Newly married, enjoying our first Christmas, I hardly dare tell you the gift I chose for her — a frying pan. Never again!

For many around the world this Christmas, the disasters are far more serious and heart-rending, and cannot be solved by a simple apology. For so many, this is a time of fear, of pain and of terrible loss. The population of Haiti is still struggling with the impact of last January's earthquake, but also facing cholera and political unrest. Some places remain large in our consciousness, like Afghanistan and Iraq, but other situations continue for decades with little reporting and no apparent solutions.

And there's much insecurity at home, too. Hopefully, not on the scale of some communities around the world, but the loss of a job, a house or good health can spell personal disaster for any of us.

It is at times like this that the life-filled words of Jesus give me fresh heart and hope. 'Peace I leave with you; my peace I give you. I do not give to you as the world gives. Do not let your hearts be troubled and do not be afraid.'

Father God, in this festive season we pray for those who are finding it hard to celebrate. May they know Your loving, peace-filled presence when times are good and when they're hard. Amen.

BROADCAST TUESDAY 28 DECEMBER 2010

December 29

Graham Forbes

After Christmas I love to read again the cards and letters that come through the letterbox. They make me think and remember. Now I find myself thinking about Basima and Nabil, and their daughters Mima and Zima. This Iraqi family was living in Edinburgh when hostilities were brewing; Nabil was studying, and their return to Baghdad was impossible. The children, aged five and seven, had no English, and yet both of them rapidly acquired Scottish accents and one of them even won the school Burns's poetry speaking competition. They were a Christian family, and we gladly invited them to join our merry throng for Christmas lunch. All the children of different ages and countries were opening presents, and I wandered around with some wine for the adults. I asked Nabil if he'd like some wine — red or white? 'Christian wine' was his reply. I paused. I wondered. Some theological gymnastics were required, and I poured him a glass of red wine. Christian wine, I rapidly realized, was, of course, the red wine of the Eucharist or the Last Supper, the red wine of the blood spilt at Calvary, the red of the martyrs from the very first martyr Stephen to the present day, the red blood of the innocent caught in the cross-fire. Christian wine reminded me of the cost of God's love, in the days after that first Christmas and beyond, and of how we are to see in the exile and the refugee the face of the child of Bethlehem.

My prayer for today?

Heavenly Father, help us to see Your Son in friend and stranger,
Bless all who are far from their homes this day
And may all of us find our true home in You.
Amen.

BROADCAST SATURDAY 29 DECEMBER 2012

December 30

Leslie Griffiths

I met some visitors from the Caribbean the other day. It's the first time they've been here and their excitement was scarcely containable. They were desperate to see snow. They've read about it, seen pictures of it, and now want to experience it. I didn't dare tell them what I think of snow — messy, dangerous stuff that I wouldn't mind never seeing again. For all that, it hasn't been snow but something they weren't looking out for at all that has really caused their jaws to drop. It's the shortness of the days. No one had told them about that. 'It's dark for breakfast and it's dark for tea,' was how one of them put it. Too true. Winter's here all right and there's plenty more to come. My dear old mother, whenever her friends grumbled about how cold or miserable it was at this time of the year, could always be counted on to offer a word of encouragement. 'Don't worry, darlings,' she'd say, 'spring's just round the corner.' Poverty stalked us as I grew up, but my mother's sublime optimism kept our spirits high. 'Hope springs eternal,' said the poet, a sentiment echoed by the Bible. Hope is one of the three great Christian virtues —faith, hope and love. They're all life-enhancing and future-oriented. We hope for what we do not yet have, life's difficulties can be endured with hope in our hearts. All things, all manner of things, can be well. And my Caribbean friends will soon see the snowdrops and the crocuses announcing that better and longer days are on the way.

Dear Lord, help us in the darkest night to sense the coming dawn; hold fast to us in love and establish us in hope, through Jesus Christ, our Lord, Amen.

BROADCAST MONDAY 30 DECEMBER 2013

December 31

❦

Kelvin Holdsworth

I'm reading and writing in a room that's just a few yards from the River Clyde in the city of Glasgow. The land all around where I am now was once an area teeming with ships. A busy place with boats coming and going from here to the farthest parts of the Earth. Goods and people arrived here and were exchanged for cargo and passengers leaving for far-flung destinations. This was, no doubt, a place of many joyful greetings and many sad goodbyes.

This evening, one year will slip into the next as we bid goodbye to the old and welcome in the new.

Here in this place, there used to be a sound that represented the New Year coming in, which people still talk about. It was the boats on the Clyde and in all the shipyards too sounding their horns and hooters at midnight. People now speak of waiting up for the bells to see in the New Year, but the cacophony and din from the river sounds a good deal more exciting to me.

I've no idea what sound you will hear at midnight tonight. Maybe it will be the sound of Big Ben. Maybe the sound of the gun fired from Edinburgh castle. Or maybe the sound of people partying. Maybe the hooting of horns. Or maybe just the stillness and peace of a time for reflecting on the New Year by yourself.

Whatever sound you hear tonight, I hope that you are blessed with love, joy and peace, not just as the year turns tonight, but every day of the year that is to come.

Eternal God, bless us through this day and bless us through tonight and fill us with hope for tomorrow. Amen.

BROADCAST SATURDAY 31 DECEMBER 2011

Biographical Index of Contributors

The Right Reverend **Alan Abernethy** was Rector at two parishes in County Down – St John's, Helen's Bay, from 1987 to 1990, and then at St Columbanus, Ballyholme – before becoming Church of Ireland Bishop of Connor in 2007. **Pages 377, 380, 383**

Bishop Dr **Joe Aldred** is an ecumenist, writer and speaker. He is Secretary for Pentecostalism and Multicultural Relations at Churches Together in England, Honorary Research Fellow at Roehampton University and a Bishop in the Church of God of Prophecy. **Pages 254, 256, 277, 280, 312, 314, 375, 378, 381**

Pastor **Lindsay Allen** was born and grew up in Belfast, and worked for FEBA (Far Eastern Broadcasting Association) before becoming Pastor of Carrickfergus Baptist Church in 1996. He retired in 2013. **Page 160**

Padre **David Anderson** is a Church of Scotland Minister. Ordained in 2002, he served as a Parish Minister before joining Her Majesty's Land Forces in 2007. He has undertaken three operational tours of duty; the most recent in Afghanistan with The Royal Scots Dragoon Guards. **Page 338**

Bishop **Angaelos** was consecrated a monk in 1990 and served as Papal Secretary until 1995. He is General Bishop of the Coptic Orthodox Church in the UK. Active ecumenically, he works extensively in inter-religious relations, youth, advocacy and development work in Britain and internationally. **Pages 14, 17**

The Right Reverend Dr **John Armes** has been Bishop of the Diocese of Edinburgh in the Scottish Episcopal Church since 2012. Previously he was Rector of the Church of St John the Evangelist, Edinburgh, and Dean of the Diocese of Edinburgh. **Page 60**

The Very Reverend **David Arnott** retired as a Minister in 2010, having held several high-profile positions within the Church of Scotland. He was appointed Moderator of the General Assembly in 2011–12. **Page 305**

The Reverend Canon Dr **Martyn Atkins** is General Secretary of the Methodist Church in Britain and Secretary of the Methodist Conference. **Pages 22, 300, 343, 384**

The Reverend **Peter Baker**, former Senior Pastor of Highfields Church, Cardiff, took over as Senior Minister of Lansdowne Baptist Church, Bournemouth, in 2013. **Pages 137, 151, 169, 207, 210, 317, 349**

Father **Tim Bartlett** is a Priest of the Diocese of Down and Connor, has been a Special Adviser to the Archbishop of Armagh and is currently Secretary to the Northern Bishops of the Roman Catholic Church in Ireland. **Page 279**

Canon **Noel Battye** served as Rector of two Church of Ireland parishes in Belfast, retiring in 2008. He was previously Chaplain of Pembroke College, Cambridge, and a member of the Chapter of the National Cathedral of St Patrick in Dublin. **Pages 42, 47, 239, 241, 309**

The Very Reverend **Mark Beach** is Dean of Rochester and formerly Team Rector at Rugby, having served at several parishes in Nottinghamshire. **Page 36**

Tina Beattie is an author and the Director of the Digby Stuart Research Centre for Religion, Society and Human Flourishing at the University of Roehampton. **Pages 56, 97, 175, 302, 306**

The Reverend **Chris Bennett** is Church of Ireland Chaplain to the Titanic Quarter in Belfast. He is a leading light at The Dock, a café and community hub. He is also Priest-in-Charge of St Clement's Church in Belfast. **Page 217**

The Reverend **Derek Boden** was Presbyterian Chaplain to the University of Ulster in Coleraine from 1975 until 1978, when he became a Minister in Dublin. From 1981 until 2012 he was Minister of Malone Presbyterian Church in Belfast. **Pages 215, 347**

Rabbi Dr **Naftali Brawer** was ordained as an Orthodox Rabbi aged 22, and for over two decades has served as the spiritual leader of congregations in the USA and Britain. He is a columnist and published author. **Pages 35, 38**

The Reverend Dr **Nicholas Buxton** is Priest-in-Charge of the Parish of St John the Baptist, Newcastle upon Tyne, and author of *The Wilderness Within: Meditation and Modern Life*. **Page 269**

The Very Reverend **John Cairns**, a former Moderator of the General Assembly of the Church of Scotland, was knighted in 2013 after retiring as Dean of the Chapel Royal. He was appointed Chaplain to the Queen in 1997. **Pages 318, 322**

Claire Campbell Smith worked for many years as a producer for BBC Religion and Ethics and Classical Music departments. She now teaches Academic Music at Chetham's School of Music in Manchester. **Pages 213, 281**

The Right Reverend and Right Honourable **Richard Chartres** DD KCVO became Bishop of London and The Dean of Her Majesty's Chapels Royal in 1995. Previously, he was Gresham Professor of Divinity and Area Bishop of Stepney. He is a notable environmentalist and Chairman of an embryo Christian University, St Mellitus College. **Pages 104, 177, 382**

The Most Reverend **David Chillingworth** is Bishop of St Andrews, Dunkeld and Dunblane and Primus of the Scottish Episcopal Church. Born in Dublin, he was ordained in 1976 and served in Northern Ireland before moving to Scotland in 2005. **Pages 107, 113, 122, 139, 141, 188, 191, 296**

Father **Paul Clayton-Lea** is a Priest of the Diocese of Armagh and is currently Parish Priest of Tallanstown in County Louth. **Page 41**

Steve Clifford is General Director of the Evangelical Alliance. He created the TIE Team (later to become DNA) discipleship course and has been active in major initiatives, such as Soul in the City, Soul Survivor and Hope 2008. **Page 386**

Mark Coffey is a teacher of religion and philosophy at The Manchester Grammar School, and a regular presenter of *The Daily Service* on Radio 4. **Pages 24, 48**

The Reverend Dr **Kate Coleman** is an author and the founding director of Next Leadership. She is Chair of the Evangelical Alliance Council, former President of the Baptist Union of Great Britain, and a Baptist Minister. **Pages 99, 248, 252**

Canon **Edwin Counsell** is Director of Education for the Diocese of Llandaff and Lead Education Officer for the Church in Wales. Ordained in 1988, he has since been a regular contributor to local and national radio. **Pages 227, 229, 232**

Dr **Catherine Cowley** is a member of the Congregation of the Religious of the Assumption. She has been Assistant Director for the Heythrop Institute for Religion, Ethics and Public Life and Secretary to the Association of Teachers of Moral Theology. **Pages 193, 196, 247, 250**

George Craig is a retired senior civil servant, and a Methodist local preacher in Cardiff. **Pages 19, 203, 206, 238, 244, 260, 299, 301, 303**

Graham Daniels joined the Christians in Sport staff in 1989 and became General Director in 2002. Graham plays football for Cambridge Veterans, is a Director of Cambridge United Football Club and is an Associate Staff member at St Andrew the Great (StAG) Church, Cambridge. **Page 249**

Shaunaka Rishi Das is Director of the Oxford Centre for Hindu Studies. He is a Hindu cleric, writer and lecturer, and Hindu Chaplain to Oxford University. Born an Irish Catholic, he joined a Hare Krishna ashram, in Dublin, in 1979. **Pages 73, 76, 237, 315, 330, 332**

Maggi Dawn is an author and songwriter, as well as Associate Professor of Theology and Literature, and Dean of Marquand Chapel at Yale Divinity School. Before moving to Yale in 2011, she served as Chaplain and taught theology at the University of Cambridge. **Pages 147, 149**

The Reverend Canon **Simon Doogan** is the Rector of St Columbanus Church, Ballyholme in Bangor. He is also Prebendary of Wicklow, representing the Diocese of Down and Dromore, on the Chapter of the National Cathedral of St Patrick in Dublin. **Pages 290, 292, 298**

The Right Reverend **Lord Eames** was elected Bishop of Derry and Raphoe in 1975. In 1980 he became Bishop of Down and Dromore, and in 1986 Archbishop of Armagh and Primate of All Ireland, retiring in 2006. He was created a Life Peer in 1995. **Page 345**

The Right Reverend **Chris Edmondson** has been the Bishop of Bolton in the Diocese of Manchester since 2008. Ordained in 1973, he has worked in a variety of parish and diocesan posts, and was Warden of Lee Abbey, Devon, from 2002 to 2008. **Pages 308, 310**

Dr **Alison Elliot** OBE has, since 2001, been Associate Director of the Centre for Theology and Public Issues at Edinburgh University. In 2004 she became the first woman to be elected as Moderator of the General Assembly of the Church of Scotland. She is an Elder at Greyfriars Tolbooth & Highland Kirk, Edinburgh. **Page 186**

Frances Finn is a journalist and presenter for TV and radio. She presents regularly on BBC Radio Nottingham and from time to time presents programmes on BBC Radio 2 and Radio 5 live. She has written movingly about a serious motorbike accident that hospitalized her in 2009. **Pages 344, 346, 348**

The Reverend **Mal Fletcher** is a Minister with the Australian Christian Churches, as well as a media/social futurist and commentator, speaker, author and business leadership consultant. He is the author of ten books. **Page 155**

The Very Reverend Dr **Graham Forbes** CBE is an Episcopolian Priest. A former Provost of St Ninian's Cathedral in Perth, since 1990 he has been Provost of St Mary's Cathedral, Edinburgh. Also, among other posts, he is Chair of the Mental Welfare Commission for Scotland and Chair of Court, Edinburgh Napier University. **Pages 9, 387**

Michael Ford has reported extensively on religion and ethics for Radio 4 and the BBC World Service. The biographer of Father Henri JM Nouwen and Father Mychal Judge, he is now involved in an ecumenical ministry of spiritual guidance and retreat work. **Pages 23, 144, 146, 187, 190, 192, 263**

The Reverend Dr **Richard Frazer** is Parish Minister at Greyfriars Kirk, Edinburgh. He is also Vice Convener of the Church of Scotland's Social Care Council and is involved with the Green Pilgrim Network. **Pages 29, 31**

The Reverend Canon **Bob Fyffe**, a Minister of the Scottish Episcopal Church, is General Secretary of Churches Together in Britain and Ireland. **Pages 65, 68, 135, 140**

Lynn Gallagher is a writer who specializes in the field of conservation. She is also a part-time lecturer at Edgehill Theological College, Belfast, and is an active member of St Finnian's Church of Ireland, Cregagh. **Page 142**

The Reverend Dr **Craig Gardiner** teaches theology at South Wales Baptist College and is an Honorary Senior Tutor at the Cardiff School of History, Archaeology and Religion. He is a member of the Iona Community. **Pages 109, 195**

The Reverend **Neil Gardner** is Minister at Canongate Kirk, Edinburgh. He has served with the Royal Army Chaplains' Department in Germany, Hong Kong, Northern Ireland, Surrey and Hampshire. **Page 295**

The Reverend Dr **Gordon Graham**, an Anglican Priest ordained in the Scottish Episcopal Church, is Henry Luce III Professor of Philosophy and the Arts at Princeton Theological Seminary in New Jersey. He has a special interest in the Scottish philosophical tradition, as well as in sacred music. **Pages 234, 240**

The Reverend Dr **Gordon Gray**, after being Minister of a Church Extension charge in Belfast, was Youth Secretary to the Presbyterian Church in Ireland from 1966 to 1973, when he became Minister of First Lisburn Presbyterian Church. He retired in 2001. **Page 117**

Andrew Graystone worked for BBC Religion and Ethics for more than a decade as a TV and radio producer. He continues to present radio programmes and researches and writes on Christian faith and digital culture. **Pages 15, 143**

The Reverend **Sharon Grenham Toze**, a former solicitor, is Lead Chaplain at HMP Bedford. She also contributes regularly to BBC Radio 2's *Pause for Thought*. **Pages 43, 61, 80, 82, 150, 165**

The Reverend Dr **Leslie Griffiths**, Lord Griffiths of Burry Port, is a British Methodist Minister and a Labour Life Peer. He served as President of the Methodist Conference from 1994 to 1995. He is President of the Boys' Brigade. **Pages 44, 172, 388**

Becky Harris is a teacher at The King David High School in Manchester. **Page 153**

Richard Hill served as a Presbyterian Minister in County Antrim and in Belfast, and in 2008 became Chair of Northern Ireland Screen Commission and of the Northern Ireland Consumer Council. He is currently a film and media consultant and a member of the Independent Press Standards Organisation. **Pages 12, 216, 220, 245, 320, 324**

The Venerable Dr **John Holdsworth** is Executive Archdeacon of the Anglican Diocese of Cyprus and the Gulf. He has spent most of his ministry in Wales, latterly as Archdeacon of St Davids. **Pages 18, 368**

The Very Reverend **Kelvin Holdsworth** serves as Rector and Provost of the Cathedral Church of St Mary the Virgin, Glasgow. He stood as Liberal Democrat candidate in the constituency of Stirling in the 2005 General Election. **Pages 10, 26, 30, 389**

Canon Dr **Ann Holt** OBE is an expert in education, as governor of several schools and consultant to Local Education Authorities, the DFE and independent schools. Since 2002 she has been Director of the Programme Team at Bible Society. **Page 92**

The Right Reverend **Nicholas Holtam** is Bishop of Salisbury. He was a Curate in Stepney, Tutor in Christian Ethics at Lincoln Theological College, Vicar of the Isle of Dogs and Vicar of St Martin-in-the-Fields, London. He is a Fellow of King's College, London. **Page 95**

Dr **Musharraf Hussain** OBE is a scientist, educator and religious scholar in Nottinghamshire. He is Chief Executive of the Karimia Institute, Chief Editor of *The Invitation*, and Vice Chair of the Christian/ Muslim Forum. **Page 243, 246, 311, 313**

The Reverend **Roger Hutchings**, a Methodist Minister, was Editor of BBC's *Songs of Praise*, and later of ITV's *Morning Worship*. He lives in retirement in Wiltshire and near Carcassonne, Languedoc, France. **Pages 84, 120, 199, 201, 329**

The Reverend Dr **Alison Jack**, now Assistant Principal of New College, Edinburgh, has throughout her academic career integrated her interest in literature with her study of the Bible. Alongside her scholarly work she has served in various parishes. **Pages 136, 138**

Father **Nicholas James** is Parish Priest of St Mary's Roman Catholic Church in Monmouth and also Parish Priest for the Parish of St Frances of Rome, Ross-on-Wye. **Page 271**

The Reverend **Clair Jaquiss** was ordained in 2008, having worked for many years as a radio producer for BBC Religion and Ethics. She is also Assistant Priest at All Saints Church, Hale Barns, not far from Manchester Airport. **Pages 74, 78, 145, 148, 182, 189, 226**

Glenn Jordan has twenty years of experience in programme development, communication and leadership in the Northern Ireland voluntary sector, and has contributed to the formation of NI community relations policy. He is a Director of the Skainos Project, a church-based project in inner East Belfast. **Pages 86, 88, 168**

Gopinder Kaur combines motherhood with postgraduate research in education. Formerly in children's publishing, she has written on Sikh heritage and participates in faith-inspired civic engagement projects fostered by the Nishkam Civic Assocation, under the tutelage of Bhai Sahib Dr Mohinder Singh. **Pages 116, 119, 179, 181, 183, 185**

Dr **Edward (Ed) Kessler** MBE, is an author and the Founding Director of The Woolf Institute, Cambridge. He is a notable thinker in interfaith relations and Fellow of St Edmund's College. **Pages 32, 261, 266, 268, 288, 291**

Monsignor **Mark Langham** has, since 2013, been Chaplain at the Cambridge University Catholic Chaplaincy. He is a Priest of the Archdiocese of Westminster and former Administrator of Wesminster Cathedral. **Page 214**

Cathy Le Feuvre is a writer, journalist and media consultant. She worked as a print and radio journalist in Jersey before moving to the UK, where she joined the media office of the Salvation Army. **Pages 130, 132, 205, 208**

The Reverend **Richard Littledale** is Pastor of Teddington Baptist Church. He served at Hertford and Purley before moving to Teddington in 1997. He works with the College

of Preachers and runs preaching workshops. **Page 96**

Leon Litvack is Professor of Victorian Studies at Queen's University Belfast, a Dickens scholar and the author of books on 19th-century literature. He has frequently contributed to BBC radio and television on arts and culture, and religion and ethics. **Page 34**

Sister **Jane Livesey** CJ is the Congregational Leader of the Congregation of Jesus, which has 1700 members in 23 countries. Her background was in education, first as a teacher and subsequently as a head teacher. **Page 287**

The Reverend Dr **Marjory MacLean** is a Church of Scotland Parish Minister in East Perthshire, and a Chaplain in the Royal Naval Reserve. She has previously served in an Orkney parish and as a Clerk of the Church's General Assembly. **Pages 178, 180, 231, 236**

Anna Magnusson has produced, written and broadcast programmes for the BBC for more than 25 years. She has been in charge of Religion and Ethics programming for BBC Radio Scotland. She is the author of three books of non-fiction. **Pages 54, 57, 64, 91, 94, 110, 112, 114, 334, 336, 339, 373, 379**

Michelle Marken OBE completed her teaching career as Principal of St Joseph's College, Belfast. She is a regular contributor to BBC Radio Ulster programmes, an enthusiast for amateur drama and a passionate educationalist, and is now volunteering with a range of charities. **Pages 369, 371**

Father **Andrew Martlew** is a former Army Chaplain who is now Vicar of St Martin's, Womersley, in North Yorkshire, and an

Honorary Chaplain of York Minster. He is one of the regular presenters of *The Daily Service* on Radio 4. **Page 184**

The Reverend Prebendary **Edward Mason** was appointed Rector of Bath Abbey in 2004. He was previously Director of Music at a Gloucestershire comprehensive school and then spent six years in Uganda with his family as Mission Partners with the Church Mission Society. **Pages 46, 101, 103**

Commissioner **Betty Matear** rose through the ranks of the Salvation Army to become Territorial President of Women's Ministries in the UK in 2006. In 2007 she became the first Salvationist to become Moderator of the Free Churches Group. She is also a published author. **Page 307**

The Reverend **Paul Mathole** has a PhD in English Literature and worked in academic publishing before entering ordained ministry in the Church of England. He is currently Associate Minister at Holy Trinity Platt Church in Manchester. **Pages 49, 51**

The Right Reverend **Nigel McCulloch** KCVO is the retired Bishop of Manchester. He is also National Chaplain to the Royal British Legion. **Pages 77, 81, 341**

Alastair McIntosh is a Fellow of the Centre for Human Ecology and Edinburgh University's Divinity School. A human ecologist, he helped set up the GalGael Trust that tackles poverty in Govan. His books include *Soil and Soul*, *Island Spirituality* and *Parables of Northern Seed*. **Page 359**

The Reverend **Johnston McKay** was Assistant Minister at St Giles Cathedral and then Minister of Bellahouston Steven Parish in Glasgow and Paisley Abbey. In 1987 he joined the BBC Religious Broadcasting Department and he retired as Editor of Religious Broadcasting for Scotland in 2002. **Pages 25, 28, 58, 111, 115, 356**

The Most Reverend Dr **Dónal McKeown** was appointed Roman Catholic Bishop of Derry in 2014. For 23 years he was a teacher, including as Principal of St Malachy's College in Belfast, before becoming Auxiliary Bishop of Down and Connor in 2001. **Pages 282, 284, 335, 337, 376**

The Reverend Canon **John McLuckie** is Vice-Provost of St Mary's Cathedral, Edinburgh. He has worked as Chaplain of King's College, Cambridge, and of the Royal Marsden Hospital, London. He writes a blog on spirituality and the arts called Justluckie. **Pages 272, 274**

Judy Merry is a freelance producer and presenter. She is also a lecturer in journalism at UCLan in Preston. **Pages 90, 93, 340**

The Reverend Dr **Katherine Meyer** first came to Northern Ireland from the United States to work with the Corrymeela Community. She was Presbyterian Chaplain at Trinity College, Dublin, before becoming, in 2007, the Minister of Christ Church, Sandymount, in Dublin. **Page 170**

Shaykh **Ibrahim Mogra**, an Imam from Leicester, is Assistant Secretary General of the Muslim Council of Britain. He is the founder and principal of Khazinatul-'llm, Madaris of Arabic and Muslim Life Studies, in Leicester. **Pages 204, 212, 362, 367, 370**

The Reverend Dr **Jeremy Morris** is Dean,
Fellow and Director of Studies in Theology
at King's College, Cambridge. He was curate
at St Mary's, Battersea, London, before
returning to Cambridge, where he was
Dean of Trinity Hall from 2001 to 2010.
Pages 123, 125, 127, 342

Shaykh **Michael Mumisa** is an author and PhD
candidate (in the field of classical Arabic
literature) and Cambridge Special Livingstone
Scholar at Trinity Hall, Cambridge. **Pages 233,
235, 242, 258, 264, 316**

Alison Murdoch is the former Director of
Jamyang Buddhist Centre, London, and of
The Foundation for Developing Compassion
and Wisdom. She is co-author of *16 Guidelines
for a Happy Life*. **Pages 159, 162, 164, 200, 202,
209, 211**

Vincent Nichols received the red hat of his
office from Pope Francis in St Peter's Basilica
on 22nd February 2014. He is Archbishop
of Westminster and President of the Catholic
Bishops' Conference of England and Wales.
He served as Archbishop of Birmingham from
2000 to 2009. **Page 385**

Father **Eugene O'Neill** is a Priest of the
Diocese of Down and Connor, and is also a
spiritual director. He works near Belfast and
contributes regularly to broadcasting and print
in the UK, Ireland and the United States.
Pages 167, 374

The Reverend Canon **Nick Papadopulos** worked
as a barrister before doing his theological
training. A former Vicar of St Peter's, Eaton
Square, London, he is now Canon Treasurer
of Canterbury Cathedral. **Page 21**

The Reverend Canon Professor **Martyn Percy**,
Principal of Ripon College, Cuddesdon,
Oxford, from 2004, is now Dean of Christ
Church, Oxford. A co-founder of the Society
for the Study of Anglicanism, he has published
many books on Christianity in contemporary
culture. **Pages 253, 255, 257**

The Reverend Dr **Michael Piret** is Dean of
Divinity of Magdalen College, Oxford;
previously he was Curate at Inverness Cathedral
in the Scottish Episcopal Church. **Pages 222,
225, 327, 333**

The Reverend **George Pitcher** is a journalist,
author and public relations consultant, and
serves as a Priest in the Dioceses of Chichester
and London. He is a contributing editor at
Newsweek Europe and leads its editorial panel.
Pages 325, 328

Andrea Rea is a freelance writer and broadcaster
working with the BBC Religion and Ethics and
Classical Music departments in Belfast. She
plays the viola and is Director of Music at
St Nicholas Church in Belfast. **Pages 50, 52,
219, 224**

Denis Rice is a retired warden of Vaughan
College, University of Leicester. He taught
ethics to social workers and medical students,
among others. He now lives in Montrose,
Scotland. **Page 20**

Pastor **Alex Robertson** is one of the Pastors at
The Lighthouse, an Elim Pentecostal church in
Salford. He is also a musician and teaches viola
at the Royal Northern College of Music.
Pages 363, 365

Philip Robinson is the former Financial
Servicers Authority (FSA) Director of Financial

Crime, having previously worked in the securities and derivatives industry. **Page 289**

Monsignor **Tony Rogers** is a Catholic Priest, currently working in Aldeburgh in Suffolk. Previously he was Priest at Our Lady and the English Martyrs Church, Cambridge. He is a regular presenter of *The Daily Service* on Radio 4. **Pages 62, 118, 121, 251**

Rabbi **YY Rubinstein** splits his time between the US and UK. He is one the most sought-after Jewish speakers in the UK and abroad. He is a columnist in several Jewish magazines and the author of eight books. **Page 37**

The Reverend Dr **Calvin T Samuel** is a Methodist Minister, currently Director of Wesley Study Centre and Academic Dean of Cranmer Hall, St John's College, Durham University. Previously he was New Testament Tutor at Spurgeon's College and Chaplain to Farringtons School in Kent. **Pages 27, 33**

The Reverend **Frank Sellar**, a Presbyterian Minister, served a congregation in Dublin from 1990 until 2007, when he became Minister of Bloomfield Presbyterian Church in the heart of East Belfast. **Page 194**

The Right Reverend **Martin Shaw** served in the Scottish Episcopal Church as the Bishop of Argyll and The Isles from 2004 to 2009. He has also served as Chaplain to King's College, Cambridge, Principal of the Institute of Christian Studies, All Saints, Margaret Street, London, and Rector of Dunoon and Succentor at Exeter Cathedral. **Pages 75, 79**

The Reverend Canon **Stephen Shipley** is a Priest in Buxton, Derbyshire, and Honorary Canon of Derby Cathedral. He is a producer for BBC Radio Religion and Ethics. **Pages 128, 171, 267, 319, 321, 323, 352**

Dr **Gemma Simmonds** CJ is a sister of the Congregation of Jesus. After a teaching career, she worked as Chaplain in the University of Cambridge. She has worked with street children in Brazil. Currently she teaches theology at Heythrop College, London, and is a volunteer Chaplain at Holloway Prison. **Pages 45, 55, 59, 63, 66, 158**

The Reverend Dr **Karen Smith** is Tutor in Church History and Christian Spirituality at South Wales Baptist College, Honorary Senior Tutor in the School of History, Archaeology and Religion at Cardiff University, and Pastor of Orchard Place Baptist Church, Neath. **Page 350**

The Most Reverend **Peter Smith** is Archbishop of Southwark. He has also served as Bishop of East Anglia, Archbishop of Cardiff, and has been Chairman of the Catholic Truth Society. **Pages 152, 156, 304**

The Most Reverend **George Stack** was installed as Archbishop of Cardiff in 2011. He was ordained Priest in 1972, later serving in Wood Green and Kentish Town, London, among other places. He has also been Administrator of Westminster Cathedral, and Bishop in the Archdiocese of Westminster. **Pages 11, 83, 105, 108**

The Reverend Canon **Mary Stallard** is Chaplain of St Joseph's Catholic and Anglican High School, Wrexham, as well as Director of the St Giles Centre for Religious Education and Faith Development in the same town. **Pages 67, 71, 129, 131, 154, 157, 297**

The Reverend Canon Dr **David Stone** became Canon Precentor and Sub-Dean of Coventry Cathedral in 2010. **Pages 124, 126**

The Reverend Canon **Patrick Thomas** is the Vicar of Christ Church, Carmarthen, and Chancellor of St Davids Cathedral, Pembrokeshire. An honorary member of the Gorsedd of Bards, he has published works in both English and Welsh. **Pages 228, 366, 372**

The Reverend Dr **Bert Tosh** was ordained to the Presbyterian ministry in 1973 and worked with congregations in Belfast, Londonderry and County Donegal before joining the BBC Religious Broadcasting Department in Belfast in 1984. He retired in 2013 but continues to produce worship programmes. In 2013 he was made an honorary Doctor of Divinity by the Union Theological College in Belfast. **Page 259**

The Venerable **Peter Townley** is Archdeacon of Pontefract, in the Diocese of West Yorkshire and the Dales. He spent the first sixteen years of his ministry in the Manchester area. Before moving to Pontefract, he was Vicar of St Mary le Tower, Ipswich. **Pages 218, 221, 223**

The late **Alison Twaddle** was General Secretary of the Church of Scotland Guild, and served that church in many ways before her death in 2013. She was a full-time mother before joining the Guild. She was a member of BBC Scotland's Scottish Religious Advisory Committee. **Pages 276, 353, 355, 360**

The late Reverend Canon **Noël Vincent** was Canon Treasurer of Liverpool Cathedral and before that a notable religious broadcaster, who was Chief Assistant to the Head of Religious Broadcasting at the BBC. Throughout the 1980s he produced hundreds of radio and TV programmes across the north of England. **Pages 163, 361, 364**

The Reverend Dr **Mark Wakelin** has served for more than 30 years with the Methodist Church as Minister in various appointments. He was President of the Methodist Conference from 2012 to 2013 and is currently a Minister at Epsom Methodist Church, Surrey. **Pages 85, 98, 161, 270, 273, 275**

The Reverend Dr **Sam Wells** is the Vicar of St Martin-in-the-Fields, London. He is also Visiting Professor of Christian Ethics at King's College, London. He is the author of twenty books on ethics, ministry, faith, mission and discipleship. **Page 331**

The Reverend **Peter Whittaker** is a retired Methodist Minister, and formerly Chair of the West Yorkshire Methodist District, and Chair of the Trustees and the Enabling Group of Churches Together in England. **Page 53**

The Reverend Canon **Jenny Wigley** is Rector of Radyr and Area Dean of Llandaff. She is a former teacher. All her ministry has been in the Church in Wales, including university chaplaincy and theological education. **Pages 13, 16, 72, 173, 176**

The Reverend Canon **Steve Williams** is Priest-in-Charge of St Gabriel's, Prestwich (in the Prestwich Mission Partnership). He is Interfaith Advisor in the Diocese of Manchester and Co-chair of the Manchester branch of the Council of Christians and Jews. **Pages 351, 354**

Rabbi **Jonathan Wittenberg** is the Senior Rabbi of Masorti Judaism UK, and Rabbi of the New North London Synagogue. He is a leading writer and thinker on Judaism. He has been involved in multi-faith chaplaincy and in efforts to establish a multi-faith school in London. **Pages 39, 286**

The Reverend Dr **Janet Wootton** is Director of Learning and Development for the Congregational Federation. Ordained in 1979, she has served in rural and city churches. She is on the editorial team for *Feminist Theology Journal* and *Worship Live*, among other publications. **Pages 106, 174, 265, 278, 283, 285**

The Right Reverend Professor **Tom Wright** is one of the world's leading New Testament scholars and from 2003 until his retirement in 2010 was Bishop of Durham. He is now Research Professor of New Testament and Early Christianity at St Mary's College in the University of St Andrews. **Page 100**

Acknowledgments

The Publishers would like to thank Bishop Richard Harries, for providing the Foreword, and Philip Billson, for the Introduction. Many thanks to Philip Billson, Sue Dickson and Vanessa Ford at the BBC for their invaluable help in producing this book.